Hot Showers, Soft Beds, and Dayhikes in
The NORTH CASCADES

SALLY O'NEAL COATES

WILDERNESS PRESS
BERKELEY

Photos and maps by the author except as noted
Design by Margaret Copeland
Cover design by Larry Van Dyke
Front cover photos:
    top: Buttercups below the Border Peaks, Mt. Baker Wilderness, WA (photo © 1996
        by John Dittli)
    bottom: WolfRidge Resort, Winthrop, WA (photo © WolfRidge Resort)
Back cover photos:
    top: Meadow at Sibley Creek en route to Hidden Lake Peaks
    bottom: Monte Cristo Inn, Granite Falls, WA
Frontispiece photo: Table Mountain

Library of Congress Card Number 97-250
ISBN 0-89997-209-8

Manufactured in the United States of America

Published by   Wilderness Press
                 2440 Bancroft Way
                 Berkeley, CA 94704
                 (510) 843-8080
                 FAX (510) 548-1355

                 Write, call or fax for free catalog

Library of Congress Cataloging-in-Publication Data

Coates, Sally O'Neal
    Hot showers, soft beds, & dayhikes in the North Cascades / Sally O'Neal Coates.—1st ed.
      p.   cm.
    Includes index.
    ISBN 0-89997-209-8
    1. Hiking—Washington (State)—North Cascades National Park—Guidebooks. 2. North Cascades
National Park (Wash.)—Guidebooks. I. Title.
    GV199.42.W22N6725 1997
    796.5'1'0979773—dc21   97-250
                                                                   CIP

For Mom and Dad,
and
for all my friends who
"walked the walk"

Contents

Areas Covered In This Book

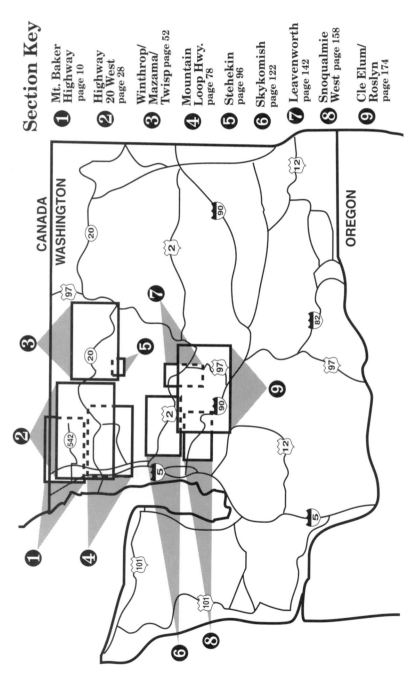

Section Key

1 Mt. Baker Highway page 10

2 Highway 20 West page 28

3 Winthrop/ Mazama/ Twisp page 52

4 Mountain Loop Hwy. page 78

5 Stehekin page 96

6 Skykomish page 122

7 Leavenworth page 142

8 Snoqualmie West page 158

9 Cle Elum/ Roslyn page 174

Introduction

Why "Hot Showers, Soft Beds?"

This book was written for the tens of thousands of us who love the wilderness but also love life's creature comforts. It's about the joy of waking up between clean sheets under a down comforter, well-rested and refreshed, with the smell of French roast coffee wafting down the hall and a day of leisure before you. Outside, miles of trails beckon, wildflowers bloom, and the mountain air is crisp and clean.

I have no problem with camping. I have done my share of sleeping on the ground, in tents, under the stars. I have backpacked and RV-camped. I have wandered Europe for weeks at a time with little more than a toothbrush, a change of underwear, and the clothes on my back, staying in cold-water flats and sleeping on sheets of dubious vintage. But I have discovered that my very favorite way to experience the outdoors is with a good night's rest behind me, a full breakfast in my belly, and the promise of a nice, hot shower at day's end.

So, together with Wilderness Press, I put together a book of great walks and hikes in the North Cascades that are true wilderness experiences, but are all within an easy walk or drive from a comfortable lodge, cabin, motel, or bed & breakfast.

Hiking from lodgings, as opposed to backpacking or dayhiking from a campsite, is practical as well as comfortable. Not everyone owns a collection of camping gear; such equipment can be expensive to acquire and maintain, and is difficult to justify if you hike infrequently. It doesn't require as much preparation time to pack for dayhiking as it does to pack for backpacking or camping out. And hiking from lodgings is a nice foul-weather alternative. Few things are more depressing than a leaky tent in a downpour. Even if you don't mind hiking in the rain, it's nice to come back to a warm, dry refuge at day's end. I would rather exercise on the trail, then relax in front of a fireplace, than get my workout packing and unpacking wet camping gear, making a mad dash to the car, and heading home early because of a storm.

Is This Book for You?

Maybe you haven't hiked in years. *Hot Showers, Soft Beds and Dayhikes in the North Cascades* can be a gentle way to "get back in the saddle" and try a few trails, all within driving distance of a comfortable overnight lodging. Included are short hikes and even easy walks of less than a mile.

Maybe you have children, or a spouse or a friend, who is new to hiking. This book will help you choose trails appropriate to their level of ambition and conditioning, and provide everyone in your party with an enjoyable wilderness experience.

Maybe you're an experienced hiker—a backpacker, even—whose idea of heaven is a week-long trudge in backcountry isolation. But you don't *have* a full week to kill every time you get the urge to hike. This book is for you—it will let you get out on the trail for a day or two when you have the chance.

Maybe you're new to the Pacific Northwest, or just visiting. In the pages that follow, you'll find an introduction to the various parts of the North Cascades. Choose the historic, topographic, and scenic features that appeal to you, and head out with confidence. Each region described has easy, moderate, and more challenging dayhike trails.

Or maybe you're like me, a Pacific Northwest native who knows a few trails and has already discovered the joy of hiking from a comfortable lodg-

Start your day with a good breakfast

ing. You need this book for its lodging and hiking descriptions, to help you make informed choices before you head out, and avoid nasty surprises.

What are the "North Cascades?"

The Cascade mountain range runs north-south from British Columbia, Canada, through Washington and Oregon, into northern California. The definition of "North Cascades" is subjective. Some might define it as the North Cascades National Park, a US National Park Service property that extends from the US-Canada border south, encompassing the Ross Lake National Recreation Area and the Lake Chelan National Recreation Area. Others might say it's the area around the North Cascades Highway (Washington State Highway 20), the scenic highway completed in 1972, the US's northernmost east-west highway in the Cascades. Others would include the part of the Cascade range that extends into British Columbia.

This book concentrates on exceptional dayhike trails near lodgings. Toward that end, our geographic area includes the mountains and foothills of the Cascade range from the US-Canada border to the Interstate 90 corridor in Washington State. This includes both the North Cascades National Park and the North Cascades Highway, but also includes parts of the Mt. Baker–Snoqualmie, Okanogan, and Wenatchee national forests and the Mt. Baker, Glacier Peak, Alpine Lakes, and Pasayten wilderness areas.

How This Book Is Organized

Hot Showers, Soft Beds, and Dayhikes in the North Cascades is organized into 9 geographic sections, beginning in the northwest corner of the coverage area, then proceeding west-to-east, north-to-south. In other words, the way you read a page of text: left-to-right, top-to-bottom. The organization follows major highways (except in the case of *Section 5, Stehekin,* where there *is* no highway; in fact, there are no roads in—you have to get there by air or water).

Section 1 - Mt. Baker Highway
Highway 542 from Maple Falls to Mt. Baker
Section 2 - Highway 20 West
Sedro Woolley to Ross Lake
Section 3 - Winthrop/Mazama/Twisp
Methow Valley, Highway 20 East
Section 4 - Mountain Loop Highway
Darrington/Monte Cristo/Granite Falls
Section 5 - Stehekin
Section 6 - Skykomish
Gold Bar to Stevens Pass, Highway 2 West
Section 7 - Leavenworth
Cascade Foothills, Highway 2 East
Section 8 - Snoqualmie West
I-90 from Snoqualmie Pass West
Section 9 - Cle Elum/Roslyn
I-90 East

Within each section, any lodging listed is within driving distance of any of the dayhikes listed (except in the case of *Ross Lake Resort, Section 2,* an isolated resort listed with its own set of trails).

About the Hikes

The walks and hikes included in this book range from short strolls of less than a mile to full-day adventures of 10 or 12 miles or more. Most are between 2 and 8 miles. All are considered "dayhikes," hikes that the moderately fit individual without mobility impairment could drive to, hike, and return to any of the lodgings in the section before dark.

Each hike begins with a listing of distance (usually round-trip), elevation gain or loss, and estimated time. Naturally, the "estimated time" is highly subjective. It is usually based on a moderately brisk pace (2 miles per hour, slower if steep), with time to stop and observe the flora and natural features of the trail.

Elevation gain is provided to help you get an idea of the steepness and relative difficulty of the hike. Experienced hikers will find this more useful than novices. For those of you new to hiking, bear in mind Sally's Elevation Rule Of Thumb: 1000 feet per mile = butt-kicker. The difficulty increases geometrically if this pitch continues for a number of miles. (Example: Section 4, Mt. Dickerman: 8.6 miles, 3700' elevation gain. 8.6 round trip = 4.3 miles each way. 3700 ÷ 4.3 = 860 feet per mile, extended over 4+ miles. In other words, this *will* be a butt-kicker to the moderately fit dayhiker.) Elevation figures in this text are sometimes rounded off, using a combination of topo map review, US Forest Service information, and, occasionally, an altimeter.

At the end of each section, *"Other Hike Notes"* is a listing of hikes which did not merit a complete write-up, either because I did not personally review them or because I do not recommended them. The descriptions of these hikes are shorter and less detailed. If a hike is not recommended, the brief description explains why.

Always obtain and use a topographical map when hiking in the wilderness. Recommended maps are listed at the beginning of each hike. Green Trails maps are excellent because their scale is large enough to show detail, but the maps are small enough to be conveniently carried. Most outdoor stores carry them. USGS topographical maps are also useful, but can be bulky. For many of the hikes, you can contact the ranger district listed at the end of that hike's section. The maps and handouts they provide, along with the detailed descriptions in this book, may be sufficient for some of the hikes. Note that the US Forest Service changed the numbering system of its roads in the early 1980's. You may run across older maps which use the old numbering system. To avoid confusion, obtain current maps.

The hikes are not rated for beauty or for difficulty. If they weren't incredibly beautiful, they weren't included. Difficulty is in the eye of the beholder (or the thighs of the hiker…). A flat 12-mile round trip might feel easier than a steep 4-miler to one hiker, but harder to another. In general, hikes in each section are listed in their approximate order of difficulty, with easy strolls and walks first, followed by easy hikes, followed by moderate hikes, followed by a challenging hike or two. Your best bet is to read the descriptions thoroughly.

While I have attempted to classify certain hikes as especially appropriate or especially inappropriate for children, it should be noted that a wilderness experience always carries with it certain dangers. Children should be mindful of the dangers posed by slippery rocks, talus surfaces, wildlife seen and unseen, rivers and streams, and drop-offs—nature does not provide hand rails and warning signs.

Be aware that hiking trails and access roads are subject to change over time: forks appear and disappear from use and disuse; washouts and other phenomena—natural and man-made—necessitate re-routing. Also note that mileage calculations vary from one source to another. Various hiking guides may differ on mileage for the same hike. Official Forest Service mileage often differs from that shown on a USGS map or a Green Trails map. Posted mileage often differs from printed information. Mileage in this book was based on a combination of Forest Service information, time/distance calculation, and use of a pedometer.

About the Lodgings

A wide variety of lodging styles were included: four-star resorts, humble cabins, charming B&B's, basic motels. Their common criteria were (1) they were located within easy access distance to the hikes in their section, (2) they were clean and comfortable, with hot showers and soft beds, and (3) they were a good value for their type of lodging in their geographic area. A $40 motel room will obviously offer a different experience than a $175 resort suite, but both can be good values.

Lodgings are not rated. If a lodging is listed under *Lodgings* and a full description is given, that lodging has been reviewed and it is recommended. Please read the descriptions and understand, while all accommodations detailed are recommended, that "rustic" is different than "elegant." In some cases, a brief listing of *Additional Lodgings* follows the detailed descriptions of recommended lodgings; these establishments were visited, but not reviewed in detail and are not endorsed by the author.

In each section, I listed lodgings in my personal, subjective order of preference. The lodgings with particular charm or uniqueness, or operated by proprietors who really went out of their way to please, are usually listed first (or second or third if there are two or three) in their section. A lodging listed farther down is still recommended, but might be more standard.

At the end of each *Lodgings* section is a grid listing objective features such as price, number of rooms or units, amenities such as swimming pool and hot tub, and policies for children and pets.

All prices and features were collected during the summer of 1996 and are subject to change. Prices are summer rates, pre-tax, and are generally for two persons unless otherwise stated. Add-on prices for additional persons are given where applicable. Advance reservations are strongly encouraged at all lodgings.

Other Information

A brief list of recommended dining establishments has been provided for each area. Other useful information, including items of historic and geologic significance, has been included, as well as contacts for Chambers of Commerce.

As this book emphasizes hiking from lodgings, information about camping is not provided. Ranger districts, listed at the end of each section, can help with this information if you plan to camp all or part of your vacation in the North Cascades.

This is not a wilderness survival text. If you plan to venture beyond the recommended routes, please check with local rangers and arm yourself with the appropriate topographic maps and other texts.

Staying Current

Every effort has been made to ensure that all lodging and trail information was accurate at press time. Always check trail and access road conditions before heading out to hike. Telephone numbers are provided in each section.

It's also a good idea to phone lodgings in advance. Rates, policies, and amenities are subject to change.

Safety and Sense

Even short dayhikes are wilderness experiences, and should be approached with caution, respect, and common sense.

Always tell someone where you're going and approximately when you expect to be back. This is another advantage to staying in a lodging: you can tell your hosts. If someone is expecting you, you won't have as long to wait should something unexpected happen along the trail. Self-registry at many trailheads is another safeguard. If you have an opportunity to sign in, do so.

Always set out with a full tank of gas and a topped-off radiator. Very few of the hikes in the book involve lengthy drives, but many are on unpaved, somewhat difficult roads, and some require your vehicle to climb steep stretches of road. Check with the local rangers as to access road conditions before you start out. Note that all hikes included in this book can be reached with a normal passenger car under normal circumstances; a 4-wheel-drive vehicle is not required.

Don't leave valuables in your car at the trailhead. Better yet, don't drive a valuable car to the trailhead. And don't assume that your trunk or your glove compartment is safe from trailhead thugs.

Anytime you venture away from town or your vehicle, you are subject to the vicissitudes of wilderness and weather. For that reason, stock your daypack with:

- Water—more than you think you need—and extra food.
- Extra clothing, including rain gear, dry socks, hat, and gloves.
- Map and compass (and the knowledge to use them).
- First aid kit.
- Flashlight.
- Sunscreen and sunglasses.
- Matches (waterproof) and fire-starter (such as a candle).
- Whistle and signal mirror.
- Pocket knife.
- Insect repellent.
- Trowel or small shovel (see *Manners*, below).

Dayhikers often underpack water. Sure, it's heavy, but running out is a nuisance, and dehydration can be very dangerous, leading to disorientation even on a dayhike, and organ damage over a prolonged period. And, no, you can't (or shouldn't) drink from sources along the trail. Giardia and other dangerous bacteria and microorganisms are odorless, tasteless, and everywhere; the only safe water is that which you pack along or purify. For dayhikes, why not just pack it in?

It's a good idea for *each* hiker in your party—child and adult—to have a basic "survival" kit on their person; often, a fanny pack will do. This provides an extra measure of safety, should you become separated. The personal kit should contain some nutrient-dense food (such as Power Bars), a whistle, and a small flashlight. Those with the knowledge to use them should have a knife, a compass, waterproof matches, and a fire-starter candle as well. And everyone should carry his or her water. Instruct children to STAY PUT if lost, to signal for help if they're able, and not to resist or hide from rescuers.

Extra clothing may seem an excessive precaution for the dayhiker. It's probably not necessary on short strolls a mile from the car, but for longer hikes, it's really a good idea to be prepared for the unexpected. A shift in weather (common in the North Cascades!) or simply a change in terrain, can change the climate of your hike. You can be on a hot, open, rocky ridge at 9 A.M., in a moist, cool, shady creekbed at

10, and crossing the remainder of a chilly, late-season snowfield at 11. And, in the North Cascades, raingear is always in order. This should not discourage your enjoyment of this magnificent wilderness; indeed, extremes in weather are part of its beauty. The person who embraces Mother Nature in all of her vagaries—from pearly overcast to tumbling thunderheads to blinding blue skies—will be the one who gets the most out of the North Cascades.

Mosquitoes and blackflies can be thick in parts of the North Cascades, especially in midsummer. While insect repellent is useful, your best defense is a sense of humor and acceptance. Expose as little skin as possible, or bring a bandanna to brush across your legs and arms as you walk. A few areas, most notoriously *Section 9, Cle Elum/Roslyn,* are also home to ticks. They don't seem to be affected by insect repellent. Check your skin and scalp thoroughly after hiking in an area with ticks.

Another item I recommend is pepper spray—and make sure you get one that is rated for bear attack, with adequate quantity and spray range (preferably 30 feet). It should have a locking device to prevent accidental spraying, and some sort of holster with a quick-release mechanism for immediate access. Using a thumb or index finger trigger, you simply aim and shoot. Black bears are common in many areas of the North Cascades, and grizzlies have been sighted. Of course, the wilderness is the bears' home, not yours, so I hope you never have to use it. Your best defense against bears is to avoid startling them. Make a bit of noise as you travel, and keep an eye peeled.

A major pepper spray manufacturer suggests the following 3-step approach:

1. If a bear approaches, shoot a cloud of pepper spray toward it when it is about 30 feet from you.
2. If it continues to advance, aim another 2 short blasts at its face when it is about 20 feet from you.
3. If it advances within 10 feet of you, spray continuously, aiming directly at the bear's face and eyes.

Pepper spray is also a good idea for women hikers, or anyone concerned about personal defense against the human element.

Rattlesnakes are another wilderness bugaboo. I have tried to indicate hikes on which these reptilian friends are particularly common. Be alert on sun-warmed, south-facing slopes. If you see one, let it pass. As with bears, the best defense is to avoid startling them. Thump a walking stick on the ground as you travel, carry on a quiet conversation, hum a little tune. In other words, be yourself. *They* don't like *you* much, either.

A walking stick, in addition to warning snakes (and other wildlife, especially if it has a little bell attached), comes in handy for stream fording. For longer hikes, or if you want to maintain a brisk pace, consider "trekking poles." These poles, singly or in pairs, are like short ski poles. An orthopedist we met en route to Hidden Lake Peaks (see *Section 4*) insisted that they are the best device ever for saving wear and tear on the knees.

Please don't be a "tennis shoe hiker." This term of derision—often referring to attitude as well as footwear—arose again and again in my conversations with rangers and veteran hikers. Hiking boots have tread and ankle support for a reason. If you're doing a paved quarter-mile stroll from your car, tennies are fine. But if a trail has any

A walking stick can come in handy for those early-season creek crossings

elevation gain, or surfaces described as "rocky" or "rooty," wear something intended for hiking. When in doubt, err on the conservative side—wear the boots. If you're new to hiking, by all means break them in by wearing them around the house, then around town, before using them on the trail.

Manners

Speaking of "tennis shoe hikers," it's a pity some people don't know how to treat the wilderness. It is a precious gift deserving our respect.

Littering is an obvious no-no. Fortunately, most travelers to the North Cascades seem to understand and respect that. For those who don't, you might want to carry an extra plastic bag along for their trash as well as yours. Plan to pack out every scrap you pack in, including orange peels, apple cores, and nut shells. The wildlife does not need your semi-edible refuse, and its introduction to their environment can be detrimental to them. And it won't "just return to the soil." Not fast enough, anyway. Just pack it out. Most trailheads don't have trash cans, so plan to take it back to your lodging with you. Never, never, put garbage in a pit toilet.

Please don't feed wildlife. Not even the squirrels and chipmunks and camp jays who come begging and might well eat from your hand. The saddest sight I saw during my research was a young doe, glassy-eyed and disoriented, at a popular highwayside trailhead, begging for "people food." Unthinking tourists of all ages and nationalities were rushing for their cameras as a family dug for their Doritos and fed this poor, formerly wild creature. I was sickened as I realized how she would die: either starving this winter, having forgotten how to forage, or getting hit by a car as she stumbled, in a sugar-induced haze, for a potential Oreo on the other side of the road.

Stay on the trail. Cutting switchbacks and trampling meadows cause erosion and flora damage that will only worsen with time.

Dispose of human waste properly. When toilets aren't available, urinate on rocks or bare soil, not on foliage. Bury feces 4–6 inches deep (here's where that trowel comes in), and use only biodegradable toilet paper (available in RV or camping stores). Always choose spots at least 100 yards from water sources.

Do not collect rocks, flowers, mushrooms, or anything else without checking beforehand with the ranger or administrative jurisdiction responsible for the area in which you are hiking.

Generally speaking, do not build fires. If your dayhike picnic plans call for something hot, consider bringing it in a thermos or packing along a camp stove. Fires in designated campsites can be an exception, but these should generally be left to the backpackers and campers.

Many of the trails in the North Cascades are for hikers only: closed to stock and/or bicycles. Be sure to check before hitting the trail with anything but your feet.

Pets are not allowed on some trails, and are required to be leashed on others. Such regulations change all the time, please check before bringing your pet.

Who You Gonna Call?

Following are a few numbers of general interest when making your plans in the North Cascades. Area-specific numbers are listed under *Contacts* at the end of each section.

NATIONAL WEATHER FORECAST, SEATTLE OFFICE	(206) 526-6087
NORTHWEST WEATHER & AVALANCHE CENTER	(206) 526-6677
OUTDOOR RECREATION INFORMATION CENTER (ORIC) (a joint Forest Service/National Park Service venture) 915 Second Ave., Suite 442, Seattle, WA 98174	(206) 220-7450
PASS REPORTS	
AAA	(206) 646-2190
WASHINGTON STATE DEPARTMENT OF TRANSPORTATION	1-888-SNOINFO
Washington State Highway Patrol	
EMERGENCY LINE	1-800-283-7808
WASHINGTON STATE PARKS INFORMATION	1-800-233-0321

Section 1—Mt. Baker Highway

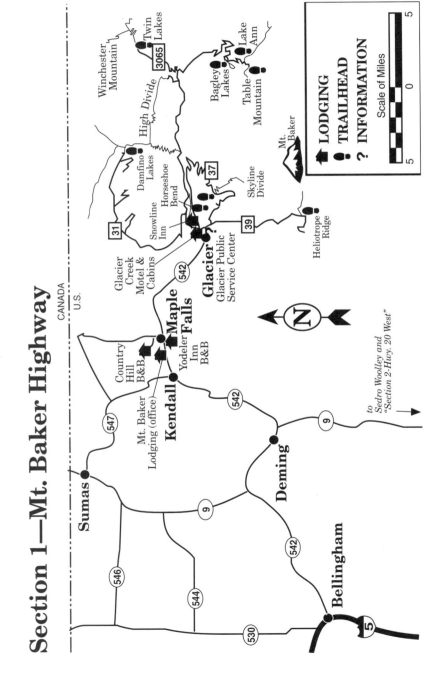

Mt. Baker Highway
(Maple Falls to Artist's Point)

Overview

Highway 542, also known as the Mt. Baker Highway, is the access route to some of the most majestic and most easily obtained vistas in the North Cascades—perhaps the world. Indeed, it's not uncommon to hear German, French, and Italian being spoken along the trails in this area as increasing numbers of Alp-weary Europeans discover the unspoiled beauty of this Pacific Northwest paradise.

To reach the Mt. Baker Highway, take Interstate 5 to Bellingham, ninety miles north of Seattle. Take Exit 255, STATE HIGHWAY 542, also known in Bellingham as Sunset Drive. Unlike Washington State Highway 20, US Highway 2, and Interstate 90, Highway 542 is not a route through the Cascades—it is a 62-mile spur highway to Mt. Baker. En route, it passes through Nugent's Corner (a scattering of services at the junction of Highway 9, 14 miles south of the Canadian border), Deming (home of the Nooksack tribal casino), and Kendall (junction with Highway 547, 11 miles south of the border) before reaching Maple Falls and the gateway to the recreation corridor.

Maple Falls, 27 miles from the I-5/542 junction, is the site of several lodgings, a family restaurant, a gas station, and two stores. The unassuming little burg has a surprisingly colorful history. With five full-scale brothels, Maple Falls was "prostitution central" in the 1800's, serving the miners, loggers, and railroad men of the region during the boom days. Much of the Town Of Ill Repute burned to the ground at the end of this heyday, and the religious folk of the neighboring town (where the fire station was located) just let it burn.

Eight miles beyond Maple Falls, you will reach the town of Glacier. The final town before Mt. Baker and road's end, Glacier is home to two motels, a few stores, and two good eateries. This area is becoming increasingly developed to take advantage of the Mt. Baker ski trade, as evidenced by several housing developments clustered around the town's few services.

The Glacier Public Service Center, a ranger station built with Civilian Conservation Corps labor in 1938, is located half a mile east of Glacier. Listed in the National Register of Historic Places and open during the summer months only, this dignified stone-and-beam structure houses an interpretive center, clean restrooms, a gift shop, and extremely helpful US Forest Service personnel.

Staying in either Maple Falls or Glacier, you will have easy access to all that the Mt. Baker wilderness has to offer. Maple Falls is just 34 miles from the highway's end at Kulshan Ridge/Artist Point, and trailheads are located all along the highway from Glacier east. With incredible views of Mt. Baker and Mt. Shuksan from virtually every trail, you'll want to have clear skies to hike this area (cloudy or rainy day alternatives include Bagley Lakes and Horseshoe Bend). If you're graced with blue skies, you'll find the "up close and personal" experience of Mt. Baker and Mt. Shuksan unparalleled. From the amazingly easy Table Mountain and Skyline Divide hikes, you can all but reach out and touch the snow-capped peaks.

But, speaking of snow…

Here's the catch. Because the Mt. Baker environs receives over 60 *feet* of snow annually (one of the heaviest averages in the nation), the prime hiking season can be unmercifully short. The road to Kulshan Ridge/Artist Point may not be open until well into August, and many of the trails remain impassable, snow-covered or icy-muddy, after that. Here, more than anywhere else, remember to check conditions before you visit the area.

Lodgings

YODELER INN B&B
P.O. Box 222, Maple Falls, WA 98244
1-800-642-9033 or (360) 599-2156

Convenient, comfortable, and cheerful, the Yodeler Inn B&B is located right on the highway at Maple Falls, 27 miles east of the I-5/Highway 542 junction in Bellingham. Hosts Jeff and Bethnie Morrison are an energetic young couple with a

Yodeler Inn B&B

genuine interest in making your stay laid back and comfortable. They anticipate your needs with pleasant little extras such as a coffee/tea bar and chocolates in your room, and shampoo and sundries in the bath. Plenty of soft fluffy towels are provided to encourage your use of the hot tub.

Accommodations at the Yodeler are simple and homey—one unit in the main house and a cottage unit out back. The main house unit has a double and a single bed, and a private entrance. The cottage, a bit more rustic and private, has a queen bed and a small kitchenette. Both units have a table and chairs, cable television, and a private bath (shower only, no tub); both are nonsmoking. Each rents for $65 for two persons; additional persons $10 each.

Guests select their own free continental breakfast items at the adjacent mini-mart, also owned by Bethnie and Jeff. Espresso drinks, coffee, tea, and juices are available, as well as a selection of bagels, croissants, scones, and other pastries, some freshly made. This little convenience store/laundry/gas station (cleverly named "Maple Fuels Wash-a-Ton"—in Maple Falls, Washington, get it?) is open 6 A.M.–10 P.M., and also offers fax and photocopy service and an ATM.

Highlight: Friendly young hosts; adjacent to well-stocked mini-mart/laundry/gas station.

MT. BAKER LODGING
P.O. Box 5177, Glacier, WA 98244
1-800-709-SNOW or (360) 599-2453

Mt. Baker Lodging manages a collection of 20 private vacation homes in developments off Highway 542. The homes vary in size, quality, and amenities, but all

Private vacation home managed by Mt. Baker Lodgings

have functional kitchens (some are more complete than others, with microwave and dishwasher) and a fireplace or woodstove. Other features may include hot tub, TV/VCR, game room, pool table, barbecue. Not all units have telephones.

Several of the homes are quite deluxe. If possible, view them before you make your selection for the best value. If this is not possible, ask for one of the newer units.

While sleeping capacity ranges from two to twelve persons, all rent for $99 for two, $10 for each additional person. Some homes are better suited to a romantic honeymoon getaway, others to families or groups. Ask for an information packet to review each home's list of amenities, then talk with manager Barbara Stein about the choice that's best for you.

Mt. Baker Lodging receives its mail in Glacier, but the rental office is housed in a trailer in Maple Falls. As you enter town heading east, watch for the sign on your left. The office is down this driveway, not visible from the road.

Highlight: A range of private vacation homes—great for longer stays!

COUNTRY HILL B&B
P.O. Box 186, Maple Falls, WA 98266
(360) 599-1049 or (360) 599-2047

Cliff and Dolores LaBounty offer a two-room suite with a private entrance on the top floor of their mountaintop home above Maple Falls. The house (some of which was originally built in 1916, but you'd never know it!) has been a work in progress since Cliff purchased it in 1963.

The B&B suite includes a country-motif bedroom with king-size bed, TV/VCR with movies, and heated towel rack, plus a sitting room with a double hide-a-bed and coffee bar (microwave and small refrigerator enable light meal preparation; dishes and utensils provided). Books and games are provided for your use, as are many toiletries and convenience items.

A generous continental breakfast delivered to your room may include fruit, muffins, yogurt, cereal, and juice.

The room, for two, with breakfast, is $75 per night on Friday or Saturday, $65 Sunday through Thursday. Additional persons may stay on the hide-a-bed at $10 apiece per night. Holiday rates are higher, and may require a minimum stay. Cash or checks only; no children, pets, or smoking.

From the Silver Lake Road and Highway 542 junction in Maple Falls, turn north on Silver Lake Road (toward Silver Lake Park, 3.5 miles from town). After 0.4 mile, turn left onto a primitive gravel drive marked COUNTRY HILL B&B, 7968 SILVER LAKE ROAD. Follow this steep, somewhat harrowing drive up, up, up another 0.3 mile until the property emerges from the forest at the top of the hill. (Truly not a road for the faint-of-heart, but the view will be worth it for many. Use extreme caution.) Continue straight ahead and park behind the house, between the rear entrance and Cliff's shop.

Highlight: Spacious suite with king-size bed and hilltop view.

Country Hill B&B has great views

GLACIER CREEK MOTEL & CABINS
P.O. Box 5008, Glacier, WA 98244
(360) 599-2991

Situated in a modest, park-like setting at the east end of the town of Glacier, this selection of 9 motel rooms and 12 cabins is open year-round. The premises are older, but clean and tidy, and conveniently located. As some of the units allow pets ($5.00 additional charge), and children are welcome throughout the property, Glacier Creek can be a useful alternative.

Motel room units start at $40 for one person, with rooms for two to four persons $42–$70. One-room cabins start at $60 for two persons. Two-bedroom cabins with kitchenettes sleep 3 to 6 persons for $75–$105. A duplex cabin with two baths and a pass-through door rents for $110 for four persons (both sides). The largest unit, a house with complete kitchen, full bath with tub, living room with wood stove, and sleeping room for up to six, rents for $115–$135. Rates may vary seasonally.

Highlight: Wide variety of motel and cabin accommodations; great for families.

SNOWLINE INN
P.O. Box 5051, Glacier, WA 98244
1-800-228-0119 or (360) 599-2788

If location is your prime consideration, and luxury is optional, consider Snowline Inn. The nearest lodging to Mt. Baker, Snowline Inn caters to the active crowd. Rooms all include equipped kitchenettes, table, chairs, and TV (although local reception leaves a bit to be desired!). Furnishings are a bit dated and worn, but the premises are clean and the managers pride themselves on keeping it quiet, even during the potentially rowdy ski season. A word of caution: each room is served by an individual hot water tank, and it's a small one. Navy-style showers (get wet, soap up with the water off, then rinse) are the only way to get a hot one.

The Inn is located one mile east of the Glacier Public Service Center, which puts it just 17 miles from the ski slopes and 25 miles from road's end at Kulshan Ridge/Artist Point.

Two types of rooms are available: studio units (most configured with a double or queen bed and a set of bunks) and loft units (various bed configurations designed to accommodate four people comfortably, on two levels). Studio units rent for $55 (summer) or $65 (winter) for two people; $5 per extra person. Loft units rent for $75 (summer) or $85 (winter) for two to four people; more at $5 if the room is appropriate for more. Weekly and special group rates available. Smoking and nonsmoking rooms available.

Highlight: Closest lodging to Mt. Baker.

Dining

The Mt. Baker Highway corridor mourned the passing of a 13-year fine dining tradition with the closure of Innisfree Restaurant in October of 1996. Operating at 9393 Mt. Baker Highway, between Maple Falls and Glacier, this destination restaurant was started as the culmination of a dream by organic farmers and culinary experts Fred and Lynn Berman in 1984, and drew rave reviews from far and wide.

The Bermans reluctantly (and perhaps temporarily) closed to pursue another restaurant project in Bellingham, but watch for a possible future re-opening.

MILANO'S MARKET & DELI
9990 Mt. Baker Highway, Glacier, WA 98244
(360) 599-2863

You can't miss this little restaurant as you drive through Glacier: it sits on the north side of the highway in the one-block strip of "downtown" Glacier. Milano's logo and brochure say "pasta fresca," and, indeed, Milano's claim to fame is its fresh pasta, made on the premises. Enjoy it tossed with pesto, alfredo, or marinara and sausage, or in more elaborate configurations such as *puttanesca* (with tomatoes, capers, olives, and hot chiles), *foriana* (with garlic, anchovies, raisins, chiles, and pine nuts), or traditional *carbonara* (with pastrami, eggs, and cream). Lasagna and a variety of ravioli are also available, as are specialties including a smoked salmon-tossed fettucine, chicken parmigiano or gorgonzola, and eggplant parmigiano. All pasta and specialty entrees at Milano's are $9.25, and include salad and bread, except the linguine *vongole* ("with clams"), available on selected weekends at $10.75. Half orders of most entrees can be selected for $6.50, and daily specials are offered.

Milano's Deli prepares fresh sandwiches, with standard favorites $4.25 on your choice of bread. Or make a meal out of their made-to-order Caesar salad. Served with bread, it's $6.95 for two, $10.95 for four. Homemade minestrone soup is also available, plus a selection of *traditionale* desserts from $1.75 to $3.25. And, of course, espresso drinks.

All menu items are also available to go, and sauces and pastas can be ordered separately to put together yourself back at your kitchenette or cabin. *Delicioso!*

Highlight: Freshly made pasta with creative sauces.

EL PAVO REAL
9989 Mt. Baker Highway, Glacier, WA 98244
(360) 599-2141

Quirky, quirky, quirky...but in a *good* way. El Pavo Real is a flung-together fresh-mex restaurant that will make you smile and fill your belly after a long day's hike—without setting your wallet back much.

Located across the street from Milano's in the sprawling one-block metropolis of downtown Glacier, El Pavo Real serves up a modest menu of Mexican fare. The most expensive item is an enchilada-style burrito for $6.50, filled with your choice of beef and beans, lime tequila chicken and black beans, spicy chicken and black beans, or mixed vegetables and beans. Tacos, $2.50 for "uno" and $4.50 for "dos," offer the same filling choices. Also available are a chicken enchilada pie and a vegetarian tamale pot pie, each for $5.50. Other choices include quesadillas, tostadas, taco salads, and some sort of daily special.

As El Pavo Real serves only beer and wine (or grab your own soda from the fridge), they offer up a unique selection of sake drinks. (Wait a minute...isn't that Japanese?) Try a sake margarita or Bloody Mary if you dare.

But it isn't just the drink menu that will crack you up. The decor at El Pavo Real runs the gamut from legitimate antiques to black velvet Elvises to Tijuana souvenirs to midwestern yard-sale chic. And watch that rubber chicken when you slam the door.

Highlight: Fun, quirky Mexican fare at bargain prices.

FROSTY INN
7461 Mt. Baker Highway, Maple Falls, WA 98266
(360) 599-2594

I'll admit it…when I saw the Frosty Inn, I almost didn't stop. Boy, would that have been a mistake. Not only are owner Eileen Foster and operators Craig and Tracy Willis (Eileen's son and daughter-in-law) some of the friendliest and most knowledgeable folks in the area, the food is terrific, too! If the building looks a bit worn around the edges, you can forgive that, too—it's part of Maple Falls' history, originally built by Charles Frost about 75 years ago.

There is nothing startling about the menu at Frosty Inn: burgers, prime rib, fish and chips, hearty breakfasts. What's startling is the preparation and care that go into this little operation. The proprietors oven-bake a fresh turkey daily, for starters. They make their soups from scratch. The vegetables are grown in their own garden. Out-of-this-world fish and chips are the result of a secret family recipe from their Welsh forefathers.

Complete dinners (chicken, seafood, hand-selected aged beef) range from $7.95 to $12.95. Burgers and sandwiches for lunch start at $3.95 including fries, soup, or salad. And those hearty breakfasts? You'll find all your standard favorites, reasonably priced, including a "Mountain Man" steak and eggs extravaganza and eggs benedict with homemade hollandaise.

Frosty's recently added pizza to its menu, too—available evenings. A large 2-topping runs $12.85, and a combo is $15.25.

Highlight: Wide variety of standard fare; friendly proprietors.

Walks and Hikes
Listed in approximate order of difficulty

BAGLEY LAKES LOOP

Map:	Green Trails #14 "Mt. Shuksan" shows the area, but only Trail #682 Chain Lakes (which forms the western second half of the loop) shows on the map; the trail as a loop is explained below
Distance:	1.5 mile loop
Elevation Gain:	None
Estimated Time:	45 minutes to 1 hour
Highlight:	Pretty, all-weather walk through heathered meadows.

Bagley Lakes is an easy loop trail through open, heathered meadows featuring two glacial tarns. You'll find it sparkling on a sunny day, and mystical in fog or drizzle.

With lake views, wildflowers, and crossings of both a picturesque stone bridge and a little dam, this makes an excellent hike with children.

Getting There

The best way to reach this hike is from an unmarked ski-area parking lot just beyond the Mt. Baker ski area. The road divides briefly into two separated lanes of one-way traffic near the ski area. Heading southeast (toward Mt. Baker), the two lanes come together again just past the ski area. One-tenth of a mile past this merge point, watch for a NO OVERNIGHT CAMPING AT HEATHER MEADOWS sign on your right. Turn into the unmarked parking lot just beyond this sign. Directions below are from this parking lot.

The Bagley Lakes Loop can also be accessed from the large parking area at the Heather Meadows visitor center, 0.6 mile farther south on the highway. This access results in a bit of a climb to reach the trail. If you choose this parking lot, you will drop down the hill below the visitor center and begin the loop at the Twin Arch stone bridge (midway through the loop as detailed below).

The Hike

Signs from the parking lot lead to WILD GOOSE TRAIL and BAGLEY LAKES TRAIL; head down the gentle slope toward the lakes trail. After 0.2 mile, follow another sign left to stay on Bagley Lakes Trail; Chain Lakes Trail forks to the right (you will be returning via the Chain Lakes Trail).

Stroll the level, crushed rock trail alongside the Lower Bagley Lake until you reach the Twin Arch stone bridge at 0.75 mile. The larger Upper Bagley Lake lies in front of you on the other side of the bridge. To make this a loop trail, cross the bridge

Mt. Shuksan

and then turn right, following the Chain Lakes Trail back. (NOTE: While this is a very easy hike, surfaces on the Chain Lakes Trail part of the loop are more uneven; those unsure of their footing might wish to turn around at the bridge and retrace their steps.)

Back at the parking-lot end of the loop (the parking lot is visible above), cross little Bagley Dam, then come to the Bagley Lakes/Chain Lakes trail junction you saw at the beginning of the walk. Ascend to the parking lot.

HORSESHOE BEND

Map:	Green Trails #13 "Mt. Baker"
Distance:	3.0 miles round trip
Elevation Gain:	Negligible
Estimated Time:	1 hour, 30 minutes
Highlight:	Easy stroll through rain-forest-style beauty alongside a wild river.

Horseshoe Bend is a magical walk through a verdant forest rife with ferns and mosses alongside a milky-white, glacier-fed river. The tumbling sight and rushing sound of the wild Nooksack River provide an exciting contrast to the tranquillity of this all-weather hike.

Getting There

Heading east (toward Mt. Baker) on Highway 542, just after crossing the North Fork Nooksack River, pull off to the right (1.7 miles east of the Glacier Public Service Center). A wide (but unsigned) shoulder provides parking for river rafters and Horseshoe Bend hikers. The well-signed Mt. Baker-Snoqualmie Forest Douglas Fir Campground is immediately across the road.

Walk back toward the bridge and you'll notice a set of steps with handrails descending to the river and the trail. A sign, not noticeable from the road, marks the trail at the top of the steps.

The Hike

At the bottom of the steps, turn left. (Going right, under the bridge, takes you into the Douglas Fir campground.) A crushed-rock trail leads you into a lush, ferny forest alongside the boiling Nooksack. Moss-hung Douglas-fir and cedar tower above, and tangled vine maple grows thick in the understory.

After a few hundred feet of walking immediately adjacent to the river, log steps lead you left and up to a higher level, still paralleling the river. Make a mental note of these steps—they are more obvious in this direction than on the return trip.

This hike provides several opportunities to get a close-up look at the Nooksack River. Obviously, caution is in order—explore this water with your eyes only. A bench is provided at water's edge at about 0.75 mile.

At about 1.0 mile, the trail bends left, and the river "follows"—one can assume this is the bend from which the trail derives its name. Another left bend follows at about 1.2 miles. At this point, the trail begins to climb, and the best is behind you. If you choose to continue, you will emerge in a field underneath telephone poles. By beating your way through the brush on the now-faint path, you will intersect an old dirt road at 1.4 miles. If you turn right on this road, you will spot the faint continuation of the trail after another 0.1 mile. At this point, the path seriously deteriorates and does not draw near the river again anytime soon.

Retrace your steps, keeping a keen eye out for a left-hand fork leading to the descending log steps a few hundred feet from the trailhead.

TABLE MOUNTAIN

Map:	Green Trails #14 "Mt. Shuksan"
Distance:	2.0 miles round trip
Elevation Gain:	600'
Estimated Time:	1 hour, 30 minutes
Highlight:	Amazing alpine views just a mile from your car!

Don't miss this hike. Those who don't hike at all should come for the views from the parking lot, and those who think a 2-mile hike is too short should think again. (Besides, the hike outlined here can be extended to a 3.4-mile loop, or even to a 10+ mile trek out Ptarmigan Ridge or down to Chain Lakes and Bagley Lakes. See the Glacier Public Service Center or the Heather Meadows visitor center for maps and information on these longer options.)

Bring your sunglasses; the combination of sun and snow is dazzling. Bring a camera; the views, the lighting, the backdrops are perfect. Bring a picnic; it's only a mile up, but you'll want an excuse to linger. And bring the kids. Sure, it's a little steep, and the ascent can be a bit of a rock scramble in places, but it's short, and they won't see views like this for so little effort *anywhere* else.

Getting There

This is the Hike At The End of The Road. By mid-August, Highway 542 is open (and paved) all the way to its magnificent end point, known as Kulshan Ridge/Artist Point. Some 31 miles past the town of Glacier, this trailhead area and vista point at 5100' draws throngs of tourists daily. Restrooms are provided. In the parking lot, you'll see everything from shorts, thongs, and bikini tops to hiking boots, packs, and Gore-Tex. The amazing thing is how few members of this crowd leave the parking lot and go up the mountain.

Don't miss the hike to Table Mountain

The Hike

The trailhead for Table Mountain may or may not be marked (a sign is usually put in place by mid-August, when the snow melts sufficiently), and the beginning of the trail is often covered in snow in the early part of the season. Ask a ranger or another hiker if you are unsure where to begin. Basically, you will be heading west toward the flat-topped "table-" looking mountain on the side of the parking lot opposite the mighty, glacier-covered flanks of Mt. Shuksan.

Cross a quarter-mile of meadow at a modest incline along the flanks of Table Mountain before ascending the switchbacks that take you steeply up its side. If snow-free, the dirt-and-gravel path is well-maintained and easy to follow. You'll want to pause often and goggle at Baker and Shuksan.

Near the top, the path contours left and around before it arrives at the table-flat top. The awesome 360° view includes far-off Baker Lake to the south and the Chain Lakes below you to the northwest.

DAMFINO LAKES TO HIGH DIVIDE

Map:	Green Trails #13 "Mt. Baker"
Distance:	6.0 miles round trip
Elevation Gain:	1100'
Estimated Time:	4 hours
Highlight:	Easiest ascent to scenic High Divide ridge; tarnlike lakes en route.

This pleasant trail leads through dense forest past marshy tarns to ridgetop views of Mt. Baker. The Damfino Lakes (pronounced with a long "i," so it sounds like a slurred "Damned-if-I-know!") are not crisp alpine jewels, but unassuming little ponds surrounded by boardwalk paths and a profusion of wild blueberries. Past the lakes are woods, an open meadow, and a moderate climb to a ridge known variously as Excelsior Pass and High Divide. Views and picnic opportunities abound along the ridge, where the hike can be extended for several miles.

Getting There

From the Glacier Public Service Center, go 1.9 miles east on Highway 542 to Canyon Creek Road (0.2 mile beyond the Douglas Fir campground). Turn left on Canyon Creek Road, which is also USFS Road 31. This road is partially paved, but can be quite rough.

Stay on Road 31. Stay left when you pass a Y-intersection with USFS Road 3130 at 7.0 miles, and left again at a Y-intersection with USFS Road 3160 at 10.1 miles. At 14.0 miles, you will come to another fork. Again, take the left fork. The trailhead is just over a mile from this final fork, with room for about 15 cars at the trailhead parking area.

The Hike

The first segment of this trail is open to equestrian, bicycle, and motorcycle traffic, but take heart—that doesn't last long. After a sharp initial ascent for a few hundred feet, the incline mellows into a gradual one for the remainder of the first half-mile, then levels off. Shortly thereafter, a trail intersects on the left. This trail, marked BOUNDARY WAY, takes all nonhikers north and uphill to the Boundary Way and Canyon Ridge trails. Continue straight ahead, through a set of uprights and steps over a log designed to discourage all but foot traffic.

The trail now descends, reaching the first of the Damfino Lakes just before 1.0 mile. An elevated boardwalk keeps you out of the marshy margins of these little lakes.

Past the lakes, you ascend again into timber. Here, as throughout this hike, the deeply shaded trail with its many creek crossings can get muddy. Boardwalk sections keep you out of the worst of it.

At 2.25 miles, you emerge into wide-open, color-dappled meadows. Traverse the hillside, cross a creek, and tackle the final short but moderately steep ascent. Reach Excelsior Pass (5300 feet) and the beginning of High Divide at 3.0 miles. Excelsior Pass Trail #670 leads south, plunging 3500 feet in a grueling 4.2-mile series of switchbacks to Highway 542. The High Divide Trail extends in front of you, tripping along the scenic ridgetop for 4.5 miles to intersect Welcome Pass Trail #698, another hellishly steep descent. Leave these alternatives to the mountain goats. Enjoy a picnic, stroll, or both at this west end of High Divide, then return the easy and scenic way you came.

SKYLINE DIVIDE

Map:	Green Trails #13 "Mt. Baker"
Distance:	5.4 miles round trip to knoll
Elevation Gain:	1800' (1400' to ridge, plus 400' to knoll)
Estimated Time:	3 hours (faster if flies are thick!)
Highlight:	Ridgetop alpine views; splendid meadow.

Beginning at 4400 feet, a steady pull up a forested hill for almost 2 miles earns you expansive views of Baker and Shuksan from a meadow-drenched ridgetop. A final climb up a beckoning knoll is the "top-o'-the-world" climax to this hike.

Getting There

From the Glacier Public Service Center on Highway 542, proceed 0.7 mile east to Glacier Creek Road (0.2 mile east of Snowline Inn). Turn right (south) on Glacier Creek Road (USFS Road 39), then almost immediately turn left on gravel USFS Road 37. Follow the North Fork Nooksack River east. At 4.85 miles, you will cross a bridge over a tributary to the Nooksack. At 5.3 miles, a sign warns NARROW, STEEP ROAD; shortly thereafter, it winds south, away from the river and uphill. After 10.0 miles, views open up and you can see how far you've really come up the mountain! At 13.4 miles, an unmarked parking pull-out on the right has room for 15 or 20 cars; park here. The trailhead is across the road, on your left, at the far end of this parking area.

The Hike

This trail, officially named Skyline Ridge Trail, is open to hikers and stock, limited to parties of 12 (counting stock). The trail-marker information sign is a couple dozen feet up the trail. It warns of bears, but says nothing of the menace you're more likely to encounter—the dreaded blackfly! At the trailhead registry just beyond the information sign, virtually every hiker in August mentioned these little pests in the "Comments" section. To minimize the effect of these biting critters, come on a cool (but not cloudy!) day if you can, preferably late in the season. If you can't, just bring lots of industrial-strength bug repellent, a kerchief to brush across your exposed skin (better yet, expose less skin), and a sense of humor. Even when the flies are at their worst, the views from the top of this hike are worth it.

Put your head down and tuck into the climb, which begins immediately at the trailhead and is unrelenting until you reach the ridge. Sometimes steep, sometimes more gradual, the trail switchbacks through forest and occasional meadow for 1.7 miles. Just when you might be thinking, "This is dumb!" (or, if you have teenagers with you, they'll inform you of same), you'll angle out onto a ridge at 5800 feet and the views explode: meadows saturated with color, Mt. Shuksan to the east, Mt. Baker dead ahead. Before you lose yourself and stumble onward into the lush carpet of color, pause to note where you entered the ridgetop. Other sources say you "can't get lost" up here, but I beg to differ. It's possible to miss the trail on the way back, choosing the wrong path from the array of boot-beaten mini-trails criss-crossing the meadowed ridge—especially if there are snow patches on the ridgetop.

This ridgetop meadow is destination enough, and some hikers might want to simply wander on this flat ridge and soak up the scenery before descending. Others will have to tackle the knoll looming another mile ahead. If you do the knoll, you'll stroll the ridgetop for about 0.7 mile, then ascend a short, steep trail to an unobstructed view of Mt. Baker.

Atop Skyline Divide

LAKE ANN

Map:	Green Trails #14 "Lake Shuksan"
Distance:	8.4 miles round trip
Elevation Gain:	800' loss, then 900' gain, then 120' loss
Estimated Time:	4 to 6 hours
Highlight:	Exhilarating full-day hike climaxing with a close-up glacier view.

The popular Lake Ann trail is a timbered, then meadowed, then rocky walk to a talus-sloped alpine lake with views of a majestic adjacent glacier. At the lake, pine grosbeaks emit their gentle, triple-whistle call. Pack a lunch and make a full day of this four-star hike.

Getting There
Follow Highway 542 to the Mt. Baker ski area. Turn right at the large roadside map. Trailhead parking is on your left 1.8 miles past the map.

The Hike
From the ample parking lot at Austin Pass, descend a narrow, pine-needled path into the forest. Lavender asters, pink monkeyflowers, and a dazzling array of mushroom varieties greet you on the wooded slopes of your initial descent. Huckleberries are abundant in September.

A sign informs you that you pass into the Mt. Baker Wilderness area about 1.0 mile into the hike. Shortly thereafter, you enter a creek-fed meadow decorated with the vibrant hues of paintbrush, fireweed, and thistles. The path, while likely to be moist if not still patchy with snow, is easy to follow.

At 2.2 miles, reach a fork in the trail. A post informs you that Lake Ann is 2.0 miles ahead via trail #600, the left fork. The right fork is Swift Creek Trail #607, leading to Baker Lake Spur Road in 8.0 miles. Austin Pass, the point from which you began, is, according to this sign, 2.0 miles behind you. (It's a *long* 2.0 miles!) A sign on a tree points to an open (no walls) pit toilet—one of the nicest views you'll ever have from a privy!

Pause here in the valley, where Swift Creek tumbles down to create Nature's perfect picnic spot.

From Swift Creek, it's all uphill, a sometimes steep, boulder-strewn, zigzagging ascent. When you reach the top, the tiny gem of Lake Ann lies 120 feet below. Stay on the main path, curving to your left around the northeast side of the lake. As you draw abreast of the lake, turn and feast your eyes on the mighty and oh-so-close expanse of Mt. Shuksan's Lower Curtis Glacier.

Other Hike Notes
These hikes not personally reviewed or not as highly recommended as the above hikes.

HELIOTROPE RIDGE

This premier 6.0-mile hike was inaccessible during the summer and fall of 1996 due to extensive road maintenance on the access road, USFS Road 39, also known as Glacier Creek Road. From the Glacier Public Service Center, go 0.7 mile east, then turn right (south) on Glacier Creek Road. Trailhead parking is 8.0 miles from the highway. Those who don't wish to hike can continue beyond the trailhead parking area to a vista point at the end of the road, another 1.5 miles. Hikers will be richly rewarded on this closest-of-all-dayhike approaches to mighty Mt. Baker. Tramp through cool and shady forest, then open, creek-fed meadow (bring a hiking stick for fording assistance!), and, finally, you're face-to-face with Coleman Glacier on Baker's northeast flank.

TWIN LAKES/WINCHESTER MOUNTAIN

Another moderately easy hike with shamelessly spectacular views. The only reason Winchester Mountain is not among the "highly recommended" dayhikes is that the driving is difficult. The trailheads for all recommended hikes in this book are all attainable in a passenger car, but Winchester Mountain really requires a 4-wheel drive, high-clearance vehicle for the last 2.5 miles. Check with the rangers on the condition of the road before attempting it, and don't let them talk you into walking the final 2.5 miles of road—if you're going to hike that far, there are better choices.

To get there, take Highway 542 for 13.4 miles east of the Glacier Public Service Center, to where you'll see a Washington State Department of Transportation maintenance complex on your left. Pull into this parking lot. On the far (east) end of the parking lot, look for a road signed YELLOW ASTER TRAIL 3, TOMYHOI LAKE TRAIL 5, TWIN LAKES 7. This one-lane, gravel road is USFS Road 3065.

Follow the gravel road 4.8 miles to the Gold Run Pass/Tomyhoi Lake trailhead; this section is easy. From here, continue via foot, mountain bike, or 4-wheel drive another 2.5 miles to Twin Lakes. The Winchester Mountain trailhead lies to your north between the two lakes. Follow the trail 0.2 mile to a fork. Take the left fork for the Winchester Mountain lookout tower. Over the next rocky mile, you'll ascend about 1000 feet, then mellow out for the final half-mile to the summit. A lookout tower, open to the public for overnight camping by reservation, is at the top, as well as views of the Picket Range, the Border Peaks (you're only 3 miles from Canada as-the-crow-flies), and, of course, Mt. Baker and Mt. Shuksan.

Contacts

BELLINGHAM/WHATCOM COUNTY VISITOR & CONVENTION BUREAU
P.O. Box 340, Bellingham, WA 98227-0340 or
904 Potter St., Bellingham, WA 98226   (360) 671-3990

GLACIER PUBLIC SERVICE CENTER
1094 Mt. Baker Highway, Glacier, WA 98244   (360) 599-2714

MT. BAKER SKI AREA   (360) 734-6771
1019 Iowa St., Bellingham, WA 98226

MT. BAKER-SNOQUALMIE NATIONAL FOREST HQ   (206) 775-9702
Forest Supervisor
21905 - 64th Avenue West, Mountlake Terrace, WA 98043

NORTH CASCADES NATIONAL PARK;   (360) 856-5700
Mt. Baker Ranger District; Mt. Baker-Snoqualmie Nat'l Forest
2105 State Route 20, Sedro Woolley, WA 98284-9394

WHATCOM COUNTY SHERIFF   (360) 676-6650

	YODELER INN B&B	MT. BAKER LODGING	COUNTRY HILL B&B	GLACIER CREEK MOTEL & CABINS	SNOWLINE INN
PRICE (1996 RATES, PRE-TAX, 2 PERSON)	$65	$99	$65–$75+	$42–$70 motel, $60–$135 cabin	$55–$85
EXTRA PERSON	$10	$10	$10	varies	$5
PAYMENT METHODS	VISA, MC, AmEx, Disc, Check, Cash	VISA, MC, AmEx, Disc, Check, Cash	Cash or checks only	VISA, MC, AmEx, Disc, Cash	VISA, MC, AmEx, Disc, Cash
# OF UNITS	2 rooms	20	1 suite	9 motel rms; 12 cabins	39 units
PRIVATE BATH	Yes	Yes	Yes	Yes	Yes
SHARED BATH	No	No	No	No	No
BREAKFAST INCLUDED?	Yes	No	Yes	No	No
COOKING FACILITIES?	1 room has sm. kitchenette	Full kitchens	Micro, fridge, coffee bar	Yes, varies	Kitchenettes
POOL	No	Yes, some units have access	No	No	No
HOT TUB	Yes	Yes, some units	No	Yes	No
CHILDREN	OK	OK	No	OK	OK
PETS	OK by arrangement	OK by arrangement	No	OK in some units; add $5	No
SEASONS OF OPERATION	Year-round	Year-round	Year-round	Year-round	Year-round

Table I. Lodgings in the Mt. Baker Highway vicinity

Section 2—Hwy. 20 West

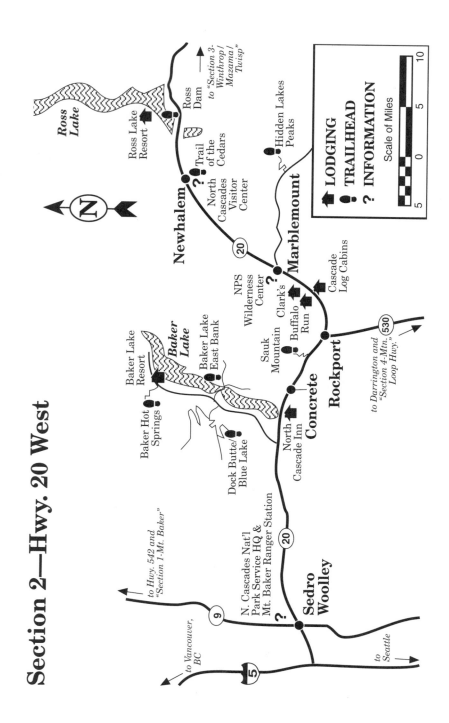

Highway 20 West

(Sedro Woolley to Ross Lake)

Overview

This is the region many folks think of when they think "North Cascades." The North Cascades Highway (Washington State Route 20), completed in 1972, provides Washington's northernmost east-west passage across the Cascade Mountain range, and is one of our nation's most scenic drives. It also provides access to dayhike trailheads, giving dayhikers the opportunity to view spectacular scenery available only to hardcore backpackers just a few short decades ago.

Reach this western part of the North Cascades Highway by taking Interstate 5 north from Seattle through Mt. Vernon to Burlington. Follow Highway 20 east 5.0 miles to Sedro Woolley, where you'll find the first US Forest Service/North Cascades National Park information station (others are located in Marblemount and Newhalem; see addresses and telephone numbers at the end of this section). Sedro Woolley is also the home of a couple of motels that make reasonable dayhike headquarters if the high country lodgings are booked up.

The town of Concrete, gateway for the hiking corridor, is 23 miles east of Sedro Woolley. Named for its primary product, produced in abundance here from 1905 until 1968, Concrete is a tiny town with a couple of watering holes, a historic main street composed of concrete buildings just north of the highway, and a uniquely constructed high school that spans Superior Ave. just south of the highway (both the downtown and the high school are visible from the highway).

Nine miles farther east is Rockport. At the confluence of the Sauk and Skagit rivers, Rockport is one of those little burgs that had more going on a century ago, when it was a stopover for the Seattle and Northern Railroad, than today. State Highway 530 intersects Highway 20 at Rockport; the town of Darrington (see *Section 4*, "Mountain Loop Highway") is 20 miles south of Rockport on 530.

The town of Marblemount is 9 miles east of Rockport. At the west entrance, a sign lacking in craftsmanship but loaded with chutzpah proclaims, WELCOME TO MARBLEMOUNT, ENTRANCE TO THE AMERICAN ALPS. It is here you will find some of the better lodging and dining options along the corridor (see *Lodgings* and *Dining*, below). In fact, if you're heading east, you'd better fuel yourself and your car in Marblemount, because there is little beyond. A small ranger station outpost here can provide trail information. Marblemount is at the junction of Highway 20 and Cascade River Road;

the latter provides access to several major high-country trails including Hidden Lake Peaks (see *Walks and Hikes,* below).

Newhalem, built as a company town for Seattle City Light, is 14 miles beyond Marblemount. A tribute to the hydroelectric power industry, the village is nonetheless worth a stop. Visit the National Park Service's North Cascades visitor center (open July and August), walk one or more of the short trails maintained by Seattle City Light, or view the old locomotive engine as you picnic in the roadside park.

Just east of Newhalem is Gorge Dam, the first of three dams that turn the Skagit River into a mighty source of electric power for the Seattle area. The second is Diablo Dam, behind which lies jade-green Diablo Lake. You may access Diablo Dam by taking a half-mile spur road off Highway 20; watch for the sign. This little road is narrow, winding, and altogether unsuitable for RVs of any kind. Drive across the dam, where you'll find the tugboat landing for Ross Lake Resort (see *Lodgings,* pp. 35-36), then backtrack to return to the highway. As you proceed uphill and east, enjoy the magnificent views of the lake below. The third and final dam, Ross Dam, forms the recreational paradise that is Ross Lake. You may hike down to the dam from the large Happy Flats parking lot at milepost 134 (see "Ross Dam Trail," p. 41). Another way to view the dams is by taking Seattle City Light's Skagit Project Tour, a four-hour extravaganza including dinner, boat cruise, powerhouse tour, and incline railway ride. Tours operate June through Labor Day and require a reservation; call (206) 684-3030 (this line begins taking reservations in May).

Section 2 in this book concentrates on dayhikes and lodgings from Baker Lake (just west and north of Concrete) to Ross Lake, an approximately 40-mile stretch of Highway 20. (See *Section 3,* "Winthrop/Mazama/Twisp" for information on the eastern segment of Highway 20.) While hikes are plentiful in this area, lodgings are comparatively scarce. In fact, I don't know which was more difficult—narrowing down the number of recommended hikes from the scores of good ones available, or finding good lodgings to recommend!

One reason for the lack of tourist accommodations is that the season is short. Highway 20 is closed from Marblemount to Mazama during the winter months. Exact closure dates vary from year to year depending upon avalanche activity. Travelers should check with the Washington State Department of Transportation for travel in the spring or fall, and expect this part of the road to be closed November through April. Within the approximately six-month band that the road is open, the actual hiking season can be as short as 6 or 8 weeks in the higher elevations, with snow still on many of the trails in late July.

Nothing exquisitely precious comes without a price, and the price for getting the most out of the Highway 20 corridor is simple: plan ahead. A person hoping to enjoy the best of this area must be willing to pick up the phone. Secure your lodgings in advance, contact the authorities regarding road access and trail conditions, try to avoid the weekends during July and August, and come enjoy!

Lodgings

CLARK'S SKAGIT RIVER CABINS
5675 Highway 20, Rockport, WA 98283
1-800-273-2606 or (360) 873-2250

This charming and eclectic collection of lodgings gets my vote for the most interesting place to stay in the area. While the address says "Rockport," the actual location is 6 miles east of Rockport, 3 miles west of Marblemount, between mileposts 103 and 104. Look for "The Eatery," the Clarks' restaurant and historical artifacts collection, on the north side of the highway (see *Dining*, below); the generous grounds and lodgings are behind it.

The Clark family has a multi-generation history in the Skagit Valley, since great-grandmother Mathilda Clark settled here in 1889. The resort was begun in 1972, and is run today by mom "Tootsie" Clark and her adult children Don Clark and Judy Clark Brooks, along with Judy's husband Bob Brooks. If you're a history buff, you'll get a special kick out of the Clarks: it seems everything and everybody from Rockport to Marblemount is connected with this family.

The resort's trademark is its bunnies—about 150 of them scamper about the property, eager for handouts.

Accommodations at Clark's range from travel trailers, which rent for $25 and up per night, to deluxe "theme" cabins up to $97 per night. In between, lodgings range from $49 (for a duplex, kitchenless unit with coffee bar) through a variety of one-, two-, and three-bedroom units with kitchens at $59 and up. The more modern the unit, the higher the price; all have kitchens with microwaves, utensils, small appliances, and stoves, and all are stocked with bedding and linens, soap, and paper sup-

Clark's "theme" cabins are outstanding

150 friendly bunnies scamper about the grounds at Clark's

plies. The property also includes tent and RV sites, a laundry facility, a large grassy yard for volleyball and lawn games, and a restroom with showers.

For the most deluxe (and highly recommended) experience, spring for one of the Clark's theme cabins. The lovely and petite Victorian Rose unit (the only theme cabin without a fireplace) sleeps two, for $69. The Mill (decorated with antiques from the area's historic mill days), Western, and Nautical units rent for $79, with room for four. The nicest units are the American Indian, Adirondack, and Hacienda. These three, each with a four-person sleeping capacity, feature beamed ceilings, gourmet kitchens, and elaborate theme decor for $97. All theme cabins look out onto the expansive grassy lawn.

All prices are based on two persons sharing one bed. Each additional person is $9; children under 10 are $8. Pets are $10 per night and must be leashed at all times. Each of the Clark's cabins, from the humblest on up, is an excellent value: clean, comfortable, friendly atmosphere. With your own kitchen and The Eatery right on the property, this resort is an excellent choice for a longer stay; weekly rates are the daily rate times six. The resort is open year-round.

Hiking access from Clark's Skagit River Cabins is good; the property is just over 6 miles west of the Sauk Mountain Trail access road, and the Clark's Skagit River Trail is just across the highway (see information on both trails, below).

Highlight: Delightful themed cabins with bunnies roaming the grounds.

CASCADE LOG CABINS
954 Alaythia Drive, Rockport, WA 98283
(360) 873-4106

Located across the highway from and a few hundred yards west of Clark's Skagit River Cabins (between mileposts 103 and 104 on Highway 20), these five cedar cabins deserve consideration. Each roomy unit is carefully constructed, clean, and attractively (although modestly) furnished. Each has two rooms: a living room/dining/kitchen combo up front and a separate bedroom in the back. Each has a private bath with shower. The front room offers secondary sleeping accommodations, which vary from cabin to cabin: futon, hide-a-bed, or additional bed. All cabins have porches, and your linens and kitchen utensils are provided.

Along with Clark's, these cabins provide one of the few really decent, clean, cabin-style accommodations in the valley. Unlike Clark's, these cabins have less of a "resort" atmosphere, being nestled on a private spot of land in the woods behind a main residence.

A word of caution: at this writing, the Cascade Log Cabins property was up for sale. I normally avoid recommending lodgings that are brand-new (unestablished) or in the process of changing hands, but this one really impressed me. Its beautiful location, the careful tongue-and-groove construction of the cabins, and the cleanliness of the property reflect well upon the owners, who seem committed to finding like-minded buyers who will continue to offer quality lodgings at a fair price. Rates have been $50 for two persons, $5 each additional, with weekly rates available upon request.

Highlight: Five comfortable cabins, conveniently located.

Cascade Log Cabins are peaceful and private

BUFFALO RUN BUNKHOUSE
5621 Highway 20, Rockport, WA 98283
(360) 873-2103 or (360) 873-2461

The Buffalo Run Ranch was born in April of 1991, when Candi Cooper asked her husband, Marshall, for a whiteface calf for her birthday. Marshall went one better, buying his delighted wife a young bull *buffalo* and two heifers. The two have been enamored with raising these majestic animals ever since. Today, their herd numbers 10 to 14 head. The Coopers also own the Buffalo Run Restaurant in Marblemount (see *Dining*, below).

The Buffalo Run Bunkhouse is a modest, single-unit studio apartment at the back of the Buffalo Run Ranch barn. Marshall and Candi built it as their own quarters while their current home, also on the property, was being built. The bunkhouse looks out onto the working ranch, and offers sleeping accommodations at $45-65 for up to six very cozy friends or family members, as follows: a full-size pullout couch, a daybed that pulls out to king size, and a one-or-two-child loft.

The single-room bunkhouse has a rough, unfinished feel, but provides all the creature comforts, including a full kitchen (microwave, utensils, four-burner propane stove, coffee maker and grinder, double sink), bath with double shower, and cable TV. No telephone. The Coopers also provide your bedding and towels, and even coffee beans for the grinder. If you don't mind close quarters and the occasional crowing of a rooster outside your room, the Buffalo Run Bunkhouse makes a nice home base for your dayhiking and touring of the North Cascades Highway. It is situated virtually across the street from Cascade Log Cabins, between mileposts 103 and 104; look for the Buffalo Run Ranch sign. The bunkhouse is available for rent year-round.

Highlight: View a working buffalo ranch from your bunkhouse window.

NORTH CASCADE INN
4284 Highway 20, Concrete, WA 98237
(360) 853-8870

If you're going to stay in a motel-type room while visiting the North Cascades Highway area, stay at the North Cascade Inn. Located right on the highway just west of the main town of Concrete, this 14-unit facility and adjacent restaurant (see *Dining,* below) provide all the fundamentals. Better yet, they do so with a smile and genuine friendliness. I never met the proprietors (although they are frequently on the premises), yet everyone who served me acted as though he or she had a stake in the place. This service-oriented attitude is rare in this type of accommodation, and I applaud both the staff and the owners for whatever they do to foster it.

The 4 smoking and 10 nonsmoking units are basic: paneled walls, synthetic bed-spreads, telephone, and cable TV. While the facility is neither new nor plush, the newer indoor-outdoor carpeting and updated trimmings, vinyls, and fixtures in some units show a commitment to maintaining a fresh and comfortable lodging. Most rooms have two beds, either doubles or queens, and one unit has three and could sleep six (although with six, there is room to do little but sleep).

Rates at North Cascade Inn are fair at $40 per person (including tax); each additional person $5. No pets. Open year-round.

Highlight: 14 unit motel with convenient restaurant.

BAKER LAKE RESORT
P.O. Box 100, Concrete, WA 98237
Reservation Line: (360) 757-2262

Operated under a special use permit from the U.S. Forest Service, Baker Lake Resort's main draw is "location, location, location." The accommodations are decidedly rustic, but the setting and the access to trails on the southern approach to Mt. Baker are unparalleled. In addition to its proximity to the Dock Butte/Blue Lake, Baker Hot Springs, and Baker Lake East Bank hikes detailed below, Baker Lake Resort is the closest lodging to such challenging and satisfying dayhike favorites as Park Butte, Railroad Grade, and Scott Paul (information available at ranger station).

If you like a deluxe accommodation with a whirlpool spa and breakfast served in your room, Baker Lake Resort is not for you. If you can handle a place that's rough around the edges and like the idea of a do-it-yourself cabin in an idyllic location on an exquisite lake, you might want to consider it. You won't have to wonder if the sheets are clean here, because you bring your own! This is the only lodging in this book that requires you to bring your own bedding and towels.

Baker Lake Resort is first and foremost a campground, and one that is geared for families, so plan on the rush and clamor of children. Nine cabins share the resort with nearly 100 RV and tent sites. Of the cabins, I can recommend only units 1 through 4. These are the ones with lakeside locations, private baths, refrigerators, and kitchens with utensils. They also have gas heaters, outdoor fire pits, and picnic tables. (Cabins 5-9 share a bathhouse with the campers, lack kitchen supplies, and do not all have refrigerators.) Cabin 1, a duplex, includes units 1A and 1B, each a single room with two double beds, renting for $55/night. Cabin 2 has two rooms, two double beds, two single beds, and a hide-a-bed, and has a gas fireplace; it rents for $75/night. Cabin 3 is similar to Cabin 2, but with three double beds and no hide-a-bed, also renting for $75/night. Cabin 4, a duplex, includes units 4A and 4B, each a single room with a loft and two double beds; each rents for $60/night. Prices as quoted include two people; additional adults are $7/night, children under 16 are $4/night additional. Pets are welcome for an additional $10/night.

To find Baker Lake Resort, take Highway 20 east from Sedro Woolley to milepost 82, 6 miles west of Concrete. Turn north on Baker Lake Road, which becomes USFS Road 11, and go 20 miles. Look for the sign on your right after milepost 20. The resort includes an amazingly well-stocked little store, a protected boat ramp for guest moorage, a playground, and a variety of watercraft available for rent. Electricity is provided by generator, which is turned off promptly at 11 P.M. and resumes at 6:30 A.M. Kerosene lamps are provided in the cabins.

There is no telephone at the resort. Reservations are made through a sometimes-reliable service off site at (360) 757-2262. Reservation hours are 7 A.M. to 7 P.M. Monday–Friday. Visa, Mastercard, and Discover are accepted, and a deposit (refundable only with two weeks' notice) of $50 per cabin is taken, $100 for holiday periods. Three-night minimum stay on holidays (Friday–Saturday–Sunday). Two-night minimum (Friday–Saturday) on nonholidays in July and August. The resort operates weekends only October 1–April 1, rates are discounted 20%.

Highlight: Best access to Baker Lake and southern Mt. Baker area trails.

ROSS LAKE RESORT
Rockport, WA 98283
(206) 386-4437 (local from Seattle)

Ross Lake Resort receives its mail in Rockport and has a phone line with a Seattle exchange, but it is located in the middle of absolute nowhere. If you want to get away from it all, this hike-or-boat-in-only resort may be your answer.

The resort consists of 10 individual cabins and 3 larger "bunkhouse" accommodations built on log floats. The entire operation, which includes docks and watercraft for rent, floats off the west bank of Ross Lake just north of Ross Dam.

All Ross Lake Resort accommodations include kitchen facilities with tableware, pots, and pans, and linens are provided. Each bears a unique moniker such as DEER SHELTER, SYMKO'S SHANTY, EAGLE'S NEST, and BROWN JUG INN. Of the cabins, eight have private baths, complete kitchens, and room for up to six. These units, referred to as the "modern" cabins, rent for $84 for one or two persons, with each additional person $10. Six of these units have woodstoves (generous wood supply provided), and two have electric heat. The two remaining cabins, referred to as the "little" cabins, have a smaller kitchen facility (no oven, smaller refrigerator), and woodstove heat, and sleep up to four. They share a bathroom and rent for $56 for one or two, with additional persons $6.

The three bunkhouse units are designed for parties of six or more. Each sleeps up to 10, with a large kitchen-dining-sleeping area. Each has a private bath, woodstove heat, full size refrigerator, and a stove (no oven). $108 for up to six; each additional person $8.

There is no charge in any of the units for children under four. Discounts of 25% apply to all cabins in June, bunkhouse cabins Sunday–Thursday in September (with boat rental), and bunkhouse and modern cabins Sunday–Thursday in October (with boat rental). The resort is closed October 31 through mid-June.

Reach the Ross Lake Resort by hiking from the Ross Dam Trail (see *Walks and Hikes*, below) or taking the Seattle City Light tugboat from Diablo Dam (locking through Ross Dam en route). As you must pack all your own food when you stay at the resort (there is no store or restaurant), most people will opt for the boat. Catch it at the parking lot on the north side of Diablo Dam; departures are 8:30 A.M. and 3 P.M. daily, and the fare is $5 per person round trip. If you hike in from the Ross Dam Trail, you may either hike all the way or call the resort's water taxi. Hiking all the way is about 2.5 miles, and rather challenging with a full pack. Take the Ross Dam Trail to the dam, cross the dam, then pick up the Big Beaver Trail, heading right (northeast) to the resort. To catch the water taxi, take the Ross Dam Trail to its intersection with the gravel road at 0.45 mile, turn *right* (*away* from the dam) and go downhill until you see a red pole labeled RESORT PHONE on your left (about 0.6 mile) Double back down the little goat path at water's edge, past an outhouse, to the telephone. A small fee of a dollar or two is charged for the water taxi across the lake.

Staying at Ross Lake Resort is a singular experience. Due to its isolation, the day-hikes detailed in the *Walks and Hikes* section below are not readily accessible. However, many other trails can be reached on foot or by water taxi from the resort (access to Big Beaver trail is right behind the modern cabins). A few of the Ross Lake area hikes are described under the heading "Ross Lake Trails" in *Other Hike Notes*, toward the end of this section.

Highlight: Remote on-the-water location; hike or boat in only.

Ross Lake Resort's floating cabins—accessible only by boat

Additional Lodgings

Because the recommended lodgings above comprise a small total number of rooms, contact information for the following lodgings is provided here. These premises were not thoroughly reviewed by the author.

THREE RIVERS INN & RESTAURANT
Hwy. 20/Hwy. 9 Jct., Sedro Woolley, WA 98284
1-800-221-5122 or (360) 855-2626
Free in-room movies, heated outdoor pool, lounge

SKAGIT MOTEL
1977 Highway 20, Sedro Woolley, WA 98294
(360) 856-6001
From I-5, take Exit 230; go 4 miles E on Hwy. 20
47 budget units, TV, phones, AC, some w. kitchens

EAGLE'S NEST MOTEL & RV PARK
206 Highway 20, Concrete, WA 98237
(360) 853-8662
12 modest units from $41/single; TV, fans, balconies; views of Skagit River in most units; Native American gift shop; not for the finicky or impatient traveler

THE TOTEM MOTEL, RESTAURANT & LOUNGE
5551 Highway 20, Rockport, WA 98283
(360) 873-4535
8 basic rooms from $40; pets, weekly rates

Dining

NORTH CASCADE INN RESTAURANT & LOUNGE
4284 Highway 20, Concrete, WA 98237
(360) 853-8870

Adjacent to the North Cascade Inn motel (see *Lodgings,* above), the North Cascade Inn Restaurant provides self-proclaimed "down-home fare" for breakfast, lunch, and dinner. In a region so laid back with respect to timing and seasons (you never know *when* things will be open around here, especially in the off-season), this restaurant is justifiably proud to maintain year-round hours of 5 A.M. to 9 P.M. Sunday through Thursday, and until 10 P.M. Friday and Saturday.

While the food at the North Cascade Inn Restaurant is good, it's the decor you'll notice first. Antiques and historic relics of every stripe are on display inside and out: household items, farm machinery, railroad and mining tools, loggers' saws, and other things that will leave you guessing. What doesn't fit on the walls is hung from the ceiling. You won't lack for amusement while you wait for your home-cooked meal.

Most full breakfasts range from $3.75 to $5.95, with a la carte offerings less and a few heftier specialties more. Lunch items (served 11:30 A.M. until closing) include an assortment of burgers from $4.25 (fries included), hot and cold sandwiches, meal-size salads, and a few all-day breakfast items. Dinner fare provides no real surprises, but the steaks ($12.95-$15.95), deep-fried seafood ($6.95-$13.95), and chicken items ($7.95-$9.95) are properly prepared and served with a smile. Save room for dessert (or come just for that)—they are especially proud of their homemade cream pies.

Group seating can be accommodated in their banquet room with prior notice, and outdoor garden dining is offered when weather permits.

Highlight: Historic memorabilia galore!

BUFFALO RUN RESTAURANT
5860 Highway 20, Marblemount, WA 98267
(360) 873-2461

Owners Marshall and Candi Cooper, who also operate the Buffalo Run Ranch (see bunkhouse under *Lodgings,* above), want to offer you a little something different along the sleepy, amenities-deprived corridor of western Highway 20. Their solution, as proclaimed on their colorful menu, is "Buffalo Run Restaurant—A Dining Adventure!"

My first thought upon entering the friendly, fresh lobby of the Buffalo Run Restaurant was, "Whew—civilization!" Marshall's food-service background and marketing savvy are evident in every aspect of the operation, from decor to menu selections. Anything other than steaks and deep-fried items is a welcome change of pace in these parts, but Buffalo Run goes a step beyond, offering such creations as "Turkey Oat Pie," a tasty and healthy meatloaf surrounded by flaky pastry, $6.50; a smoked-trout sandwich with remolade sauce, $6.50; surprising New Zealand greenshell mussels, $5.95 a half dozen. Vegetarians will heave a sigh of relief, with choices including the $9.25 "Garden Boat" (whole-wheat loaf filled with tempeh and veggies and topped with mushroom sauce), the $4.95 "Super Spud" (a giant baker topped with steamed veggies and cheese) and the $6.50 "Latino" (tortillas filled with potato, cheese, mushrooms, and onion, with salsa and guacamole on the side). Other rare-in-these-parts choices include a decent Caesar salad, quiche, and linguine with shrimp, clams, or bratwurst.

But Buffalo Run Restaurant's true specialty is exotic meats. Ostrich, venison, and, of course, buffalo are all on the menu. Steaks, chops, burgers—you can even have a buffalo patty with your morning eggs or eggbeaters.

You'll find Buffalo Run at milepost 106, right on Highway 20 in the middle of Marblemount. Breakfast starts at $3.45, with most choices $4-$7; most luncheon options range $4.95 to $6.95. Dinners run the gamut: you can get full for not much more than $5.00, but a buffalo T-bone steak dinner will set you back $24.95; most choices are $9.25 or $10.95. Kids' menu is offered, as is a selection of beer (including microbrews), wine, and cocktails.

Highlight: Exotic meats including ostrich, venison, and buffalo.

THE EATERY
5675 Highway 20, Rockport, WA 98283
(360) 873-2250

This restaurant and museum combo is part of the Clark's Skagit River Cabins complex just west of Marblemount. You can't miss the cheerful structure on the north side of the road. A take-out espresso/snack kiosk is attached to the front, with the main restaurant behind.

All the locals rave about The Eatery, or simply, "Clark's." "Oh, yeah, they got the best cinnamon rolls." Indeed, they do. Other fare includes varied and hearty breakfasts, burgers, Gardenburgers, sandwiches, and a nightly dinner special. For entertainment, take a cast-off pancake, tortilla, or slice of bread from the "for the bunnies" bin in front of the take-out window and feed a few of the rabbits frolicking on the adjacent lawn.

Highlight: Local favorite; museum-and-restaurant in one.

Walks and Hikes
Listed in approximate order of difficulty.

TRAIL OF THE CEDARS

Map:	None needed, but can be obtained from the National Park or Seattle City Light information centers (see *Getting There*, below)
Distance:	0.3 mile loop
Elevation Gain:	None
Estimated Time:	30 minutes
Highlight:	Easy walk, with six others nearby.

A pleasant, level walk through a mighty cedar grove adjacent to the Skagit River and community of Newhalem. Interpretive plaques explain the area's history and ecosystem. For more easy walks ranging from 330 feet to 1 mile, see *Newhalem Area Strolls* under *Other Hike Notes* at the end of this section.

Getting There

The tiny village of Newhalem is home to two separate visitor centers. The North Cascades National Park visitor center, an impressive and well-staffed (in the summer) facility adjacent to several trailheads, is situated off Highway 20. To reach this center, watch for the large monument sign at the west end of Newhalem, turn south across the concrete bridge over the Skagit River, passing the ranger station and the Newhalem Creek Campground. The Seattle City Light Information Center sits right on the highway on a cross street across from the convenience store and the park with the "Old No. 6" locomotive. To walk Trail of the Cedars, find the Seattle City Light Information Center and park nearby.

"Now that's a big tree . . ." One of the giants along Trail of the Cedars

Walk south, away from the highway, and cross the suspension footbridge at the end of the road. The trail begins on the far side of the bridge.

The Walk
You can't get lost on this well-maintained loop trail through giant cedars. Accompanied by the rushing sounds of the Skagit River, stroll through a shady grove and learn about the forest and its history from the interpretive plaques. The Newhalem Creek Powerhouse marks the halfway point, near the confluence of Newhalem Creek and the Skagit River.

BAKER HOT SPRINGS

Map:	None needed (Green Trails #14 "Mt. Shuksan" shows the approximate location of the springs, and #46 "Lake Shannon" shows access roads)
Distance:	0.5 mile round trip
Elevation Gain:	None
Estimated Time:	20 minutes, plus soaking time
Highlight:	20' x 20' natural hot springs pool.

A short stroll on a wide, shady path through old-growth forest to a nearly 20' x 20' pool formed by the hand-dredging and damming of a natural hot springs. The path is hard to find, but well used. Bathing suits are a point of contention here; local custom has long eschewed them, but tourists have expressed alarm at the nudity. Use discretion when children are present.

For your best chance at relative solitude, come early in the morning. Bring a towel for yourself and a litter bag for the clueless who may have preceded you. When visitors are conscientious, this is a pretty little stroll, and the hot spring itself, albeit sulfurous, is a good one. The roomy pool is a couple of feet deep, and the water ranges from a 98°-99° at the far side of the pool to about 104° at the source.

Getting There
From Highway 20, take Baker Lake Road north 20 miles. Just across from the entrance to Baker Lake Resort (see *Lodgings*, above), turn left on USFS Road 1144. A bumpy, badly potholed 3.2 miles later, find an unmarked pull-out on the left. A short, steep little goat path (also unmarked) leads to the trail.

The Walk
There's no trailhead marker per se, but at the top of the steep little access path you'll be greeted by a sign giving the decay cycle of common litter items. According to the junior scientist responsible for the sign, it takes one to two years for an orange peel to return to the earth, five years for a cigarette butt, a million years for a glass bottle. And plastic?—well, that's "indefinite." A nice reminder; too bad not everyone heeds it.

Turn left at the sign and follow the ferny path past a few awesome old giant trees to the soaking pool at the end.

ROSS DAM TRAIL

Map:	Green Trails #48 "Diablo Dam"
Distance:	2.0 miles round trip to cross dam
Elevation Loss:	About 550' in 0.4 mile (steep!)
Estimated Time:	1 hour, 15 minutes
Highlight:	Short, steep descent to mighty Ross Dam.

This rather steep trail begins at the Happy Flats parking lot at milepost 134, about 5 miles east of the Colonial Creek campground. It's all downhill on the way to the dam, and you'll be entertained by the assortment of tennies, sandals, dress shoes, and, yes, even thongs that people think are appropriate for such a walk. Such is the ambiance of a trailhead right on the highway.

The trail is pretty beat up from the amount of foot traffic, and can be dusty. Due to the steep pitch of the first 0.4 mile, those with breathing or heart conditions, or difficulty with footing, might think twice about this walk. But if time is no object, almost anyone without significant mobility impairment can take this hike. Shade and attractive creeklets provide respite en route, and the dam is impressive. Fit hikers will want to hop out of the car and take this jaunt as a quick leg-stretcher.

This is also the route to take if you are hiking or taking the water taxi (not to be confused with the tug boat) to Ross Lake Resort (see *Lodgings*, above).

Getting There

The Happy Flats parking lot is on the lake side of Highway 20 at milepost 134 (on your left if you're heading east, on your right if you're heading west). Ample parking is provided, and toilets at the trailhead.

The Hike

Descend through open Douglas-fir forest along a heavily trampled dirt path beside a creeklet. Switchbacks, dust, and crowds might make you wonder what you're doing here. Then you'll see the dam below and think, "gosh, this *is* pretty neat!"

Just past 0.4 mile, intersect a gravel road. If you are staying at Ross Lake Resort and don't wish to hike all the way in, turn right here and walk down the hill to the water-taxi telephone. If you wish to continue to Ross Dam, turn left on the road.

Shortly (at 0.5 mile) the road intersects another; make a hairpin switchback to your right to continue down toward the dam. As you walk along this final stretch of one-lane gravel road, you pass through a striking channel about 150 feet long, where solid granite walls ascend steeply on either side.

Emerge from the rock channel to the southeast end of the dam at 0.6 mile. Cross the dam, with views of Diablo Lake to your left and Ross Lake to your right, for a total walk of about 1.0 mile. You can see Ross Lake Resort uplake on your left. Intrepid hikers can continue north on the Big Beaver Trail on the far side of the dam. Ross Lake Resort is about 1.5 miles farther along Big Beaver, and the trail continues for many miles beyond that. Most of us will cross the dam, say "Gee whiz!" a few times, then climb back to the parking lot.

BAKER LAKE EAST BANK

Map:	Green Trails #46 "Lake Shannon"
Distance:	Your choice, up to 28.0 miles round trip (including a beautiful and satisfying 2.0 mile round trip)
Elevation Gain:	None
Estimated Time:	Your choice
Highlight:	Lush, green, all-weather hike.

A flat, well-engineered and maintained path along the green and scenic east bank of beautiful Baker Lake. This is a rewarding walk for all ages and abilities, and is suitable for all weather. In fact, the giant firs dripping with moss look particularly spectacular and haunting on a good, juicy rainy day.

For years, this trail went only 4.0 miles, to the hike-or-boat-in-only Maple Grove campground. It has recently been lengthened to about 14 miles, with plans to eventually bridge the Baker River at the north end of the lake and connect with other trails.

Getting There

From Highway 20, take Baker Lake Road, which becomes USFS Road 11, 14.5 miles north to gravel USFS Road 1106. Turn right (east) on 1106. Pass a left turnoff for Horseshoe Cove campground, but continue straight, following the sign for WATSON LAKES TRAIL and ROAD OVER DAM. At 1.5

Big, moss-hung cedars make fine dens for all sorts of critters

miles from Baker Lake Road, you come to the top of the dam. The road makes a sharp right, crosses the dam (Baker Lake is to your left as you cross, Lake Shannon is below and to your right), then makes a left. At 2.2 miles from Baker Lake Road, turn left onto USFS Road 1107, following the signs for EAST BANK TRAIL and WATSON LAKES TRAIL. The well-signed trailhead is on the left side of the road in 0.8 mile. (Continuing on this road takes you to the Anderson/Watson Lakes trails. See *Other Hike Notes*, below.)

The Hike

Drop very gently down into a forest primeval: ferny, mossy, and lush. The trail is wide and well-graded, and many little boardwalk bridges (over a dozen in the first mile!) have been built to make your stroll as comfortable as possible. First-time hikers will marvel at the rain-forest environment, and everyone will enjoy the incredible old-growth Douglas-fir: monsters 4, 6, and 8 feet in diameter everywhere you look.

While this is not a "view" hike—making it especially suitable for a cloudy or rainy day—you do catch some views out over the lake, beginning at about 0.3 mile. On a clear day, you'll also see a lot of majestic Mt. Baker as you continue along the path on this, the deep side of Baker Lake.

An unmarked campsite provides a good rest, snack, or turnaround spot at about 2.0 miles; watch for a trail forking off to the left to it. Continuing on the main trail (signed MAPLE GROVE at the fork), you'll come to Maple Grove campground, another turnaround or picnic spot, just before 4.0 miles. This is the best and easiest place to access the lakeshore, and as far as most people will go for a dayhike, but the trail does continue north for a total of about 14 miles.

SAUK MOUNTAIN

Map:	Green Trails #46 "Lake Shannon"
	(#78 "Darrington" shows Highway 20/Sauk Mountain Road jct.)
Distance:	4.2 miles round trip
Elevation Gain:	1200'
Estimated Time:	2 hours
Highlight:	Wide-open hike up a colorful meadow to a panoramic vista.

Let your car do most of the climbing to this mountain summit. From a 4300-foot trailhead (scenic in its own right), climb through a colorful, butterfly-filled meadow and around a bouldered ridge to the 5500-foot summit and former site of a lookout tower. Because there is very little forest cover, this can be a hot hike, but the views are great all the way. An optional 1.5 mile (each way) spur trail leads down to Sauk Lake at the 1.5-mile point, but the 1200-foot descent and subsequent ascent turn this moderately easy hike into a fairly difficult one, and for little gain.

The Sauk Mountain trail is open to hikers only, so no stock, bikes, or other vehicles will spoil your experience. But don't expect solitude—this is a popular one, even for families with small children (although the climb could prove a challenge for little ones, and there are drop-offs near the top). *Do* expect black flies and other pests in peak season; bring repellent.

Getting There

Take Highway 20 east of Concrete to milepost 96. Watch for USFS Road 1030, also called Sauk Mountain Road, on which you will turn north. (If traveling east on Highway 20, it will be the first left after well-marked Littlefield Road intersects on the right. If traveling west, it will be the first right after Rockport State Park.)

Take this steep, narrow, dirt and gravel road up, up, up, gaining views over the Skagit River valley en route. Stay right when USFS Road 1034 forks off to the left at 6.8 miles. After this junction, the road curves sharply east and you get your first good views of the craggy, bare rock bulk of your destination: Sauk Mountain. Its green flanks and massive crags are a beautiful contrast to the ugly, scarred clearcuts off to your left.

At almost 8 miles from the highway, turn right on USFS Road 1036. The road ends at the trailhead, in 0.2 mile. There is room for a dozen cars at this scenic trailhead, and a pit toilet at the beginning of the trail, making this a reasonable spot for a tailgate picnic for nonhikers.

The Hike

From the trailhead at the southeast corner of the parking lot, enter a thick meadow, immersing yourself in the feast of wildflower color you have been viewing alongside the road on the drive up: white daisies, lavender asters, orange paintbrush, pink fireweed, purple thistles, and red-orange and yellow columbines. The meadow growth is so lush that you stand a good chance of getting wet from the dew, and gaiters will do you no good unless they come up to your armpits. On an especially damp day, consider rain gear, at least from the waist down.

Most of your altitude is gained in the initial 1.5 miles, as you climb the 26 (but who's counting?) switchbacks through the meadow on the southwest side of the mountain, with views out over the wild, winding, turquoise snake of the Skagit River below. On a warm day, you'll welcome the brief dips into a small patch of forest on the east edge of the slope as you ascend. At about a mile, you'll be treated to views of snow-capped Glacier Peak dead ahead, with majestic Mt. Baker 180° behind you, and the confluence of the Sauk and Skagit rivers below.

Nearing the 1.5-mile point, the trail contours around behind the mountain, and views expand to the north to include Eldorado's snowy ridge. At 1.5 miles, a narrow trail with a tiny sign descends east to Sauk Lake, a 1200-foot drop in 1.5 miles, and worth it only if you feel like the extra exercise or a bit of fishing (Washington state fishing license required).

As you head north and west on the approach to the summit, you'll pass a couple of nice picnic sites, then have a view down over the tiny aquamarine gem of Sauk Lake, with Bald Mountain rising on the opposite side. Don't be surprised to find snow patches on this side of the mountain, even in the heat of August. A final rocky scramble takes you to the summit and former lookout-tower site. Your reward awaits: Mt. Baker, to the northwest; the Picket Range to the north; Eldorado to the northwest; Glacier Peak and the jagged fingers of Mt. Pugh to the southeast; and Whitehorse to the south, all rising above the picture postcard of the Skagit and Sauk river valleys.

DOCK BUTTE/BLUE LAKE

Map:	Green Trails #45 "Hamilton" (#46 "Lake Shannon" helps for access roads)
Distance:	4.4 miles round trip (includes 0.5-mile spur to lake)
Elevation Gain:	1100'
Estimated Time:	3 hours
Highlight:	Incredible 360° views and a lake side trip, too.

An awesome view hike for comparatively little effort, and a spur to a charming lake to boot. This is a good family hike for sturdy-legged pre-teens and vigorous grandparents, because it has it all—namely, both the butte view and the lake access. And for those who would like part of the experience but would rather not climb the rather steep final 500 feet to the butte, a nice meadow at midpoint makes a fine turnaround (or a stop-and-wait point while the rest of the party continues, if the blackflies aren't too feisty). Another short hike option (also a rainy-day option, if clouds would obscure

the view from the butte), is
to do the 0.8 mile each way
to the lake and skip the butte
climb. The trailhead, however, is not attractive, so leave
the nonhikers at home for
this one, and be sure to pick
a clear day so you'll be
rewarded for your efforts.

The Dock Butte summit
is at 1.7 miles, and the 360°
panorama it offers makes it
a great place for a lunch
stop. It takes about an hour

The amazing view from atop Dock Butte

to get there, and you'll want to allow plenty of time on top.

Getting There

From Highway 20, take the Baker Lake Road, which becomes USFS Road 11.
Shortly after crossing the National Forest boundary (at 12.6 miles), turn left on USFS
Road 12 (at 12.8 miles). Follow Road 12 for 7 miles, then turn left on USFS Road 1230.
Drive 4 more miles to the trailhead parking lot. The sad scar of a recent clearcut
greets you straight ahead, but, thankfully, the trail doesn't go that way. Look for the
BLUE LAKE trailhead sign on the west side of the parking lot.

The Hike

A brief descent into lush forest takes you almost immediately to a Y; take the
right-hand fork and begin a modest ascent. Footing is good on this popular trail, and
the filtered sunlight (you are near the top of the hill from the beginning) ensures a
fairly dry tread most of the year.

Reach a signed fork in the road at 0.3 mile; take the right fork toward Dock Butte
(return this way and take the walk to the lake at the end). The climb becomes a bit
steeper and steady, turning to a quarter-mile stretch of switchbacks at about 0.5 mile.
Glimpses of Mt. Baker—a preview of the treats ahead—spur you on.

At 0.75 mile, break out into open meadow and a view of the jigsaw-puzzle contours of Loomis Mountain to your right. Follow the ridgetop, which descends briefly
into a saddle before climbing to your final assault on the butte. More than one path
leads to the top; I recommend the long and relatively gentle switchbacks across the
northwest face. Whichever trail you pick, take care to stay on it as you cross the rocks
ascending the butte.

The summit is sublime. Once you've conquered it, at 1.7 miles, you'll be able to
answer the question, "What's Up Dock?": 360° views of the Cascades from Rainier
to Baker, Lake Shannon, the remnants of a lookout tower. A weathered old foundation stone appears to read, FRED THORNE, ROY EVANS, AND BILL BENEKE, FOUNDATION
BUILDERS, INC.

Return the way you came, reaching the signed BLUE LAKE/DOCK BUTTE fork at 3.1
miles. Take the fork right to Blue Lake, descending gently on the wide, well-worn

path to this popular lake. Stay on the main trail, even as it ascends and you wonder how you'll ever reach the lake below. You'll see your first glimpses of the lake and its talus-covered opposite banks at about 3.5 miles. The path bends left and takes you to the lakeshore at 3.6 miles.

HIDDEN LAKE PEAKS

Map:	Green Trails #48 & #80, "Diablo Dam" & "Cascade Pass" (#47 "Marblemount" shows access roads)
Distance:	8.4 miles round trip
Elevation Gain:	3290'
Estimated Time:	5+ hours (3 up and 2 down; plus time at the top)
Highlight:	Marmots, meadows, mountains—magnificent!

This awesome, underrated hike is a swell alternative to nearby and overused Cascade Pass. A variety of terrain is packed into its relatively short 4.2-mile length: forest, meadows, talus slopes, and bouldered ridges, culminating in breathtaking vistas from the 6890-foot lookout cabin.

The hike may be difficult for some, especially the final 300-foot ascent to the lookout cabin. If you are uncomfortable with a steep rock scramble, or if the day is cloudy, or if the final approach is snow-covered, you may wish to settle for the perfectly exhilarating views from the 6600-foot saddle at about 3.75 miles. If you are able to go all the way to the top, bring your maps to identify the many peaks visible on a clear day. The lookout cabin, no longer used for fire protection, is maintained as a backpacker shelter and sleeps four.

Expect to see marmot, pika, hawks, Ptarmigan, hummingbirds, and perhaps an eagle or two en route. We were detained a good half hour by a pair of plump, furry marmots who appeared as curious about us as we were them. (These were not the sad product of too much tourism, begging for handouts, but a healthy pair who viewed us from a safe distance at the mouth of their burrow.)

This trail and its access road have a short season; both are prone to washouts. Be sure to check with the ranger station at Marblemount for current conditions.

Getting There

In Marblemount, Highway 20 takes a 90° bend north, while Cascade River Road goes across the Skagit River and follows the course of the Cascade River east. Take Cascade River Road, a popular hiking access road that leads to the Cascade Pass and Lookout Mountain trails as well as Hidden Lake Peaks.

About 0.6 mile past the bridge, the Rockport-Cascade Road intersects on the right; continue straight ahead. At 5.6 miles, the road turns to gravel (this road is prone to washouts, but is repaired quickly due to its heavy use). Pass Marble Creek Campground on the right at 8.7 miles. At 10.2 miles, turn left onto USFS Road 1540. A narrow road, steep in places, 1540 ends at the trailhead, 4.9 miles from Cascade River Road.

The Hike

Begin the hike on a rocky-surfaced forest trail, beneath a tunnel-like canopy of greenery, flanked by ferns and wild berry bushes. There are many creek crossings; indeed, the trail itself initially has the character of a creekbed.

After about 0.3 mile, the thick surroundings give way to more open forest. The trail switchbacks gently, climbing steadily through a large stand of bare, sentinel-like conifer trunks, with a canopy of needles overhead but a wide-open understory, like the forests of western Europe. The surface here is a carpet of pine needles. Around 0.75 mile, let your ears lead you off to the left of the trail to view a waterfall along the East Fork Sibley Creek. Continuing on, boardwalks help you across some of the muckier drainage areas where forest meets meadow.

Emerge into an open meadow just after a mile. Fiddlehead ferns and cow parsnips line the path, and rocky outcroppings loom above. Cross Sibley Creek and head east through the meadow and up along the course of the creek. As you ascend (this trail is prone to damage and washouts, but was in excellent repair when I hiked it), switchbacking through lush meadow, the kaleidoscope of color expands to include thistle, monkeyflower, ragwort, fireweed, bluebells, paintbrush, penstemon, and old man of the mountain. Views south across the creek basin reveal a myriad of little waterfalls down the face of the opposite rock walls. Allow plenty of stop-and-gawk time in this meadow (also catch-your-breath time; it's deceptively steep!)

As you near the top, after about 2 miles, the switchbacks tighten. This is marmot heaven; watch for burrows. The path turns south to recross the creek, then bends sharply to the southwest at about 2.25 miles. Here, you leave the lush meadows behind and enter a boulder-strewn alpine landscape with heather ground cover. The path leads over and around granite rock (and, often, snow patches until mid-August) for another mile and a half, finally rounding a bend at about 3.75 miles and giving you your first good view of your goal: the twin gothic spires of the Hidden Lake Peaks. The lookout cabin is on the left-hand peak.

During much of the season, the final half mile is snow-bound and inaccessible, and it is always a steep climb. If you're pooped, the 3.75-mile point is a reasonable turnaround. For the hearty, ascend to the cabin and enjoy views of Forbidden

A marmot patrols the ascent to Hidden Lakes Peaks

Peak, Sahale Mountain (east), Snowking Mountain, (south), and many others. On a clear day, you can see Mt. Baker to the north and Glacier Peak and Mt. Rainier to the south. You'll also see Hidden Lake, some 1100 feet below. The truly intrepid can scramble down; it's about half a mile—but, why? You can't beat the view from the top.

Other Hike Notes
These hikes not personally reviewed or not as highly recommended as the above hikes.

NEWHALEM AREA STROLLS

North Cascades National Park, in cooperation with Seattle City Light, offers seven easy day strolls around Newhalem. The latest maps and trail descriptions are available at any of three locations: the North Cascades National Park visitor center south of Highway 20 at the west end of Newhalem, the North Cascades visitor center in Sedro Woolley, and the Seattle City Light Information Center on Highway 20 across from the Skagit General Store next to the park in Newhalem. Trails include the 330-foot, wheelchair-accessible Sterling Munro boardwalk trail, suitable for all ages and abilities, the more adventuresome 1.0-mile River Loop Trail, and the steep but short 0.4-mile Ladder Creek Falls Trail, featuring flower gardens, a suspension bridge, and colored lights at night.

CLARK'S SKAGIT RIVER TRAIL

Just across from The Eatery (see *Dining*, above) and the access drive to Clark's Skagit River Cabins (see *Lodgings*, above) is a little sign for RIVER TRAIL. Follow it to a pleasant, 1.5-mile trail that meanders along the banks of the Skagit River. Suitable for jogging as well.

ANDERSON/WATSON LAKES TRAIL/ANDERSON BUTTE

More good options if you're staying in the Baker Lake vicinity. Follow the directions for the Baker Lake East Bank trail (above). Continue past the East Bank trailhead 10 more miles on USFS Road 1107, then turn left on a 0.5-mile spur road to the trailhead. The main trail, to Anderson Lake, is 2.5 miles each way, gaining 600 feet to a junction with the Watson Lake trail, then dropping 300 feet to the lake. For Watson Lake, also 2.5 miles, take the left fork here, which also descends 300 feet to its lake. Those wishing a shorter, steeper hop, can take the 1.5-mile hike up Anderson Butte. This trail makes a left fork off the main trail just before 1.0 mile, then climbs steeply for a total gain of just over 1100 feet. Nice views for such a short hike.

ROSS LAKE TRAILS

Guests at Ross Lake Resort can pick up the Big Beaver Trail right behind the cabins. A short stroll to the northeast takes you to Green Point; a slightly longer walk to the southwest leads to Ross Dam. The intrepid hiker might want to try Sourdough Mountain. From the resort, it's a little over 7.0 miles each way, and punishingly steep. Take Big Beaver northeast past Green Point to a junction with Pierce Mountain Packway. Double back southwest, where you'll ascend about 4400 feet over the next 6 miles to a nearly 6000-foot summit. There are panoramic and photogenic views from the site of a lookout tower (the tower itself is not open to the public). The summit can also be reached via an equally difficult trail from Diablo Dam, to the south.

Several other trails are accessible via water taxi from Ross Lake Resort. Pick up Big Beaver at the Big Beaver Campground just a few miles uplake and enjoy a nice, flat 4-hour walk (2 hours each way) to a forest of 1000-year-old cedars. Or walk in Jack Kerouac's bootsteps to Desolation Peak, where the beat-generation poet worked as a fire lookout in 1956. You can access the 9.4-mile, moderately steep trail from a water-taxi stop about a dozen miles uplake from the resort.

PARK BUTTE/RAILROAD GRADE/SCOTT PAUL

These popular trails are a part of the Mt. Baker National Recreation area, located northwest of Baker Lake, on the southern slope of Mt. Baker. From Highway 20, take Baker Lake Road, which becomes USFS Road 11, for 12.8 miles, then turn left onto USFS Road 12. Proceed 3.5 miles to USFS Road 13 and turn right. Continue to the end of the road (about 6.0 miles) and the trailhead (total mileage from Highway 20: 22.3). Park Butte is a scenic 7.0-mile round-trip trail that passes through Schrieber's Meadow, crosses a suspension bridge, then switchbacks up a forested slope to Morovitz Meadow, ending at a historic lookout tower. Total elevation gain is 2800 feet. Those wishing a short sample of this area can stop at Schrieber's Meadow, only about a half mile from the trailhead. Railroad Grade is a signed 1.0-mile spur that leaves the Park Butte trail after 2.0 miles, climbing a moraine to come face-to-face with Easton Glacier. Scott Paul is a newer trail that also begins as a spur off the Park Butte Trail. A loop trail constructed in the memory of a Forest Service ranger, this 6.0-mile trail gains 2000 feet.

CASCADE PASS/SAHALE ARM

Leave this one to the clueless weekenders. Yes, it's a beautiful trail, especially for those willing to go beyond the pass and up the arm of the glacier. But, because it is so gorgeous, and so easy, Cascade Pass reminds me of an aging showgirl who has been around the block a few too many times. The several hundred pairs of boots that traverse her flanks each day have left their mark. The Forest Service is scrambling valiantly to preserve the area: reforesting like crazy, building deck areas to handle the heavy traffic, etc. So, yes, it's a stunning trail, but let's give the poor old girl a break. Take the Hidden Lake Peaks trail instead (see above), or ask the rangers about the Thornton Lakes or Lookout Mountain/Monogram Lake trails.

Contacts

CONCRETE CHAMBER OF COMMERCE
P.O. Box 743, Concrete, WA 98237

MT. BAKER-SNOQUALMIE NATIONAL FOREST HQ   (206) 775-9702
Forest Supervisor
21905 - 64th Avenue West, Mountlake Terrace, WA 98043

NORTH CASCADES NATIONAL PARK;   (360) 856-5700
MT. BAKER RANGER DISTRICT;
Mt. Baker-Snoqualmie National Forest
2105 State Route 20, Sedro Woolley, WA 98284-9394

NORTH CASCADES NATIONAL PARK WILDERNESS CENTER   (360) 873-4500
Ross Lake National Recreation Area
728 Ranger Station Road, Marblemount, WA 98267

NORTH CASCADES VISITOR CENTER   (206) 386-4495
Newhalem

SKAGIT COUNTY SHERIFF   (360) 336-9450

WHATCOM COUNTY SHERIFF   (360) 676-6650

"The Bear" in uptown Concrete

	CLARK'S SKAGIT RIVER CABINS	CASCADE LOG CABINS	BUFFALO RUN BUNKHOUSE	NORTH CASCADE INN	BAKER LAKE RESORT	ROSS LAKE RESORT
PRICE (1996 RATES, PRE-TAX, 2 PERSON)	$25–$97	$50	$45–$65	$45	$55–$75	$56–$84 Bunkhouses $108 for up to 6
EXTRA PERSON	$9 (children under 10: $8)	$5	Included	$5	$7 (children under 16 $4)	$6–$10 (kids under 4 free)
PAYMENT METHODS	VISA, MC, AmEx, Disc, Check, Cash	Call	VISA, MC, AmEx, Disc, Check, Cash	VISA, MC, AmEx, Disc, Check, Cash	VISA, MC, Disc, cash	VISA, MC, Check, Cash
# OF UNITS	26	5 cabins	1 studio unit	14 motel rooms	9 cabins	10 cabins, 3 bunkhouses
PRIVATE BATH	Yes	Yes	Yes	Yes	No	Yes, 8 cabins & bunkhouses
SHARED BATH	No	No	No	No	Yes, 5 cabins	Yes, 2 cabins
BREAKFAST INCLUDED?	No	No	No	No	No	No
COOKING FACILITIES?	Yes; most with full kitchens	Yes, full kitchens	Yes, full kitchen	No	Yes, some units	Yes; full kitchens (some without ovens)
POOL	No	No	No	No	No	No
HOT TUB	No	No	No	No	No	No
CHILDREN	OK	OK	OK	OK	OK	OK
PETS	OK $10 per night	Call	Call	No	OK, $10 per night	No
SEASONS OF OPERATION	Year-round	Call	Year-round	Year-round	Year-round; weekends only Oct 1–Apr 1	Closed Oct 31–mid-June

Table 2.
Lodgings in the Highway 20 West vicinity

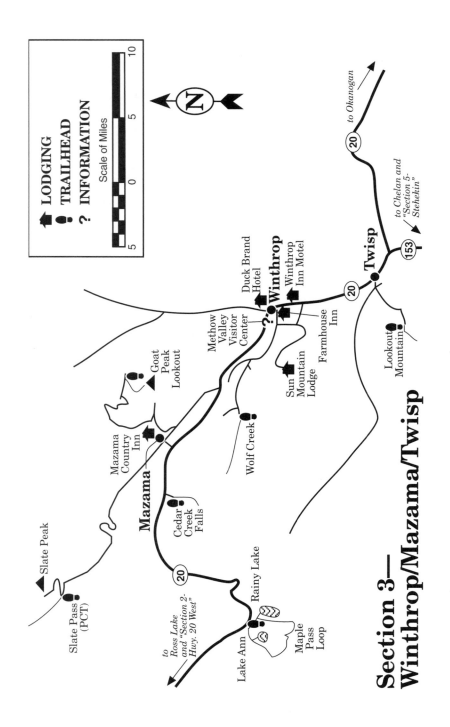

Winthrop/Mazama/Twisp
(Methow Valley, Highway 20 East)

Overview

At the east end of the North Cascades Highway lies the Methow Valley, a four-season recreational paradise inhabited by residents equally committed to preserving the environment and to providing a tourist-friendly recreational experience. The area's answer to eco-tourism is an emphasis on "trail-based recreation": hiking, horseback riding, mountain biking, and cross-country skiing. While this commitment is not embraced wholeheartedly by everyone in the valley (the specter of downhill skiing raises its head periodically, and is systematically shot down), it seems to be the prevailing sentiment.

The Methow Valley Sport Trails Association (MVSTA), backed by the money and the muscle of many powerful valley residents in cooperation with the US Forest Service, has constructed an incredible network of multi-use trails throughout the valley. When snow is present, these trails are groomed and closed to all but cross-country skiers, but when dry, they are open to hikers and mountain bikers. You may choose to walk these trails, but be aware that the width required for snow-grooming machinery makes them feel more like roads than wilderness trails. However, the overall gentle slopes and good grading make them a good choice for families with children or others wanting a gentle, predictable route. For more information on the MVSTA, write P.O. Box 147, Winthrop, WA 98862.

As the eastern gateway to the North Cascades Highway, the Methow Valley, specifically the communities of Winthrop and Twisp and the hamlet of Mazama, is also an ideal staging area for accessing nearby Okanogan National Forest trails. The Okanogan National Forest encompasses 1.7 million acres, and administers an additional 200,000 acres of the adjacent Mt. Baker-Snoqualmie and Wenatchee national forests. Hiking is excellent here on the less populated and sunny eastern slopes of the Cascades.

Wildlife indigenous to the area includes several types of deer and a prodigious selection of butterflies, both of which you will have trouble *not* spotting. Less commonly seen are elk and moose, Canadian geese in season, and black bears (bears are most commonly seen in the fall, when the berries are ripe). Rattlesnakes are a factor on trails east of the Methow River, especially those with south-facing, sun-warmed slopes. Curiously, the locals insist the reptiles are never found on the west side of the river. Trails most prone to rattlesnakes are noted and are usually signed at the trailheads.

The town of Winthrop is worth a visit even for nonhikers. When the North Cascades Highway (Highway 20) opened in 1972, a cooperative effort by local merchants gave the community a "Wild West" theme, complete with boardwalks, hitching posts, and false storefronts. Several historical buildings remain, among them pioneer Guy Waring's 1879 log cabin, the centerpiece of the Shafer Museum, which also includes cabins built in 1889 and 1910. Browsers will enjoy shopping for antiques, arts and crafts, and unique gifts in Winthrop's shops. Treats including espresso drinks, fresh juices, and ice cream are always close by. The old west pioneers never had it so good.

Twisp, 9 miles south of Winthrop on Highway 20, is a little farther into the "dry side" of the state. It is an unpretentious town not given over to impressing tourists, but nonetheless offers good shopping and a couple of fine eateries (see *Dining, below*).

Mazama, 13 miles northwest of Winthrop on Highway 20, is the "last stop on the block" for those heading west into the North Cascades. A tiny outpost with lodgings and a store/cafe, it is the closest spot to the best of the hiking trails.

Reach the Methow Valley from Seattle by taking Interstate 5 north to Burlington, then Highway 20 east 120 miles. Highway 20 is closed from November until mid-April. When it is closed, use Highway 2. From Seattle, take I-5 north to Highway 522, and on it pass through Bothell and Monroe to reach Highway 2. From Bellingham and points north, take I-5 south to Everett to connect with Highway 2. Take Highway 2 east to Wenatchee, then, following the signs to East Wenatchee/Okanogan, cross the Columbia River, and turn left at the junction, heading north on Highway 2/97/151 for Pateros and Okanogan. Stay on 97/151, bearing left at Orondo, where Highway 2 turns toward Spokane. Just before Pateros, turn left onto Highway 153 toward Twisp/Winthrop. From Spokane, take Highway 2 east to Orondo (at the Columbia River), then turn north onto 97/151 and continue toward Pateros as above.

Lodgings

SUN MOUNTAIN LODGE
P.O. Box 1000, Winthrop, WA 98862
1-800-572-0493

One cannot write about lodgings in the Methow Valley, or in the North Cascades, without mentioning Sun Mountain Lodge, one of the crown jewels of fine lodging in Washington state. The seclusion and pampering of this all-season mountaintop resort will make you feel as though you'd been helicoptered into the middle of a James Bond movie. Sun Mountain Lodge is the only resort in the entire state to earn AAA's 4-Diamond award for both the lodgings and the restaurant.

Begun by a wilderness-loving visionary named Jack Barron in 1965, Sun Mountain Lodge has expanded in scope and amenities steadily over the years. The lodge was purchased by a German concern in 1987. Their investment of tens of millions of dollars has resulted in a world-class experience that remains true to Barron's original vision of a deluxe retreat reflecting the Methow Valley wilderness experience. Rock and timber are the predominant decor themes, with accents utilizing the skills of local artists and craftsmen.

The main lodge includes 50 guest rooms. Those with views of Mt. Gardner (referred to as "Mountain View" rooms) range in price from $105 to $165 most times of year. "Valley View" rooms in the main building range from $95 to $155. The lodge also encloses the restaurant (see *Dining,* below), gift shops, activities center, library and other common areas. The activities center (currently planned for expansion), offers seasonal rental equipment (cross-country skis and mountain bikes) and coordinates the lodge's many activities, including guided hikes, naturalist retreats, rafting trips, horseback rides, and fly fishing. Many special programs are available just for children. For a memorable family experience, ask about the Cowboy Camp Dinner or Buckaroo Breakfast: a horseback or hay-wagon ride to a hearty country meal at an old homestead.

The Gardner Building, adjacent to the main lodge, has 28 deluxe rooms with the feel of studio apartments. Each Gardner room has a fireplace, a wet bar with minifridge and coffeemaker, and a sitting area, and all look out on a view of the mountain. These rooms range from $120 to $195. Both the main lodge and the Gardner building also offer suites, with separate sleeping quarters, ranging from $175 to $260.

A selection of cabins is also available for rent at Patterson Lake, just down the mountain from the main lodge. These range in price from older units renting at $105 to $165 to newer, larger units renting at $175 to $260. All cabins include kitchen facilities. Rowboats, paddle boats, canoes and fishing gear are available for rent to make your Patterson Lake experience complete.

All prices quoted are for two adults. Kids 12 and under stay free with parents; add $16 for additional persons 13 and over. Holiday periods are slightly more and

Sun Mountain Lodge, crown jewel of the Methow Valley

require a 3-night minimum. Weekends require a 2-night minimum. Special reduced rates apply during Spring and Fall Value periods: approximately mid-March to mid-April and early November to mid-December.

In the winter of 1996-1997, Sun Mountain opened its latest advance in luxury: the Mt. Robinson wing. Situated in a private glen a short distance beyond the Gardner Building, the 24 Mt. Robinson guest rooms have incredible views, whirlpool tubs, and enough "elbow room" (500 sq. ft.) for a comfortable extended stay. Call for prices. These ultra-deluxe rooms run $160 to $235; 2 bedroom suites $330-$490.

To reach Sun Mountain Lodge, turn west on Twin Lakes Road off Highway 20 just south of the Methow River bridge at the southeast end of downtown Winthrop. After 1.6 miles, turn left on Patterson Lake Road. Continue up this road for 6.4 miles, passing Patterson Lake and following the signs for Sun Mountain Lodge.

Highlight: Four-star mountaintop lodge overlooking the Methow Valley.

WOLFRIDGE RESORT
Rt. 2 Box 655, Wolf Creek Road, Winthrop, WA 98862
1-800-237-2388 or (509) 996-2828

Sun Mountain Lodge may take your breath away, but Lou and Gabrielle Childers' WolfRidge Resort will steal your heart. Combining a tremendous amount of energy and a dedication to trail-based recreation, the Childers family began construction of this unique retreat in 1989. The ever-evolving facilities are an obvious labor of love.

Lodgings at WolfRidge Resort consist of a series of modular-use fourplex cabins and one free-standing cabin unit. The fourplex units offer the flexibility of combining rooms with suites for larger parties. Hotel-style rooms start at $59 for two persons, with one-bedroom suites at $93 and two-bedroom, two-bath townhouse combos at $139 for four persons. The Wolf Hollow Cabin In The Woods is an 1100-square-foot custom home with loft bedroom and main floor bedroom that rents for $149 for four persons. All units are smartly designed and situated on the ample grounds to

Staying at WolfRidge is like staying with family

give a feeling of privacy. Sleeping areas in all units have both queen and single beds; suites also offer queen sofa sleepers in the living rooms. Adults beyond the two or four mentioned per unit are $10 additional, and kids are $5 additional. Discounted rates are offered for extended stays and during certain off-season/midweek periods.

A lovely footbridge on a nature trail near WolfRidge

WolfRidge suites and the Wolf Hollow Cabin each have fully equipped kitchens plus decks with barbecues. All WolfRidge rooms have TV's, telephones, coffee makers and a comfortable rustic yet contemporary ambiance enhanced by log-beam ceilings, tasteful decor, and the Childers' own handcrafted log furniture and accessories. (Yes, these folks "do it all!" Be sure to ask for a brochure about their other business, WolfRidge Log Furniture & Accessories. You'll admire the craftsmanship as well as the environmentally conscious methods of timber harvest and construction.)

Situated on 60 beautiful acres, the WolfRidge Resort's grounds include a heated swimming pool, hot-tub gazebo with changing room, playground, picnic areas, and a recreation room with outdoor fireplace that doubles as a centrally located "warming hut" for cross-country skiers on the MVSTA trail network (see *Overview*, above). The grounds include trails and are adjacent to the People Mover cable tram (see *WolfRidge Resort Trails* under *Other Hike Notes*, below).

Best of all, despite all the amenities—the cathedral ceilings, the mountain grandeur—staying at WolfRidge Resort is like staying with family. Lou and Gabrielle manage to be warm and accommodating in the extreme, without being intrusive in any way. They have anticipated the needs of the privacy-seeking, nature-respecting, adventure-loving traveler, and met those needs from the design up.

To reach WolfRidge Resort, turn west on Twin Lakes Road off Highway 20 just south of the Methow River bridge at the southeast end of downtown Winthrop. Go about 1.5 miles and turn right onto Wolf Creek Road. Follow Wolf Creek Road until you come to a fork and the pavement ends. Take the right fork; after one mile, turn right at the WolfRidge Resort sign.

Highlight: Private cabin suites with kitchens are the perfect couple, family, or group getaway.

MAZAMA COUNTRY INN
HCR 74 Box B9, Mazama, WA 98833
1-800-843-7951 or (509) 996-2681

A "rustic-chic" lodge at the eastern gateway to the North Cascades Highway, Mazama Country Inn offers 14 guest rooms. All rooms are clean and well cared for, with oak furniture, quilts, newer carpets and vinyls. Common areas, including the lobby, upstairs sitting room, and restaurant, have hand-peeled log beams and generous, polished woodwork.

The 10 rooms in the main lodge have more of a quaint, "hunting lodge" feel, with wood wainscoting and wallpaper accents, while "The Back 4" rooms by the hot tub are more modern. All rooms have queen beds and ceiling fans, and are stocked with shampoo, conditioner, lotion, and extra towels for use with the hot tub and sauna.

Rooms 1, 2, and 3, downstairs in the main lodge, are the smallest. They share a deck across the back of the building that connects them conveniently with the hot tub/sauna area. They rent for $75 on weekends, $70 week nights. Rooms 4, 5, 6, and 7 in the main lodge (4 and 5 upstairs, 6 and 7 down) are larger, with two queen beds, chairs, and a small table, and bathrooms with tub as well as shower (all other rooms have shower only). They rent for $85 on weekends, $80 week nights. Rooms 8, 9 and 10, upstairs in the main lodge, are configured as loft rooms, with the queen bedroom up a narrow staircase, and a small sitting room with built-in bunk below. These rooms have a small private balcony and rent for $80 on weekends, $75 weeknights.

The Back 4—rooms 11, 12, 13, and 14—are on the ground level. A bit roomier, they each include a table and chairs, private deck, and spacious bath, and two of them have an additional single bed. They rent for $85 on weekends, $80 on week nights.

Rates listed are for two persons per room; additional person $15. Discounts of $10 per night are offered for midweek stays of four or more nights. A 50% deposit is taken at the time of reservation. No smoking, no pets. Children are allowed except during the winter season.

Things change at the Mazama Country Inn during the winter, which, for them, usually runs mid-December through mid-March. This is peak cross-country season, and, being situated along the MVSTA trail network, it's a busy time for the inn. Room packages, including three meals per day for two people, run $160–175 per night, with discounts for longer stays. Additional people sharing a room are $50 per night, and single persons are $20 less than the two-person rate. Meals are served family style, with lunches self-packed "to go" on the trails. No children under 13 during ski season, but inquire about a selection of nearby cabins that can accommodate families.

The Mazama Country Inn—rustic chic

To find the Mazama Country Inn, take the Mazama turnoff from Highway 20. Cross the Methow River bridge, then come to an intersection with Lost River Road (Mazama Store is on your left). Proceed straight ahead onto the dirt road through the gateway in front of you. Then stay left, watching for signs to the inn and restaurant.

Highlight: "Rustic-chic" lodge with restaurant.

DUCK BRAND HOTEL
P.O. Box 118, Winthrop, WA 98862
(509) 996-2192

The Duck Brand is a 6-unit traditional hotel over a restaurant (see *Dining,* below), located just west of the Methow River bridge, on the east edge of historic downtown Winthrop.

Rooms at the Duck Brand range from $55.50 for one queen bed to $65.50 for two. All rooms have private baths, TV and air conditioning; a rollaway bed is available for $6.00 additional. Rooms are simple and clean, with rustic pine furnishings and touches of country decor. All are accessed from the back of the property and have views overlooking the charming, "old west" main street of Winthrop. As parking can be a zoo in front of the restaurant during tourist season, park in the lot above and behind the building for best access to your room.

The hotel is nonsmoking, and offers discounts in the winter. No pets, please. Its country ambiance places the Duck Brand Hotel in a category above common hotel lodgings, and its downtown location makes it attractive for those who plan to shop and stroll the streets of Winthrop.

Highlight: Charming hotel overlooking "old west" Winthrop.

THE WINTHROP INN MOTEL
P.O. Box 265, Winthrop, WA 98862
1-800-444-1972 or (509) 996-2217

A newer, 30-unit motel in the eastern section of town, the Winthrop Inn offers a quiet night's sleep in air-conditioned comfort and a hot shower to start or end your day. Other amenities include a small swimming pool, year-round hot tub, satellite TV, and hot coffee in the morning. Managers LeRoy and Carlene Johnson are helpful with information about local sites and activities, and maintain a sparkling, if standard, facility inside and out. Plenty of dining options nearby, but no connecting restaurant or lounge, which makes for an even quieter room. Room rates range from $50 to $75, with seasonal variations. The motel is located on the east side of Highway 20, south of the Methow River bridge.

Highlight: Clean, modern motel with pool and spa.

Dining

SUN MOUNTAIN LODGE RESTAURANT
P.O. Box 1000, Winthrop, WA 98862
1-800-572-0493

When I visit the Methow Valley, I always budget for one dinner at Sun Mountain. While that's no mean feat—a full dinner for two without alcohol can easily set you back $80.00—this *is* the place to splurge. From the moment your appetizer hits the table (if not before), you'll understand why this restaurant has earned the AAA 4-Diamond rating. And for a view that's beyond any ratings system, do whatever it takes to get a window seat (dining early or late helps, as does a midweek reservation).

Sun Mountain serves a fresh, seasonally inspired menu that changes three or four times a year. Choices always include fresh and unusual seafood, pastas, and vegetarian options. You will find traditional beef, pork, and/or poultry as well, but there's nothing traditional about the preparation. The chef is a master of sauces: curries, peppercorn, pestos, mustards, and whatever the ethnic trend of the day might be. I ate my first cactus at Sun Mountain Lodge when Tex-Mex was king; other fashions masterfully interpreted in recent years have included Thai, east Indian, and, of course, Pacific Northwest cuisine. The menu on my most recent visit featured an outstanding marlin, and three vegetarian dishes using half a dozen different mushroom varieties. Special requests and dietary restrictions graciously honored. Plan to spend $20-$30 per entree, which includes soup or salad, and $3.50–$10 for most appetizers.

Perhaps best of all, everyone—from the host to the waitstaff to the chef—seems to genuinely enjoy working here. That may go a long way toward explaining why this is truly a premier dining experience.

Highlight: Top-notch, seasonally inspired cuisine suitable for a celebration meal.

DUCK BRAND CANTINA
P.O. Box 118, Winthrop, WA 98862
(509) 996-2191

After a long day of hiking, nothing hits the spot like a heaping plate at the Duck Brand. With indoor seating as well as a spacious and inviting deck, the casual atmosphere makes this a natural choice for the active crowd. Relax with a cold beer or soft drink and enjoy complementary chips along with the Duck Brand's signature hot sauce as you wait for your entree.

Prices range from $7 to $13 for entrees including south-of-the-border specialties, monster salads, steaks, poultry, fish, and pasta. Vegetarians will find Mexican options and a stir-fry sans meat. In homage to the name "Duck Brand" (for the cattle brand of town founding father Guy Waring), a few dishes include roast duck or a duck-breast option in lieu of chicken. Desserts are as massive as the dinners, with home-baked pies taking center stage.

The Duck Brand Cantina is also a great place to start the day. Unique and filling breakfasts offer options to please any palate. It's hard to decide between the egg creations and the fresh bakery goods. (And, believe me, you won't have room for both.) Espresso drinks are available, but stick with the outstanding fresh ground coffee.

Highlight: Heaping plates of Mexican and American specialties in a cantina atmosphere.

RIVERSIDE GRILL
Winthrop, WA 98862
(509) 996-2444

Just down the block from the Duck Brand, on Winthrop's main street, Denise and Mike Pruett offer two restaurants in one at the Riverside Grill. In the summer, the

Riverside Grill is a casual eatery specializing in hefty 1/3-pound burgers and hand-crafted pizzas. In the winter, they retro-fit the entire facility into a quality bistro with an emphasis on continental cuisine and fine wines, complete with fireplace and white table cloths.

Most hikers will visit the Riverside Grill during burger season, and they'll find plenty of choices: buffalo burgers, garden burgers, lamb burgers, salmon burgers, or plain ol' beef burgers with a variety of toppings. Other standards include a few chicken items, salads, deli sandwiches, and he-man daily specials that range from ribs and steaks to more chicken choices. The proprietors are especially proud of their pizzas, with homemade crusts and oven-roasted sauce. Top-of-the-line is the Gourmet, featuring artichoke hearts, roasted garlic, and sun-dried tomato pesto; a large is $17.95. Other entrees range from $5 to $9. Beer and wine are served, including specialty beers, ales, and Northwest microbrews. Draft beer, soft drinks, and lemonade are available by the pitcher or glass.

Highlight: Casual burger-and-pizza eatery in the summer, continental bistro in the winter.

CINNAMON TWISP BAKERY
116 N. Glover, Twisp, WA 98856
(509) 997-5030

A glorious surprise! The Cinnamon Twisp Bakery, situated one block north of Highway 20, across from the Branding Iron restaurant and next door to Glover Street Market Natural Foods, is a feast for lovers of whole-grain baking. From the signature "Cinnamon Twisps" (flaky pastry twists) to savory filled pastries, everything I sampled from this bakery was sublime.

Pema Bresnahan and the others at the Cinnamon Twisp bakery exude a positive attitude and take a caring, mindful approach to their products. They use organically grown local whole grains and flours from Okanogan County's Windsong Farms (but don't let the "whole grain" label scare off the white-flour aficionados in your party—tasty sweet glazes and rich fillings will satisfy even a jaded teenager's palate!). Breakfast treats on any given day might include poppyseed scones, Morninglory Muffins, and orange honey buns. Generous loaves of bread come in such inspired varieties as fig-cashew, basil-garlic, and hazelnut. Savory luncheon empanadas (perfect to pack along on your hike) have such tasty and heart-healthy fillings as hummus and black bean with cheese.

Highlight: Whole-grain heaven! Don't miss this healthy gourmet bakery.

ROADHOUSE DINER
202 Methow Valley Highway (Highway 20), Twisp, WA 98856
(509) 997-4015

For a place that proudly displays "Road Kill Cafe" T-shirts, the food at the Roadhouse Diner is surprisingly good! Don't be put off by the atmosphere—big, dark rooms with high ceilings and exposed beams—this is the kind of place where everybody from meat-n-potatoes types to vegetarians can find a tasty and filling meal at breakfast, lunch, or dinner.

Anabel and Tony Andres are the warm and accommodating proprietors of this multi-faceted diner. Omelettes and other specialty breakfasts start around $5. Lunches, with an emphasis on "Killer Sandwiches," start at $3.95. Dinners (chicken, beef, pasta) start around $8, with a Cornish game hen at $10.

The Roadhouse Diner serves cocktails, including the meal-in-a-glass "Roadhouse Mary"; team this with a giant $18.95 "Roadhouse Platter" of assorted (mostly fried) appetizers for a filling snack. Other good bets at the Roadhouse are desserts (their forté) and the Sunday brunch buffet, a bargain at $6.95.

Highlight: All around diner, featuring bargain Sunday brunch.

Walks and Hikes
Hikes are listed in approximate order of difficulty.

RAINY LAKE

Map:	Green Trails #50 "Washington Pass"
Distance:	2.0 miles round trip
Elevation Gain:	Negligible
Estimated Time:	1 hour or less
Highlight:	Barrier-free trail suitable for any hiker.

This broad, paved, almost level path is one of the premier handicapped-accessible trails in the North Cascades, leading along a forested path to a lake-viewing platform.

Getting There

From the Mazama turnoff on Highway 20, go 22.7 miles west on Highway 20. Turn left into the RAINY PASS PICNIC AREA. (Coming from the west, go 50 miles east of Marblemount, turning right into the picnic area.) On the way to the parking area, you will see the shared trailhead for Rainy Lake and Lake Ann on your left; continue on to the parking area and walk back to the trailhead. The ample parking lot (also a pass-through point for the Pacific Crest Trail) includes information kiosks and restrooms.

The Hike

From the trailhead map, go left on the paved path. The path is hiker-only, no stock, and no mechanized or motorized vehicles except wheelchairs and similar conveyances for mobility-impaired hikers. Stroll through spruce and hemlock forest; pass a pleasant waterfall at 0.2 mile, and the intersection with the Maple Pass Loop trail at 0.5 mile. There are benches and "passing lanes" en route, along with a few interpretive signs explaining the ecosystem.

A landing at 1.0 mile is paved and ringed with logs and benches, providing a close-up view of the lake. Frisco Mountain's Lyall Glacier broods on the opposite shore, and waterfalls cascade down to the lake.

CEDAR CREEK FALLS

Map:	Green Trails #51 "Mazama"
Distance:	4.0 miles round trip
Elevation Gain:	500'
Estimated Time:	1 hour, 45 minutes
Highlight:	Easy hike to a mighty waterfall.

The Cedar Creek Trail (Okanogan National Forest Trail #476) actually extends 9.5 miles from the trailhead, climbing from a starting point at 3200 feet to a high point over 6500 feet, eventually intersecting the North Creek Trail. Most folks venture only as far as the falls, a mere 2.0 miles up the trail. This Cedar Creek Falls segment of the trail is well-maintained and popular, a gently inclining trek through young forest requiring just enough exertion to make the falls an apt reward. As such, it is a good hike for children. When runoff is high, you can hear the creek for the entire length of the hike, but see it only after about 1.8 miles. The rest of the time, the scenery is young conifers and canyonside greenery, with one nice glimpse of Goat Peak near the start of the hike. The falls are beautiful and peaceful, but not particularly photogenic, so you might want to save weight and leave your camera home.

Getting There

On Highway 20, go west 4.3 miles past the Lost River Road/Mazama turnoff (about 18 miles west of Winthrop), to the signed Cedar Creek turnoff. Follow gravel USFS Road 5310-200 about a mile to a gravel pit and the signed trailhead for Okanogan National Forest Trail #476.

The Hike

The trail begins with a couple of somewhat steep but short sections. Let the kids burn off that energy here, as the rest of the hike is only at a gentle incline. The trail heads toward the west bank above the creek (which you can hear but not see), then south.

The first time a view opens up to your left, at about 0.2 mile, turn to see Goat Peak in the distance to the northeast. If you miss it on the way up, don't sweat it—you'll see it easily on the way down.

At 1.8 miles the sound of rushing water increases in volume and you know you're getting close to Cedar Creek. Indeed, if you look to your left at this time, you can at last "see der creek."

A butterfly graces hikers' hats at Cedar Creek Falls

At 2.0 miles, you arrive at the falls. Cedar Falls is not a "postcard view" waterfall, in that you cannot step back and get a picture looking up at the falls. Rather, you are above and beside the falls, and very close to them. Several vantage points afford good options for viewing parts of the falls, and for picnicking and resting up for the return trip. Relax atop the boulders and enjoy the music of the falls. Watch young children near the edge, as it is steep and footing can be unsure.

Return to the trailhead, watching for Goat Peak as you near the end.

SLATE PASS (PACIFIC CREST TRAIL)

Map:	Green Trails #50 "Washington Pass" (also, #51 "Mazama" shows access from Mazama, and #18 "Pasayten Peak" shows trail continuing past the first 1.5 miles to Windy Pass and beyond)
Distance:	4.0 miles round trip (more or less if desired)
Elevation Gain:	200'
Estimated Time:	2 hours (more or less if desired)
Highlight:	Wide-open ridge hike; drive to highest road in state.

Nowhere in the North Cascades is a "top o' the world" experience more easily attained. The *drive* can be harrowing for those nervous about heights, but the hike is a nearly level, wide open, well-maintained delight, traversing high meadows along a ridge just 30 miles from the Canadian border.

Bring the whole family for this one, even those who don't hike. The drive up and the trailhead views are worth it.

Getting There

The drive to Slate Pass (also known locally as the drive to Harts Pass and Slate Peak) is an experience all its own. Plan at least an hour each way. The route is one-lane, steep in places, and has drop-offs. It is *safe* (check with the ranger station for current conditions, of course) but can be nerve-wracking for some. Use extreme caution on corners, and expect two-way traffic on a summer day. Finally, if you meet a truck hauling horses (the only large-scale vehicles allowed on this road), local custom asks that you allow the truck to pass on the *inside,* regardless of who's on the right or left, if at all possible.

From Highway 20, take the Mazama turnoff. Cross the Methow River bridge, then come to a T intersection with Lost River Road. Turn left, toward the Mazama Store. It's a good idea to fuel yourself and your vehicle here—this is the last civilization you'll see for several hours. Top off your radiator, too; it's a long, steep pull to the top.

Follow Lost River Road, which crosses Lost River bridge at 6.8 miles and loses pavement at 6.9 miles, then becomes Harts Pass Road (the point at which the name changes is not clear). You will follow this road 19.2 miles. Along the way, you'll pass infamous Deadhorse Point at 12.0 miles, a narrow stretch of this one-lane, gravel road that winds precariously around the edge of a sheer cliff. Use extreme caution, as the outside edge of the road tends to crumble away in big chunks here!

At 19.1 miles, USFS Road 5400/500 intersects on your left, going to Meadows Campground and Pacific Crest Trail access. At 19.2 miles, reach Harts Pass. A campground with a pit toilet is on your left, a little ranger hut is on your right, and USFS Road 5400/700, a rough and not always passable road signed CHANCELLOR 9, goes straight ahead. (The Pacific Crest Trail crosses Chancellor road a few dozen feet past this intersection). Turn right, around the ranger hut, onto USFS Road 5400/600, which is signed SLATE PEAK 3.

Pass a set of restrooms and an unloading area for horse trucks on your left 0.4 mile past Harts Pass. A mile and a half past Harts Pass, on your left at the crook of a hairpin turn, is the parking lot for the Pacific Crest Trail at Slate Pass, from which this hike begins.

Before or after your Slate Pass PCT hike, you'll want to drive the additional mile up the road to its end at Slate Peak. (Pass the trailhead for Buckskin Ridge on your right en route.) At 7440 feet elevation, Slate Peak is the highest point attainable by road in Washington state. Park at the gate at road's end, about 0.25 mile from the lookout tower and viewpoint at the top. Enjoy the panorama from the parking area or take the short, steep stroll to the top.

The Hike

From the Slate Pass parking lot (1.5 miles north of Harts Pass, see above), follow the dirt path past the SLATE PASS/PACIFIC CREST TRAIL trailhead sign. This short path connects you with the PCT proper in less than fifty yards. Proceed to your right (north) on the PCT. (To your left, the trail drops a mile or so to Harts Pass. This mile is steeper and less visually rewarding than the trail from Slate Pass north.)

A well-defined, well-maintained (even graveled in some places) trail, this section

of the PCT takes off across high, heathered meadows, contouring around the side of Slate Peak. Views to the southwest across Slate Creek basin reveal row after row of Cascade peaks receding into the distance; you are above many of them, strolling unencumbered along this amazingly flat, wide-open trail.

A creek-fed meadow at about 1.75 miles is a splendid place for a catnap on a sunny day. At 2.0 miles, after a slight incline, you can see the buildings of Barron below, an old mining area. From there, if you choose to continue on, the trail drops 150' to Windy Pass at 3.75 miles.

Pacific Crest Trail access point at Hart's Pass

LAKE ANN

Map:	Green Trails #49 & #50, "Mt. Logan" & "Washington Pass"
Distance:	4.0 miles round trip
Elevation Gain:	700'
Estimated Time:	2 hours, 30 minutes
Highlight:	Easily attained cirque lake.

The second of three hikes from the same trailhead (see easier "Rainy Lake," above, and more difficult "Maple Pass Loop," below), Lake Ann is a moderate hike through lush forests and glacier-carved meadow basins to the banks of a beautiful cirque lake.

Getting There

From the Mazama turnoff on Highway 20, go 22.7 miles west on Highway 20. Turn left into the RAINY PASS PICNIC AREA. (Coming from the west, go 50 miles east of Marblemount, turning right into the picnic area.) On the way to the parking area, you will see the shared trailhead for Rainy Lake and Lake Ann on your left; continue on to the parking area and walk back to the trailhead. The ample parking lot (also a pass-through point for the Pacific Crest Trail) includes information kiosks and restrooms.

The Hike

The Lake Ann trail is hiker-only, no stock, mechanized or motorized vehicles. From the trailhead map, go right, up the steep dirt path that immediately begins a switchbacking ascent. The trail surface is rocky and rooty as it ascends through lush forest. Surrounding foliage includes ferns, vine maple, devil's club, and wild berries. Bracket and gill mushrooms, as well as coral- and sponge-like fungi, are abundant along the trail, in colors from lemon to mustard yellow, burgundy to brown, copper to steel gray.

After 0.5 mile, the trail opens up into an avalanche-chute meadow, affording views east across the valley toward Whistler Mountain. Thistles, bluebells, asters,

Pristine Lake Ann

and elderberries provide color; camp jays chatter inquiries as to the contents of your day pack. Over the next mile, the trail winds in and out of the forest, passing a waterfall, open areas, and views to your left of small tarns in the east end of the Lake Ann cirque.

Section 3 • Winthrop/Mazama/Twisp

As you near the signed Lake Ann turnoff at 1.5 miles, you'll see where wilderness rapists have beaten their own "shortcuts" to the meadowed cirque below. Wait for the LAKE ANN sign, which points you down a trail to the left. Descend through the forest and into a meadow; the ponds you see are not Lake Ann, not yet. The meadow is alive with color and moisture. Watch for the deep-blue mountain bog gentians, which are striking indigo flowers that line the paths late in the season just before the first snows, and late-season dwarf huckleberries.

Lake Ann finally reveals itself, blue-green and pristine. Approach its banks gently, mindful of the thousands who do likewise each summer. An island pokes up in the lake's southwest corner; the ridge of Maple Pass rises above the opposite shore.

Returning through the meadow, your view is dominated by Whistler Mountain, front and center in the distance. To its right, the cracked peak of Liberty Bell; to its left, Cutthroat Peak.

LOOKOUT MOUNTAIN

Map:	Green Trails #84 "Twisp"
Distance:	3.0 miles round trip
Elevation Gain:	1200'
Estimated Time:	A little over an hour up, a little under an hour down
Highlight:	Short, steep, early-season climb to a lookout tower and 360° view.

Here's a short, steep, fun little climb to a ramshackle (and inaccessible) fire-lookout tower. Well-maintained trail offers early-season opportunity and pretty forest scenery throughout. The payoff is a 360° panorama over the Methow Valley and views of the Sawtooth Ridge.

Rated by the Forest Service as one of the area's "easiest" hikes due to its short length, Lookout Mountain is actually a pretty good climb for the less fit hiker. Gaining 1200 feet in a little over a mile can feel like quite a bit if you're not used to it. So bring the teens and ambitious older children along, but leave the pre-schoolers and those with creaky knees behind.

The likelihood of spotting wildlife is high, especially deer and butterflies. (En route to the trailhead, our pace car was a showy swallowtail.)

Getting There

From Highway 20 in Twisp, turn west on Twisp River Road, following the signs toward the Twisp River. After 0.3 mile, fork left onto gravel Lookout Mountain Road. The road leads uphill and southwest (not to be mistaken for the other gravel road that intersects at the same spot and leads southeast). The trailhead is 6.6 miles from this intersection.

Lookout Mountain Road is rated as an all-weather gravel road, and is well-graded with a pretty good surface (can be washboardy in places). When cleared and graded, it is passable in a regular passenger car.

Beginning your ascent, you will wind past a few homesites (including one with a charming warning: "This area patrolled by shotgun three days a week—you guess which three!") Watch for a few hairpin turns including a double at 2.7 miles and a signed one at 5.1 miles. You will pass forks and intersections with a few less-developed roads (most notably a fork with USFS Road 200 at 4.75 miles), but always stay on the main gravel road. Sweeping views to your right over the Methow Valley at 6.4 miles indicate you are almost at the top.

At 6.6 miles, pull off to the right and park. A short section of road doubling back and uphill to the left is passable with most vehicles, but this is the best parking spot.

The Hike

Begin by walking up the short stretch of road that doubles back to the left (south). The trail forks off on your right after less than 0.1 mile.

Follow the well-maintained trail uphill along a ridge, with valley views to both sides. A cattle guard grating

Lookout Mountain lookout (from the Department of Redundancy Department?)

takes you through a barbed wire fence at about 0.3 mile. The climb is steady throughout this hike, gaining 1200 feet in less than 1.5 miles with a minimum of switchbacks.

At half a mile from the trailhead, views to the northeast over Twisp show just how high you've come. A few switchbacks just before the mile mark give you a push, and at 1.3 miles you break out into a meadowed hillside with dramatic views of the Sawtooth Mountain Range to the west. Possible snowcaps in view include Mission, Hoodoo, and Star peaks and Spirit Mountain. The high desert vegetation and the sometimes broiling sun at this point remind you that you are on the east side of the Cascades.

A final ascent curves around the tip of Lookout Mountain to the ramshackle (and inaccessible) fire-lookout tower. A sign (from the Department of Redundancy Department?) says, "Lookout Mountain Lookout, Elevation 5692."

The trail is attractive and forested, but the ridge is exposed and can get pretty hot in the summer, making this a good early-season jaunt as soon as the snow is gone.

WOLF CREEK

Map:	Green Trails #83 & #84, "Buttermilk Butte" & "Twisp"
Distance:	Various, up to 23.4 miles round trip
Elevation Gain:	800' first 4.2 miles; 1400' the next 4.4; 1200' the final 3.1 miles to Gardner Meadows

Estimated Time:	Varies; allow one hour per each 2 miles
Highlight:	Cool, green, shady walk along a creek draw.

Wolf Creek Trail, Okanogan National Forest Trail #527, is a deeply green, peaceful hike that is seldom overpopulated due to the abundance of other, "showier" trails nearby, and to the fact that it does not connect with any other through trails for backpacking loops. For hikers seeking panoramic alpine vistas, this won't be a satisfying trail. But those who live in cities or desert climates will appreciate the way this cool, green, shady stroll brings you close to the earth.

Other benefits of this hike include spectacular views on the drive to the trailhead, and the fact that you can choose a little or a lot of walking. The trail doesn't change much except to become a bit more wild as you go deeper into the canyon. Watch for bears.

Getting There

From the Methow River bridge at the southeast end of downtown Winthrop, make the first turn off of Highway 20, onto Twin Lakes Road. Go about 1.5 miles and turn right onto Wolf Creek Road. Follow Wolf Creek Road until you come to a fork and the pavement ends; WolfRidge Resort (see *Lodgings*, above) is one mile farther on the right fork, but you want to stay left for the Wolf Creek trailhead, which is 4.8 miles from this fork. (Subsequent mileages to the trailhead are given from this fork.)

Follow this narrow dirt road as it winds up the side of a rather steep hill. At 0.5 mile, there is another fork in the road. Take the right fork, following the sign for the Wolf Creek Trail; the road levels out. After 1.4 miles, pass over a cattle guard. The road continues to climb steeply, opening up into meadowed areas and affording exceptional views of the valley below, including a great view of Sun Mountain Lodge to the south at 3.7 miles. At 4.2 miles is another fork; stay left, following the sign to the Wolf Creek Trail, and begin descending to the trailhead, where ample parking and a spacious, clean (for a pit toilet) restroom are available.

The Hike

A soft, earthen trail leads you gently down from the trailhead to the north bank of east-flowing Wolf Creek. At 0.25 mile, the trail begins winding in and out of numerous draws as streams and creeklets flow down to join Wolf Creek. This hike is as much an auditory experience as a visual and a physical one; the lullaby of the creek and its feeder streams ebbs and flows with the turns of the path: first distinct, then muffled, never loud but never completely beyond earshot. Punctuating the symphony are calls of dozens of types of birds, and the chattering of squirrels. Greenery is lush in the canyon, and views across the valley are pretty and peaceful. This is a good early-season hike because of its sheltered location and low elevation; the early season also is the best time to see the valley's thick carpets of wildflowers and a more intense version of Wolf Creek, swollen with snowmelt runoff.

After gently descending for the first 0.75 mile, you will almost welcome the first ascent. Soon after, a field of giant boulders to the right of the path changes the landscape briefly and offers a potential stopping point. Above, towering extrusions of basalt show the likely origins of these boulders. This is also the first point where you can see the creek to your left.

At about 1.0 mile, you come close to the water's edge for the first time, at an overlook some 20-30 feet above the creek. The next time you draw so near the creek will be at 2.5 miles, after which a grassy meadow offers a good picnic spot on a cool day.

Choose as much or as little a hike as you like; then retrace your steps to the trailhead.

GOAT PEAK LOOKOUT

Map:	Green Trails #51 "Mazama"
Length:	5.0 miles round trip
Elevation Gain:	1400'
Estimated Time:	2 hours, 30 minutes
Highlight:	Manned lookout tower; great views.

Vistas, vistas everywhere. You'll see Silver Star and Gardner mountains, plus sweeping panoramas of the Methow Valley and Pasayten Wilderness, all from atop an isolated 7000-foot fire-lookout peak. The lookout tower is still active, and likely to

be manned by gregarious Lightnin' Bill Austin and his faithful companion Lookout Turk. Take a few minutes to chat with Bill; you may learn something, or at the very least feel as though you've made a friend. Ask about his painting and his poetry, participate in his photo album, and slip him a buck or two for film. Guys like Bill make you feel good about the Forest Service.

The Goat Peak hike can be hot and dry. Take it early or late in the day, or early or late in the season if the road is open. If you're lucky enough to catch it in the fall, the tamaracks may be turning gold and losing their needles—a curious sight. This is one of the few areas in the North Cascades where these nonevergreen conifers grow.

Lightnin' Bill and Lookout Turk—guardians of Goat Peak

Nonhikers might enjoy the drive, and could hang out on some big flat rocks just a few hundred feet up the trail. The rest of the hike is steep, and that, combined with the altitude, could leave first-time hikers gasping.

Getting There

From Highway 20, take the Mazama turnoff. Cross the Methow River bridge, then come to a T intersection with Lost River Road. Turn right. After 2.0 miles, you'll see a BIKE ROUTE sign indicating a left turn. Turn left here, doubling back into a hairpin turn onto USFS Road 52. As you ascend, you'll see snowmobile and cross-country skiing signs; the MVSTA trail system crosses this road. Pass a Sno-Park at 0.3 mile from Lost River Road. Cross Goat Creek on a one-lane bridge at 1.2 miles from Lost River Road. At 2.8 miles from Lost River Road, turn left, doubling back and ascending on a road signed GOAT PEAK L.O. TR 9/USFS Road 5225. From this junction, it is 9.2 miles to USFS Road 5225/200, a spur road that intersects on your right. Turn right here, following the sign for GOAT PEAK L.O. Stay on this road for 3.0 miles, passing a junction with spur road 5225/230. A parking area at the trailhead provides room for 8–10 cars. Trailhead is signed simply, TRAIL.

The Hike

Start off at 5600 feet on a wide dirt trail, exposed and dusty, with a definite dry and sunny "east side" character. After a short, moderate climb through sparse timber, you emerge onto a ridge with a high desert feel: exposed rock and sage-like shrubbery. As you climb, you alternate between stands of trees and open desert.

At 0.75 mile, the climb gets earnest as switchbacks begin. Grouse scramble about in the increasingly dense underbrush beneath stands of tamarack.

At about 2.0 miles, you attain the final ridgetop. Straight ahead, across the yawning Methow Valley, you are greeted by the jagged peaks of Silver Star Mountain, the highest of which is 8876 feet. Here, the trail bends left (south), following the open ridge for 0.5 mile in a moderate ascent to the lookout tower at 7019 feet.

MAPLE PASS LOOP

Map:	Green Trails # 49 & #50, "Mt. Logan" & "Washington Pass" (full loop trail does not show)
Distance:	7.5-mile loop (add 1.0 mile for spur to Lake Ann, add another 1.0 mile for spur to Rainy Lake)
Elevation Gain:	2000'
Estimated Time:	All day (4.5 to 6 hours)
Highlight:	Spectacular and challenging loop trail overlooking two mountain lakes.

One of the finest, most exciting hikes in the North Cascades, this loop trail takes you to the best of everything: alpine cirque overlooks, low and high meadows, wildflowers, ridgetops, expansive snowcap vistas. It's challenging, topping out at 6800 feet, but the views are incredible and ever-changing. Plan a full day, including the spurs to both Lake Ann and Rainy Lake (resulting in a 9.5-mile hike), and two or three snack stops.

As the Maple Pass Loop is a new trail, the trailhead map may not show it clearly. In the past, Maple Pass was an out-and-back trail that followed the route to Lake Ann, continued on to the pass, then returned the way it went out. Now, hikers can make a loop out of it, returning on a path that overlooks Rainy Lake, then intersects with the paved Rainy Lake trail a half mile from the trailhead. For the best effect, go counterclockwise.

Getting There

From the Mazama turnoff on Highway 20, go 22.7 miles west on Highway 20. Turn left into the RAINY PASS PICNIC AREA. (Coming from the west, go 50 miles east of Marblemount, turning right into the picnic area.) On the way to the parking area, you will see the shared trailhead for Rainy Lake and Lake Ann on your left; continue on to the parking area and walk back to that trailhead. The ample parking lot (also a pass-through point for the Pacific Crest Trail) includes information kiosks and restrooms.

The Hike

From the Rainy Lake/Lake Ann trailhead map, head to your right, up the steep little dirt trail toward Lake Ann. This is a hiker-only trail, no stock, or mechanized or motorized vehicles.

The first 1.5 miles of this trail are also the Lake Ann Trail, detailed on pp. 66-67. At the Lake Ann turnoff, either take the left fork down to Lake Ann (adding 1.0 total miles to your hike), or continue straight ahead on the main trail to Maple Pass.

From the Lake Ann trail intersection, the Maple Pass Trail continues up through the forest, breaking out shortly onto an open, rocky hillside overlooking Lake Ann. Gently inclining, the trail continues far above the north shore of the lake for half a mile, then switchbacks north and up toward Heather Pass. At 2.5 miles from the trailhead, a fork in the path gives you the option of wandering a few hundred feet off to your right on the meadow trail at Heather Pass, or continuing straight ahead on the main trail toward Maple Pass. Heather Pass is a beautiful spot, but the vistas it provides of Lewis Lake and the next valley will also be seen from the switchbacks ahead on the main trail.

As you continue climbing, Corteo Peak looms in the distance. Switchbacks provide the promised views to the northwest of Black Peak and tiny Lewis Lake. Soon you emerge, like the mountain goat you have become, above the treeline to the land of marmots and heather.

A sign informs you when you reach Maple Pass, a long 3.1 miles, at 6600 feet elevation. Here, the views go on forever, including that drama queen, Glacier Peak, in the distant southwest. Follow the ridgeline south, passing a few wind-sheltered depressions that make prime picnic spots. Continue climbing, topping out along a shoulder of Frisco Mountain. Keep an eye out for a low MAPLE PASS LOOP sign at the hike's high point, 6850 feet. From here, the trail drops over the edge to the east, switchbacking down toward a basin some 1000 feet below (the little pond in this basin is not Rainy Lake, but feeds into it).

After about a mile of descent, Rainy Lake comes into view on your right. At several points, the hillside on your left dips low enough that you can see Lake Ann, far below on your left, and Rainy Lake, even farther below on your right, simultaneously.

The next 2.0 miles are a steep descent through dense forest; mushroom spotting is excellent. The trail finally intersects with the paved Rainy Lake trail at about 7.0 miles. To finish, turn left and stroll the paved, level 0.5 mile to the parking lot. To see Rainy Lake up close and personal, turn right and walk an additional half a mile to the viewpoint before returning to your car, adding an easy mile to your hike.

Other Hike Notes
These hikes not personally reviewed or not as highly recommended as the above hikes.

WOLFRIDGE RESORT TRAILS

Because WolfRidge Resort is centrally located on the MVSTA trail network, nature trails and hiking paths are right outside the doors of the resort. A short stroll (just a few hundred feet) from the Wolf Hollow Cabin on a clearly marked trail takes you to the banks of the Methow River through a green and shady path decked with wild roses and tiger lilies in season; a different route takes you back to the main meadow and the fourplex cabins. For longer walks, use the cross-country skiing/mountain bike trails to find a nice level walk of any length (NOTE: do not walk on the trails when snow is present, they are reserved for skiers). Lou and Gabrielle Childers, hosts at WolfRidge Resort, can provide maps and information on the nearby trails.

While exploring the trails around WolfRidge Resort, don't miss the most unique way ever to cross a river: the People Mover pedestrian cable tram. Using towers recycled from the Squaw Valley Winter Olympics of 1960, this hand-crank system

Crank your way across the Methow River

was engineered exclusively for users of the Methow Valley trail-based recreation system. The sturdy metal basket has room for four, plus hooks for mountain bikes and a basket for skis. To use the system, leave one person on shore for safety and crank your way across the mighty Methow River to the trails on the other side. The system opened to the public in the winter of '96-'97, but, as a prototype, is subject to closure for retooling from time to time.

SUN MOUNTAIN LODGE TRAILS

Public trails ranging from strolls of less than a mile to hikes 4.5 miles and longer await you right outside the lodge; maps are available at the desk. Guided, naturalist-led hikes are available to Sun Mountain Lodge guests through the lodge's activities center.

LOST RIVER TO EUREKA CREEK

This is a nice, shady creekbed hike with modest elevation gain, utilizing the first four miles of the Monument Creek trail. Use Green Trail maps #50 "Washington Pass" and # 51 "Mazama" to locate. Drive from the Mazama Store northwest on Lost River Road. Pavement ends at 6.9 miles from Mazama, just after crossing the Lost River bridge. Turn right onto USFS Road 015 0.2 mile after pavement's end, following the sign for MONUMENT TRAIL #484. Proceed 0.1 mile uphill to parking area and trailhead, signed EUREKA CREEK 4. Due to a healthy population of rattlesnakes, this hike should be undertaken during the cooler parts of the day. Remember, they really are more afraid of you than you are of them. If you see one, let it go its way.

PIPESTONE CANYON

And speaking of rattlesnakes…here's why we buy guidebooks! If you have a problem with these reptilian friends, you'll want to avoid Pipestone Canyon at all costs. A 3-mile stretch running roughly parallel to Highway 20 about 5 miles east of it "as the crow flies," this is a popular mountain-bike trail, especially in the early spring before the other trails open. After things heat up, all but the heartiest locals simply advise hikers, "Don't go there!" Despite all that, Pipestone Canyon does have an unusual biosphere. Its sculpted canyon walls rising over sun-bleached sand and sage will make you feel more like you're in Arizona than Washington.

NORTH TWENTYMILE PEAK

This one is supposed to have a lookout tower on top, but I never got there. Here's a hike only for mountain goats and masochists. It's not so much the 5000-foot-plus elevation gain in five miles that turned me off, as the fact that the scenery was boring and the south-facing slope offered the worst of both worlds weather-wise: broiling hot and dry for the first two to three miles, then a brief period of cool and muddy before the trail became too snow-covered to traverse and yet return dry. And that was mid-June! There isn't a time of year when this hike is comfortable bottom-to-top, and the elevation gain makes it a pain in the calves (and other places) besides. Call this an "anti-recommendation." Still not convinced? Access this trailhead by going north from Winthrop on East Chewuch Road (as though you were going to Pearrygin Lake). Continue north, crossing the river, until the road becomes USFS Road 51. Turn east at Camp Four campground, crossing the river again. Follow signs to Road 700 and North Twentymile Trail.

Contacts

METHOW VALLEY SPORT TRAILS ASSOCIATION P.O. Box 147, Winthrop, WA 98862	(509) 996-3287
METHOW VALLEY VISITOR CENTER (operated by US Forest Service)	(509) 996-4000

METHOW VALLEY CENTRAL RESERVATIONS
  In WA
  Outside WA
	1-800-422-3048
	(509) 996-2148

OKANOGAN NATIONAL FOREST Forest Supervisor 1240 S. Second Ave., Okanogan, WA 98840	(509) 826-3275
TWISP CITY HALL	(509) 997-4081
TWISP INFORMATION CENTER & CHAMBER OF COMMERCE P.O. Box 565, Twisp, WA 98856	(509) 997-2926
U.S. FOREST SERVICE METHOW VALLEY RANGER DISTRICT Twisp Administration Office P.O. Box 188, 502 Glover St., Twisp, WA 98856	(509) 997-2131
WINTHROP CHAMBER OF COMMERCE P.O. Box 39, Winthrop, WA 98862	(509) 996-2125
WINTHROP CITY HALL	(509) 996-2320

	SUN MOUNTAIN LODGE	WOLFRIDGE RESORT	MAZAMA COUNTRY INN	DUCK BRAND HOTEL	WINTHROP INN MOTEL
PRICE (1996 RATES, PRE-TAX, 2 PERSON)	$95–$195+ suites to $260 cabins $105– $260	$59–$149 for up to 4	$70–$85	$55.50–$65.50	$50–$75
EXTRA PERSON	$16 (children 12 & under free)	$10 (children $5)	$15	Included (roll-away bed $6)	$5
PAYMENT METHODS	VISA, MC, AmEx, Checks, Cash	VISA, MC, Check, Cash	VISA, MC, Disc, Check, Cash	VISA, MC, AmEx, Cash	VISA, MC, AmEx, Disc, Cash
# OF UNITS	102 rooms plus several cabins	4–5 fourplexes, 1 cabin	14	6	30
PRIVATE BATH	Yes	Yes	Yes	Yes	Yes
SHARED BATH	No	No	No	No	No
BREAKFAST INCLUDED?	No	No	No	No	No
COOKING FACILITIES?	Rooms, no Cabins, yes	Yes, except smallest rooms	No	No	No
POOL	Yes	Yes	No	No	Yes
HOT TUB	Yes	Yes	Yes	No	Yes
CHILDREN	OK	OK	OK (except winter)	OK	OK
PETS	No	OK, $5 fee	No	No	Small pets OK in some rooms
SEASONS OF OPERATION	Year-round	Year-round	Year-round	Year-round	Year-round

Table 3. Lodgings in the Winthrop/Mazama/Twisp vicinity

The grounds at Sun Mountain Lodge

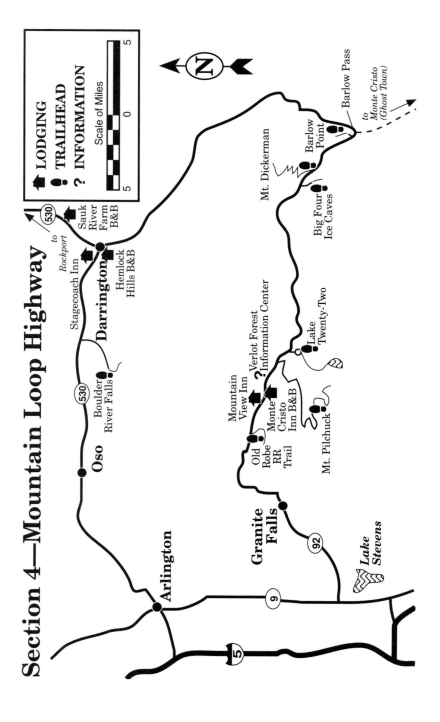

Section 4—Mountain Loop Highway

LODGING
TRAILHEAD
? INFORMATION

Scale of Miles

5   0   5

N

Barlow Pass

to
Monte Cristo
(Ghost Town)

Barlow
Point

Mt. Dickerman

Big Four
Ice Caves

530

Sauk
River
Farm
B&B

to
Rockport

Stagecoach Inn

Darrington

Hemlock
Hills B&B

Oso

530

Boulder
River Falls

Verlot Forest
Information Center

Lake
Twenty-Two

Mountain
View Inn

Monte
Cristo
Inn B&B

Mt. Pilchuck

Old
Robe
RR
Trail

Granite
Falls

92

9

Arlington

Lake
Stevens

5

Mountain Loop Highway
(Darrington/Monte Cristo/Granite Falls)

Overview

The Mountain Loop Highway is a 50-mile National Scenic Byway stretching from Highway 92 at Granite Falls to Highway 530 at Darrington. Less well-known than its showier cousin, the North Cascades Highway, Mountain Loop is a delightful pocket of adventure for the dayhiker. The highway itself is scenic, lined with wildflowers in the summer, berries and autumn colors in the fall. Dayhikes accessed along the highway range from easy, level strolls to challenging 5-hour-plus excursions, and trailheads are easy to access—many are right on the highway.

From Seattle, take Interstate 5 north to Everett, then Highway 2 east to State Highway 9 and Lake Stevens. Just north of Lake Stevens, take Highway 92 east to Granite Falls. Continuing east from Granite Falls, you will be on the Mountain Loop Highway.

The valley formed by the South Fork Stillaguamish River, today the southern lobe of The Mountain Loop Highway, was first opened as a railroad right-of-way in the 1800's. This controversial route for the Everett and Monte Cristo Railway was put in place to carry ore from the Monte Cristo mines west to Everett. It was a direct route, but involved a 5-mile stretch through a steep canyon that was prone to violent flooding; service was often interrupted as the tracks were torn from their moorings in spectacular landslides. (Vestiges of this route can be viewed on the *Old Robe Railroad Trail,* p. 88).

Not as confusing as it looks—just turn left in Granite Falls to access the Mountain Loop Highway

The southern lobe of the Mountain Loop Highway stretches east from Granite Falls through the area known as Robe (home of the Monte Cristo Inn B&B and the Mountain View Inn, see *Lodgings,* below) to Verlot (pronounced "VAYR-lot", with the "t," not "ver-LOE" like "merlot"), a wide spot in the road where the Verlot Forest Information Center is located. Trailheads are abundant in the Robe and Verlot areas and all points east and north on the Mountain View Highway.

Twenty miles east of Verlot, you come to Barlow Pass. At this point, a spur road to the mining ghost town of Monte Cristo heads southeast and the "highway" heads north and loses pavement. The next 14 miles of the highway are a scenic but sometimes-harrowing stretch of gravel with sharp turns, steep dropoffs toward the South Fork Sauk River, and potholes galore. It's nothing a passenger car can't handle, but don't plan on making good time. A continuing controversy about whether to pave this section was revived in 1996, when spring floods closed the popular road through July. Check with the Verlot or Darrington ranger station for current conditions before driving this part of the loop.

Continuing north, pavement resumes at White Chuck. The next town you'll reach is Darrington, home of Sauk River Farm B&B, Hemlock Hills B&B, and the Stagecoach Inn motel (see *Lodgings,* below). From Darrington, Highway 530 leads north to Rockport (see *Section 2,* "Highway 20 West") and west to Arlington. Highway 530 from Arlington through Darrington to Rockport is a route many take to access the North Cascades Highway (State Highway 20).

The area that is now reached by the Mountain Loop Highway has long been recognized as a scenic and recreational paradise. Before the road was built, the visionary Rucker brothers, investors out of Everett, built the grand Big Four Inn resort as a tourist stop on their railroad line (see *Big Four Ice Caves,* pp. 85-86). Nothing remains of the inn today, but a few quality B&B's and motels do their best to support today's tourist trade.

Lodgings

MONTE CRISTO INN B&B
32410 Mountain Loop Highway, Granite Falls, WA 98252
(360) 691-4851

No lodging in the North Cascades rivals Cliff and Harriett Duncan's Monte Cristo Inn for overall warmth and generosity of spirit. They designed their custom home on the banks of the Stillaguamish River with family and friends in mind, and that's how you'll feel when you walk in the door—like family.

"Bring your favorite slippers," encourages their brochure, and you'll want to comply. Their shoeless policy (also no smoking, no kids, no pets) maintains both a homey atmosphere and an immaculate premises.

Monte Cristo Inn offers two guest rooms. The Wildflower, on the main floor, is a small room with a double bed. The Azalea, upstairs, is a bit larger and offers a more secluded feeling. Each room has a private bath.

Shared areas include the cozy loft sitting room, with books, TV and excellent video library; the great room, with river-rock fireplace and expansive views; and the spacious deck, with lawn furniture and the cleanest, most inviting hot tub in the northwest. Relax and soak up the atmosphere of their private, park-like 3-acre lawn on the Stillaguamish at the base of Mt. Pilchuck.

Rooms at the inn are $70–$85 per night. A deposit of one night's rent is requested within 7 days of your reservation, with balance due upon arrival.

While the mailing address is Granite Falls, the inn is actually located in the Robe Valley, 10.5 miles east of Granite Falls. As you head east, watch for the little oval MONTE CRISTO INN BED & BREAKFAST sign on the right just past the Mountain View Inn, restaurant, and convenience store. Coming the other way, it's 0.9 mile west of the Verlot Forest Information Center.

As if the house and beautifully landscaped grounds weren't special enough, the food at Monte Cristo Inn is outstanding. Harriett's healthy gourmet breakfasts are both abundant and attractive. Other treats, including popcorn and beverages to go with your movie, or homemade desserts straight from heaven, might appear if you ask (or just look hungry enough…!) As you are sharing Cliff and Harriett's home with them, they tend to anticipate your needs, being amazingly accommodating without ever being intrusive. Box lunches can be prepared upon request.

If you can bear to tear yourself away from the deluxe digs and the warm hospitality, you'll find that Cliff and Harriett can help with your recreational plans as well. Experienced outdoorsfolk themselves, they can offer tips about hikes, bike rides, and cross-country ski routes from their personal experience. The Duncans chose this area for their home because they love the Monte Cristo area as much as you will after staying with them.

Highlight: Immaculate adult-only B&B in exquisite setting.

Monte Cristo Inn—one of the finest B&B's in the state

SAUK RIVER FARM B&B
32629 State Route 530 NE, Darrington, WA 98241
(360) 436-1794

While quite different from the manicured Monte Cristo Inn, Sauk River Farm is another highly recommended B&B experience in the Mountain Loop Highway area. The casual, old farmhouse puts you at ease immediately, and the rambling 19-acre grounds give you room to roam if you don't feel like traveling to formal hiking trails.

Delightful Sauk River Farm B&B

From Darrington, take Highway 530 north as though heading toward Rockport and State Highway 20 (Highway 530 takes a right-angle turn north at a gas station/convenience store in Darrington). Proceed 3.5 miles from the convenience-store intersection, watching for the sign on your right (third driveway past milepost 52). Turn right into the driveway, then immediately right again through the open gate.

Proprietors Leo and Sharon Mehler offer two rooms with a shared bath in the main farmhouse. The Victorian Room is small, ruffled, and charming, with a queen brass bed, for $55 per night. The Native American Loft—actually the entire upstairs of the house—features an enormous king-size bed, skylights, small sitting area with potbellied stove, and a collection of Northwest artifacts; two youth cots are available. This room rents for $65. Ask about the possibility of a third room with futon and limited kitchen facilities apart from the main house for about $45. (Prices and policies continue to evolve; this project is a labor of love and a work in progress.)

You can invite the resident kitty in for a nap if you wish at Sauk River

Breakfasts are homemade and heart-smart, with specialties including a you'd-never-know-it's-low-fat granola and Leo's wonderful German puff-pancakes. Fruit, yogurt, and creative carbs will stoke the active person's engine for a day of hiking. In the evening, relax with a book, video, or music of your choice in the living room, or soak in the funky old wood-fired hot tub beneath a gnarled apple tree in the backyard.

The Sauk River Farm property includes an expanding network of on-premises trails, with the ever-present possibility of wildlife viewing, including beaver, raccoons, Columbian black tail deer, and bald eagles (December–February). The Mehlers also provide Mongoose light-duty mountain bikes for your use and rubber boots for mucking about in inclement weather. Leo and Sharon are a delightful couple; you'll be reluctant to leave. When you do, be a sport and participate in their semi-mandatory photo session: one for their album, and one for you, arriving in the mail a few weeks later as a pleasant reminder of your stay.

Highlight: Rambling old farmhouse and grounds with character.

HEMLOCK HILLS B &B
612 Stillaguamish, Darrington, WA 98241
1-800-520-1584 or (360) 436-1274

A third B&B alternative in the Mountain Loop Highway area, Hemlock Hills provides a family friendly atmosphere in which children are welcome. Dale and Elaine Hamlin's home is located on a quiet, deadend street with an acre and a half of landscaped grounds within walking distance of several informal hiking trails near Squire Creek and Beaver Lake.

A European-style B&B, Hemlock Hills offers two rooms with a shared bath, each for $50 per night. Rooms are decorated in a country motif with cozy quilts. Guests also have access to a game room with pool table and a parlor area.

Price includes a full breakfast, with fare that might include a cheese soufflé one day, baked blueberry French toast the next. Apple pancakes and crepes are other specialties, and every day includes plenty of fruit.

Highlight: Quiet, family-friendly B&B with shared bath.

MOUNTAIN VIEW INN
32005 Mountain Loop Highway, Granite Falls, WA 98252
(360) 691-6668

A single-story motel adjacent to a restaurant and a convenience store, this historic structure is under the new ownership of Vince and Diane Henry. The Henrys are an energetic couple with longtime roots in the Robe Valley. They took over the facility in a property swap with former owners Bob and Phyllis Thomas in 1996.

Six simple rooms each rent for $40 per night. Each room has a private bath and can accommodate up to 4 persons. The facility is older, but well-maintained, and Vince and Diane are excellent resources for local information. A casual, laid-back place to stay, the Mountain View offers great access to trailheads and the convenience of an on-premises restaurant (see *Dining*, below) and store. Located 10 miles east of Granite Falls.

Highlight: Simple, inexpensive rooms adjacent to café and convenience store.

STAGECOACH INN
1100 Seaman St., Darrington, WA 98241
(360) 436-1776

A basic motel with 21 units, Stagecoach Inn provides an option if the B&B's are full. Rates are $69 for rooms with one queen bed, $78 for rooms with two queens. Five of the rooms have kitchenettes: stove, mini-fridge, and sink. All bathrooms have tubs as well as showers, and all rooms come equipped with telephone and TV. Kids and pets welcome; pet fee is $6 per night.

Dining

If fine dining is your #1 priority, think twice about Darrington. At the time of my research, the local restaurants were, to put it gently, "in a state of flux." Due to family circumstances, vague remodeling plans, and other personal problems uninteresting to the hungry traveler, there was literally no place to eat dinner in Darrington after 9:00 P.M., and precious little before. This situation is likely to remedy itself as the area gains popularity as a tourist destination, but at this writing I can recommend no eateries in Darrington or on the upper lobe of the Mountain Loop Highway. Your best bet is to talk with the Chamber of Commerce or your B&B hosts in advance, or plan to drive the 28 miles west to Arlington or 20 miles north to Rockport for dinner.

Granite Falls, gateway to the lower lobe of the Mountain Loop, is a bit better than Darrington in terms of dining opportunities. At first glance, the only choices seem to be those typical of Small Town, Washington: a mind-numbing blur of burgers, with espresso outlets outnumbering restaurants 5-to-1, and every restaurant marquee loudly proclaimed the availability of red meat. But a bit of determined sleuthing resulted in the following solid recommendations.

THAI EXPRESS
206 E. Stanley St., Granite Falls, WA 98252
(360) 691-4787

This unassuming little place proved the most exciting culinary discovery in Granite Falls. You'll find it on your right, across from the Post Office, on the main drag as you drive through Granite Falls toward the Mountain Loop Highway. Don't blink, or you'll miss it. I *think* it's called Thai Express—even after studying the exterior and interior signs, and the menu (headlined: THAIGRANITEFALLSEXPRESSCUISINE BBQ & TERIYAKI) I could not be sure.

Apparently specializing in take-out, their seating consists of a wall counter with a few stools. Entrees begin at $3.99, including chow mein, teriyaki chicken, and fried rice with your choice of meat. The most expensive item on the menu is a barbecued boneless chicken marinated in coconut milk and herbs, served with rice and vegetables, for a whopping $5.00. Over 20 other entrees, mostly $4.25 and $4.50, include Chinese standards and Thai specialties. My vegetarian Pahd Thai (not on the menu, but cheerfully accommodated), was excellent, filling, and delicately spiced, and it set me back about $5.00, including fragrant jasmine tea. Browse the Thai magazines and travel brochures and listen to country western music while you await your custom-prepared lunch or dinner. You gotta love this place.

Highlight: Authentic, economical Thai cuisine.

OMEGA PIZZA & PASTA
102 S. Granite Ave., Granite Falls, WA 98252
(360) 691-4394

Offering an Italian menu with an Aegean slant, Omega is another low-on-atmosphere, high-on-taste recommendation in Granite Falls. Unlike at Thai Express, there is plenty of seating at this clean, cheerful, family-friendly restaurant.

The menu falls into three basic categories: pizza, Italian dishes, and oven-baked subs. Pizzas come with your choice of garlic white sauce or regular red sauce, and toppings are inventive. Five featured specials include the Gyro Pizza (with gyro meat, feta cheese, and fresh tomatoes) and Popeye's Pizza (a veggie delight with spinach, natch). Thirty-one other numbered combos include all the standard ingredients plus a few less common ones like smoked oysters, chicken, and shrimp. A single-topping large runs $12.80; the most expensive combo is $19.30.

Italian dinners come complete with a tasty mixed salad and generous helping of garlic bread. The pasta dishes, over a dozen, start at $5.95. Veal parmesan, chicken cacciatore, and beef spare ribs, served with pasta, are $8.95. Hot subs and gyros start at $4.75.

Highlight: Greek-Italian menu includes pizza, subs, and pastas.

MOUNTAIN VIEW INN RESTAURANT
32005 Mountain Loop Highway, Granite Falls, WA 98252
(360) 691-6668

Operated by jacks-of-all-trades Vince and Diane Henry (see *Mountain View Inn*, p. 83), the Mountain View Inn Restaurant serves homestyle fare including burgers, steaks, and sandwiches. Soups, sauces, gravies, and dressings are homemade.

Breakfasts at the Mountain View are hearty affairs. Choose a standard meat and egg combo or go out on a limb with the Mountain View Special: pan-fried rainbow trout with your eggs, hashbrowns, toast, and jelly. Prices are reasonable, with omelettes starting at $5. Dinner choices include steak, chops, chicken, ribs, and seafood (steamed clams, snow-crab legs, and trout are available in addition to the standard selection of fried fare). All entrées include soup or salad bar, and beer and wine are available. Prices top out at $12.95 for steak and prawns. If you can, save room for a slice of homemade pie for $2.50.

The back room is a tavern and general gathering place, where you can relax with locals and fellow tourists over a beer and a game of pool at the end of the day.

Highlight: Hearty home-style fare on the Mountain Loop Highway.

Walks and Hikes
Listed in approximate order of difficulty.

BIG FOUR ICE CAVES

Map:	Green Trails #110 "Silverton"
Distance:	2.0 miles round trip
Elevation Gain:	None
Estimated Time:	1 hour
Highlight:	Short, pleasant family hike to genuine ice caves.

This popular, short trail begins at the site of the Big Four Inn, a grand hotel opened in 1921 and burned to the ground in 1949. Today's tourist can only mourn the loss of such a fine facility. In its day, amenities included a 9-hole golf course, a man-made lake, tennis courts, putting and bowling greens, ski slope, and recreation room with dual fireplace. All that remains is the fireplace and parts of the original sidewalks.

Suitable for all ages and nearly all fitness levels, the one-mile stroll from the large parking lot to the year-round ice caves is the most popular trail in the area. Up to 2000 hikers may visit the caves in a single weekend. Bring a smile and a friendly attitude, and expect lots of human and canine company. Ranger-guided tours are offered here during the summer months.

Please note that the caves themselves are NOT SAFE TO ENTER. The idea of this hike is to take a pleasant walk and *view* the ice-cave phenomenon from *outside* the caves. By their very nature, ice caves are unstable and can collapse at any time, causing injury or death. You will see people ignoring this and entering the caves; don't add to the problem.

Getting There

Heading east on the Mountain View Highway, watch for the Big Four sign on your right about 15 miles east of the Verlot Forest Information Center. A short spur road leads to the large parking area and trailhead.

The Hike

From the ample parking area, with dual pit toilets, follow the signs to the trail. Stroll along the historic Big Four Inn sidewalks, cross marshland on a safe and well-constructed boardwalk, then hike an easy 15 minutes through the woods.

At 0.5 mile, you will emerge from the forest into a field of glacial scree. The ice caves, different every year, are visible across the field in the distance. You can walk right up to the caves and feel the chill of the icy air wafting from their interior. If you're tempted to ignore the warnings and go inside the caves, just remember how they are formed: snow and ice *fall* from the steep cliffs above. Suddenly. Without warning.

Those wishing to linger might want to bring a picnic lunch and hop atop some of the big rocks a few hundred feet to the right of the caves. This little ridge makes a good place to catch some rays, people-watch and observe the caves from a respectful distance.

Big Four ice caves

BOULDER RIVER FALLS

Map:	Green Trails #77 & #109, "Oso" & "Granite Falls"
Distance:	2.5 miles round trip to falls (8.4 miles round trip to campsite at trail's end)
Elevation Gain:	250'
Estimated Time:	1 hour, 30 minutes (4 hours to trail's end)
Highlight:	Ferny, old-growth hike to twin waterfalls.

A gentle, well-maintained walk through old-growth timber to a pair of waterfalls and a pleasant picnic stop. Those wishing a longer walk can continue on some or all of the maintained trail along the Boulder River to a campsite turnaround at 4.2 miles.

Getting There

From Arlington, take Highway 530 east 20 miles; from Darrington, take the same highway 8 miles west. Just east of milepost 41, turn south on (possibly unmarked) USFS Road 2010, following signs toward French Creek Campground. Follow this bumpy, potholed, single-lane road 4.0 miles to its end, where you'll find the trailhead for Boulder River Trail #734.

The Hike

This stroll is an easy way to get an "up close and personal" look at a low-elevation section of old-growth forest. Begin on an old roadbed, which narrows to a trail after 0.5 mile. If runoff is high, you may be able to hear the waters of Boulder Falls below the trail at about 1.0 mile. (These falls are too far below the trail to be seen; instead, you will be viewing two unnamed falls at 1.25 miles.)

The trail is lush and ferny, attesting to the Darrington area's higher-than-Seattle's annual precipitation. This is a pretty hike rain or shine, and makes a good early- or late-season hike because the elevation is only 1000 to 1250 feet. Watch for banana slugs on wet days!

Just before the twin falls come into view, a side trail leads to the river and a few camping sites. The falls can be seen across the river; they are at their most dramatic early in the season. If the river is low, scramble down the embankment for a picnic site at water's edge before your turnaround. Those continuing on toward Boulder Ford Camp will see basically more of the same: forest, ferns, and slugs.

BARLOW POINT

Map:	Green Trails #111 "Sloan Peak"
Distance:	2.5 miles round trip
Elevation Gain:	950'
Estimated Time:	1 hour, 45 minutes
Highlight:	Short, steep hike with peaceful valley views at the top.

Barlow Point Trail #709 is a short, steep, exhilarating little climb to a peaceful viewpoint overlooking the Stillaguamish Valley. Since Barlow Point is not as popular as some trails in the area, you might catch a measure of solitude here.

Getting There

Take the Mountain Loop Highway 19.4 miles east of the Verlot Forest Information Center. This area, known as Barlow Pass, is where the gated road to Monte Cristo goes off to the right (south) and the main road (Mountain Loop Highway) makes a hairpin turn to the left to head north along the Sauk River. This is also the point where the highway loses pavement and turns to gravel heading north.

A short driveway to the left just before the highway turns to gravel leads to a parking lot for the trailhead. The dozens of cars you'll see here on a typical summer day probably belong to backpackers and mountain bikers who have headed south toward Monte Cristo.

The Hike

The sign at the head of this hiker-only trail reads BARLOW POINT - 1, OLD GOVERN- MENT TRAIL - 0.5. Barlow Point is more like 1.25 miles. The other trail, Old Government, which forks off of Barlow Point Trail at about 0.3 mile, is a section of the old Monte Cristo Railroad bed that parallels the highway and includes interpretive plaques explaining the railway history.

Head into a timbered area with a high canopy and open understory. Initially flat, the pine-needled trail begins rolling after 0.1 mile. At 0.25 mile, a trail signed RAIL-ROAD GRADE forks off to the left. Barlow Point Trail goes straight ahead and begins ascending. Very shortly thereafter, the Old Government Trail goes off to the left toward the highway. The Barlow Point Trail switchbacks off to the right, climbing the steepening grade in earnest.

Near the top, the switchbacks tighten and the trail deteriorates to a narrow goat path. You'll know you're almost there when a short spur path takes you off to the right for a view from a cliff top over the Sauk River valley to the north. Be careful at the edge—it's a three-screamer to the bottom.

Returning to the main path, you reach the summit within a few dozen yards. A sign declares BARLOW POINT, ELEV. 3300'. Several flat rocks and the flattened area where a lookout tower once stood provide rest points. Wander out to the northwest point and enjoy the best view: the verdant, undulating Stillaguamish Valley.

On your return, stay left at the junctions with the other trails if you wish to return to the parking lot; it's easy to get diverted onto the old railroad grade (on the other hand, the latter is a short walk, and the interpretive plaques are interesting).

OLD ROBE RAILROAD TRAIL

Map:	Green Trails #109 "Granite Falls" (trail does not show on the map)
Distance:	3.6 miles round trip
Elevation Loss:	200'
Estimated Time:	2 hours, 30 minutes
Highlight:	Old railroad tunnels; rushing whitewater.

A trail of historical as well as aesthetic significance, this hike takes you to the former route of the old Everett and Monte Cristo Railroad. This controversial section of the tracks was routed through a steep and wild section of the South Fork Stillaguamish River gorge, and was so prone to washouts as to render the railroad unfunctional; it closed after a few short years.

The trail is mostly flat, after an initial descent. Older children will love this hike, but footing can be difficult; it is not recommended for toddlers or first-time hikers. Sights along the way include the sometimes raging whitewater of the South Fork Stillaguamish River and passage through two old railroad tunnels.

Getting There

From Granite Falls, the trailhead is 7.3 miles north and east on the Mountain Loop Highway; from the Monte Cristo Inn and Mountain View Inn, it's 3.0 miles west. Look for the brick OLD ROBE TRAIL sign on the south shoulder of the road. Park along the shoulder.

The Hike

Leaving the road behind you, enter a natural tunnel of greenery, from which you will emerge on the edge of an open valley after 0.1 mile. A short path to your right leads to views over the valley; the main path goes to the left. Descend 200 feet along an open hillside decked with fireweed and foxglove in a series of half a dozen switchbacks to the marshy valley floor, where you again enter a canopy of greenery.

At a bit past 0.5 mile, you will come to a junction and a sign pointing toward the tunnels. Follow the trail and the sounds of the Stillaguamish River and proceed to the right. You will reach the river at 0.75 mile and begin walking west along its course.

After the waterfall at 1.0 mile, you can spot remnants of the railroad in the form of concrete, stone, and occasional timbers along the way. The power of nature is eloquent here: these fragments of man's ingenuity, a mere century old, have been thoroughly destroyed by water and reclaimed by soil and plants.

Descend into the basalt-lined river gorge, where the South Fork Stillaguamish rages below and the cliffs rise above. Shortly, you will spy the entrance to the first of the abandoned railroad tunnels. The trail passes through this 300-foot tunnel, as well as a shorter one 0.25 mile farther. This second tunnel marks the end of the trail.

The wild Stillaguamish River alongside the Old Robe Railroad Trail

LAKE TWENTY-TWO

Map:	Green Trails #109 "Granite Falls"
Distance:	5.0 miles round trip
Elevation Gain:	1500'
Estimated Time:	3 hours
Highlight:	Unmolested old growth forest and cirque lake; waterfall near trailhead for nonhikers.

A popular trail through a protected section of old-growth forest to a fragile cirque lake. Suitable for sunny, cloudy, or even rainy days. A waterfall view at 0.1 miles makes this a good destination for nonhikers as well.

Getting There

Heading east on the lower lobe of the Mountain Loop Highway, the signed turnoff to the Lake Twenty-Two trailhead is 2.1 miles past the Verlot Forest Information Center; turn right. A short access road takes you across the South Fork Stillaguamish River and to a roundabout parking lot with a pit toilet.

The Hike

The trailhead is clearly marked: LAKE TWENTY-TWO TRAIL, #702. A well-engineered, wide gravel path leads you to a creek crossing (the first of several), then within the first 0.1 mile to a view of a beautiful, rushing waterfall off to your left (nonhikers can hang out here). Keep your eyes peeled for at least two more waterfalls in the first 1.5 miles.

The first 0.5 mile is flat to gradually ascending, until the Twenty-Two Creek bridge, where switchbacks begin. After about a mile, you break out into a meadowed hillside, where wild berries abound. (Huckleberries may be in season as early as mid-July—and they are delicious!) Enjoy views to the north across the Stillaguamish River valley.

Continue switchbacking up this open hillside (actually the lower north flank of Mt. Pilchuck) to reach the lake at about 2500 feet. Tread lightly on this overused lakeshore, enjoying its delicate beauty.

MT. PILCHUCK

Map:	Green Trails #109 "Granite Falls"
Distance:	6 miles round trip
Elevation Gain:	2200'
Estimated Time:	4 or 5 hours
Highlight:	Popular trail to open lookout tower.

This is not an easy hike. It's steep, often muddy, with difficult footing and tedious boulder-field scrambling. In the fog (which is frequent), it's a marginal choice, and in the rain, forget it. But it's popular. On a summer weekend, the lookout tower at the top can seem like a fraternity party. And the black flies can be horrendous.

So why include it as a recommended hike? Two reasons. First, the lookout tower is a marvel, perched seemingly precariously atop an improbable pile of rubble. Second, on a sparkling, clear day, you can see almost forever from the top.

Getting There

Take the Mountain Loop Highway 1.0 mile east of the Verlot Forest Information Center. Turn right, following the sign to Mt. Pilchuck. The road immediately forks; take the left fork, following the sign to Mt. Pilchuck and Heather Lake. After 0.25 mile, the road turns to gravel. At about 1.4 miles, you'll pass parking and access to the Heather Lake Trail. Pavement returns at 5.5 miles, but don't let that lull you into a false sense of security—potholes can be large enough to swallow small cars.

At 7.2 miles from the highway, a sign reads MT. PILCHUCK RECREATION AREA (Pilchuck was once home to a downhill ski area); immediately afterward, reach the trailhead parking lot. You have gained about 2000 feet in your car.

The Hike

The trailhead is clearly marked with an information signboard. The route begins on the remnants of an old logging road. An outhouse is on your left just a couple dozen feet up the trail; a footpath on the right leads to a campsite.

Between 0.1 and 0.2 mile, the road forks; take the right fork. Here, the route loses its logging-road character and becomes more of a trail. (NOTE: Significant trail reconstruction was underway as of this writing; details of the first mile may change. As this is a very popular trail, hikers can count on the route being easy to follow.) Pick your way carefully up the roots and rocks; this is *not* a tennis-shoe hike.

Cross two fields of rocky scree as you wind around the north flank of the mountain, heading east. Around the 2.0-mile point, you begin to see little orange paw prints painted along the route to help you find your way. As the route turns to boulder field and continues to climb, these markers—sometimes just dots, sometimes a color other than orange—are even more helpful.

The path climbs the boulder field south toward a peak sometimes known as Little Pilchuck, then turns east toward its goal. A sign near the top offers an alternate route, a shorter, steeper scramble. I'd stick with the old trail, which drops down briefly, contours along the southern side of the

Mt. Pilchuck Tower has been restored for hiker use—the final scramble is a doozy

peak, then ascends a final 0.3 mile to the top. The last hundred feet or so is a hands-and-feet scramble; use caution.

The lookout tower is an absolute piece of work; cables jut every which way to anchor it into the pile of rock upon which it perches. It's exhilarating to climb the staircase to the top. Volunteer mountaineers have fixed up the former fire lookout as a hiker shelter, with a deck on all four sides. Inside is historic and geographic information and a logbook for guests to sign. The 360° view includes Mt. Baker, Mt. Shuksan, Whitehorse, and Three Fingers to the north; White Chuck, Mt. Pugh, Glacier Peak, and Big Four to the east; Mt. Stuart, Mt. Index, Mt. Rainier, and Mt. St. Helens to the south; Puget Sound, the Olympic peninsula, and the city of Everett to the west.

MT. DICKERMAN

Map:	Green Trails #111 "Sloan Peak"
Distance:	8.6 miles round trip
Elevation Gain:	3700'
Estimated Time:	5 or 6 hours
Highlight:	A tough climb with 360° rewards.

No two ways about it—this is a tough booger. But it's also one of my favorite hikes in the book.

If you think that 3700 feet of elevation in 4.3 miles is unlikely to be a walk in the park, you're right. Leave the kiddies and wimps home for this one. But if you're feeling your animal instincts, and the forecast is for clear skies, go for it. The summit is awe-inspiring and the route, while unrelenting, is well-engineered, never requiring hand-scrambling or special mountaineering skills. Carry plenty of water and a good attitude.

Getting There

Take the Mountain Loop Highway 16.6 miles east of the Verlot Forest Information Center and watch for the trailhead on the left (as you head east). The roadside pullout has room for half a dozen cars.

The Hike

The trail to Mt. Dickerman is for hikers only; no equestrian or mountain-bike use. From the clearly marked trailhead, you'll begin your steep ascent immediately, passing through deadfall, tall old timber, and a ferny understory. The trailhead information sign and hiker registration box are about 50 yards up the path.

Switchback through the forest accompanied by the sounds of largely unseen creeklets rushing down the mountain. The valley ecosystem is given to mosses, nurse logs, and humus soils; the pungent smells of cedar decay surround you as you climb. The woods contain shade-loving Indian pipe, coral root, and Canadian dogwood, and are home to curious camp jays and an occasional snake.

After about a mile and a half, breaks in the trees begin to provide views across the valley to the south. At 2.2 miles, you emerge into a meadowed hillside dotted with columbine, tiger lily, and wild rose. Rocky and improbably steep Dickerman rises above you, and views of the valley expand; Big Four mountain is soon visible to the southwest. After 2.5 miles, the ascent is less steep, as the trail contours around the southwest side of the mountain through meadows. The forest is below you now, and wide-open views all around except those blocked by Dickerman herself. Just when you think you might be getting your breath back, begin the final steep mile, heading east and up toward the summit.

At the top, choose either of two viewpoints, a couple of hundred feet apart, for a jaw-dropping 360° panorama. Nearby Mt. Forgotten and Mt. Pugh are easy to spot to the north, with Three Fingers just to their left.

The author enjoys the great view from Mt. Dickerman

In the distance, also north, are Mts. Baker and Shuksan. Glacier Peak is the largest snow-cone in the distant east. You can still see Big Four just to the southwest, and Mt. Pilchuck. Beyond them, the waters of Puget Sound and, with luck, the Olympics beyond are visible. On a clear day, mighty Mt. Rainier stands tall on the distant southern horizon.

Have a snack, take a nap, goggle at the peaks. The summit of Dickerman is one of the best in the North Cascades on a sunny day.

Other Hike Notes

These hikes not personally reviewed or not as highly recommended as the above hikes.

GREEN MOUNTAIN

Steep and pretty, this 8.0 round-trip hike rises 3000 feet above the Suiattle Valley for dramatic views, green meadows, and more mountain peaks than even the most ardent map junkie can identify. It would be a recommended hike if access weren't so difficult. The route from the main highway is long, poorly surfaced in places, and prone to slides. When it is not closed, it is often suitable only for four-wheel-drive vehicles, which makes it unsuitable for recommendation in this book. Check with the ranger district, and go for it if the roads are open and you want a good workout with big-league rewards.

From Darrington, take Highway 530 north toward Rockport. After 7.5 miles, cross the Sauk River bridge. Less than 0.2 mile after the bridge, you will turn right onto USFS Road 26, the Suiattle River Road. Follow this road 19 miles to USFS Road 2680, Green Mountain Road, onto which you turn left. Switchback up this road, gaining about 2500 feet in 5 miles. At road's end, find the trailhead sign for Trail #782.

Climb through verdant forests, then lush meadows, past two small ponds and ever-expanding views. The tower at the 6500-foot summit has been both a wartime sentry station and a fire lookout.

KENNEDY HOT SPRINGS

I'm very partial to natural hot springs, but this one is rather a dud in terms of temperature (not hot enough), size (not big enough), and popularity (who wants to wait in line?) The 10.2-mile round trip is a nice enough hike, with only a 1000-foot gain in elevation, but there are others more interesting in the area. If you need to get naked with Mother Nature, opportunities abound without sitting elbow-to-elbow with strangers in this 4'x4' bacteria pit.

Still not convinced? Take the Mountain Loop Highway south out of Darrington or east, then north, from the Verlot Forest Information Center. Just south of a Sauk River crossing, about 10 miles south of Darrington, turn east on USFS Road 23, White Chuck River Road. Go 11 miles to a parking area at the end of the road. Use White Chuck Trail #643, continuing straight ahead when the Pacific Crest Trail forks off to the left just before 5.0 miles.

MONTE CRISTO TOWNSITE

Historic? I suppose, but you'll find better ghost towns elsewhere, and the "hike" in is strictly bogus. It's actually just a really rough road—too wide to be a good trail, yet not accessible to cars. If you want to see the site of the old Monte Cristo mines, the best way to do it is by mountain bike. It's over 8 miles round trip. Access from Barlow Pass, 20 miles east of the Verlot Forest Information Center.

Contacts

DARRINGTON RANGER STATION 1405 Emmons St., Darrington, WA 98241	(360) 436-1155
DARRINGTON CHAMBER OF COMMERCE P.O. Box 351, Darrington, WA 98241	(360) 436-1177
DARRINGTON CITY HALL	(360) 436-1131
MT. BAKER-SNOQUALMIE NATIONAL FOREST HQ 21905 - 64th Avenue West, Mountlake Terrace, WA 98043	(206) 775-9702
VERLOT FOREST INFORMATION CENTER 33515 Mountain Loop Highway, Granite Falls, WA 98252	(360) 691-7791

	MONTE CRISTO INN B&B	SAUK RIVER FARM B&B	HEMLOCK HILLS B&B	MOUNTAIN VIEW INN	STAGECOACH INN
PRICE (1996 RATES, PRE-TAX, 2 PERSON)	$70–$85	$45-$65	$50	$40 for up to 4	$69–$78
EXTRA PERSON	N/A	$5	N/A (Family rate $75 for both rooms)	N/A	N/A
PAYMENT METHODS	VISA, MC, Check, Cash	Check, Cash	Check, Cash	VISA, MC, Cash	VISA, MC, AmEx, Disc, Check, Cash
# OF UNITS	2	2–3	2	6	21
PRIVATE BATH	Yes	No	No	Yes	Yes
SHARED BATH	No	Yes	Yes	No	No
BREAKFAST INCLUDED?	Yes	Yes	Yes	No	No
COOKING FACILITIES?	No	Possibly in 3rd unit	No	No	5 kitchenettes
POOL	No	No	No	No	No
HOT TUB	Yes	Yes	No	No	No
CHILDREN	No	OK over 12, otherwise OK by prior arrangement	OK	OK	OK
PETS	No	No	No	OK	OK, $6/night
SEASONS OF OPERATION	Year-round	Year-round except October	Year-round	Year-round	Year-round

Table 4. Lodgings in the Mountain Loop Highway vicinity

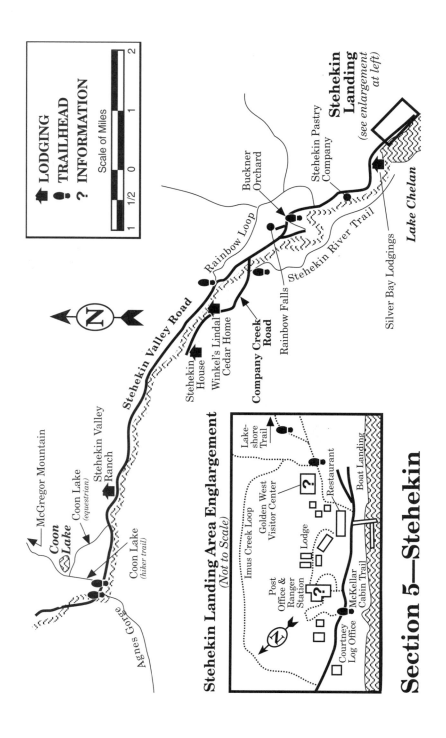

LODGING
TRAILHEAD
? INFORMATION

Scale of Miles

1   1/2   0   1   2

Buckner Orchard

Stehekin Pastry Company

Rainbow Loop

Stehekin Landing
(see enlargement at left)

Stehekin River Trail

Rainbow Falls

Lake Chelan

Stehekin Valley Road

Stehekin House

Winkel's Lindal Cedar Home

Company Creek Road

Silver Bay Lodgings

McGregor Mountain

Stehekin Valley Ranch

Coon Lake
(equestrian)

Coon Lake

Coon Lake
(hiker trail)

Agnes Gorge

Stehekin Landing Area Englargement
(Not to Scale)

Lake-shore Trail

Imus Creek Loop

Golden West Visitor Center

?

Restaurant

Lodge

Boat Landing

McKellar Cabin Trail

Post Office & Ranger Station

?

Courtney Log Office

McKellar

Section 5—Stehekin

SECTION 5

Stehekin

Overview

One of the most remote places you can visit in Washington state without a multi-day backpacking trip is Stehekin. Accessible only by water and air, Stehekin nestles at the head of Lake Chelan. Its residents (and its tourists) do without malls, fast food, and even telephones (the National Park Service recently installed one satellite phone for the entire area's use; even this created controversy).

Lake Chelan (from the Native American "*Tsillan*," meaning "deep water") itself is a marvel. Many assume this long, skinny lake is man-made, but it is not. The glacial gorge is one of the deepest in the nation—far deeper than the Grand Canyon. In its bottom is a vast natural lake: 55 miles long and 1486 feet deep. The lake's bottom is nearly 400 feet below sea level and its depth has been augmented by a mere 17 to 20 feet by a dam built in 1920.

At the headwaters of Lake Chelan is the tiny, isolated village Native Americans named *Stehekin*—"the way through." Lake Chelan, and the Stehekin Valley and Cascade Pass to the north and west of it, provided a way through the mountains for trading, and, later, a way to the mountains for tourists.

Stehekin has been a tourist destination for a long time—remember, travel by water was easier than travel by land a century ago. The original Lady of the Lake (ancestor to today's Lady of the Lake II) made trips uplake as early as 1900, and the 50-room Field Hotel, built near the site of today's Silver Bay Inn in 1905 and torn down in 1920 when the dam at Chelan Falls raised the level of the lake, was a destination resort. In fact, the resident population of Stehekin was greater at the turn of the century than it is today.

Beautiful, historical, geographically unique—Stehekin is all of these things, but perhaps its most remarkable feature is its people. What could possess folks to live and thrive in such an isolated area? Those of us in cities, caught up in the pace of our hectic lives, might fantasize that we'd *love* to move to a place like Stehekin. But could you really live in a little valley where the only "road" in and out is a 55-mile lake? Where a trip to the store for a gallon of milk or a loaf of bread must be planned at least a day in advance? Where the only telephone is down the road—maybe 6, 7 or 10 *miles* down a mostly one-lane, mostly gravel road? It's fine in the summer, but what about the winter, when the valley floor receives 4 to 6 *feet* of snow, beginning before Thanksgiving and lingering into April?

Drawn by a yearning for such isolation or, for those who grew up here, by a sense of tradition, Stehekin Valley residents seem to be among the happiest, friendliest people I have ever met. For the two or three months out of the year when tourists run amok through their little valley, Stehekin folks young and old offer nothing resembling resentment or hostility—just a friendly wave when they pass you on the road or a piece of information if you ask (or, sometimes, even if you don't!).

Small-town trust abounds between neighbors in Stehekin. Valuable historical buildings are left unlocked and unattended for use by residents and tourists alike. Gasoline purchases are made on the honor system. Perhaps most startling of all, keys are left in cars and cars are left unlocked. "Someone might need to use it," a resident explained to me simply. Besides, where would a thief go? No roads leave Stehekin!

You can't come to Stehekin without coming into contact with the Courtney family. By some estimates, these brothers and their relatives comprise 30% of the valley's population. They also provide some of the area's most-needed services. Cliff Courtney's family runs Stehekin Valley Ranch and shuttle service, plus river rafting and bike rentals. Cragg Courtney's family runs the pastry company and the original family business, Cascade Corrals trail rides (fit one of these in if you can; write Box 67, Stehekin, WA 98852). Tom Courtney's presence may affect you less directly, but he provides crucial tug, barge, and construction services, as well as selling the gasoline for valley residents' cars and boats.

To reach Stehekin from Seattle, first find Wenatchee. Take Highway 2 east (begin with Interstate 405 north to Bothell, then Highway 522 northeast to Monroe) to Wenatchee, or take Interstate 90 east to Highway 970 at Cle Elum to Highway 97 north, which merges with Highway 2 fifteen miles west of Wenatchee. From Wenatchee, take Highway 97 (east of the Columbia River) or Alternate Highway 97 (west of the Columbia River) north to Chelan.

From Spokane, take Highway 2 west to its junction with Highway 97 at Orondo, then take Highway 97 north to Chelan.

From Chelan, the most common method of reaching Stehekin is by one of the boats operated by the Lake Chelan Boat Company. The Lady of the Lake II runs May through October, departing at 8:30 A.M. daily. It reaches Stehekin in 4 hours, stays 90 minutes, then departs at 2 P.M. to return to Chelan at 6 P.M. The faster Lady Express operates almost year-round (no service for two weeks in October), with departures at 8:30 or 10 A.M., making the trip uplake in about 2 and a half hours. Lady of the Lake II round-trip fare is $22; Lady Express round-trip fare $41 May–October, and $22 November–April. A combination round-trip ticket is also available for $41 May–mid-October, allowing passengers to take the Lady Express up and the Lady II back, resulting in a longer layover in Stehekin. Bicycles may be taken aboard for $13 round trip. For a brochure or clarification, call the Lake Chelan Boat Company at (509) 682-2224.

A parking area is provided for passengers on the Lady II or Lady Express in Chelan; a fee is charged. By driving about 30 minutes outside of town along the southwest shore of the lake to Fields Point Landing, passengers can save about 50% on the parking fee and about an hour's time on the boat. Boat fares are the same from Fields Point as from Chelan.

Another transportation option between Chelan and Stehekin is Chelan Airways. Operating a de Havilland Beaver and a Cessna 185, this small air-transportation company offers a basic round-trip airtaxi service for $90 per person, with a 2 person minimum. Flightseeing tours are also offered from Stehekin and from Chelan, from $60 to $120 per person. Discounts for children. Call (509) 682-5555 for more information.

For those who wish to use their own boat to reach Stehekin, moorage fees at the Stehekin boat landing are reasonable.

Arriving at Stehekin Landing, you will find a minimum of services, many of which are open May–September only: a tiny store, the North Cascades Lodge and restaurant, a craft shop, an outdoor supply store, a photo and stationery store, a ranger station, and the Golden West Visitor Center. Marina services, gasoline, and bicycle rentals are also available at the landing. You can access the McKellar Cabin Trail, Imus Creek Nature Trail, and Lakeshore Trail from the landing area.

One road leads out of the landing area and up the valley. This road, Stehekin Valley Road, leads to all other services and points of interest. Within the first 4.3 miles, this road takes you to Silver Bay Road (site of Silver Bay Lodgings), the Stehekin Pastry Company, Buckner Lane (access trail for Buckner Orchard), Rainbow Falls, the southern trailhead for the Rainbow Loop Trail, and the old and new Stehekin schools. It connects with the other road, Company Creek Road, 4.3 miles upvalley from the landing at the Harlequin Bridge. Company Creek Road leads to the Stehekin River Trail, Winkel's Lindal Cedar Home, and Stehekin Vacation Rentals' Stehekin House.

Continuing upvalley on Stehekin Valley Road, you will reach the northern trailhead for the Rainbow Loop Trail, Stehekin Valley Ranch, and High Bridge, site of the Agnes Gorge and Coon Lake trailheads. In years past, this road also continued upvalley several miles to other campsites and trailheads. Flooding in 1996 closed the road north of High Bridge indefinitely.

Lady of the Lake—the way to get to Stehekin

Lodgings

You might be puzzled (as I was) over how lodgings in a place with no telephones can have telephone numbers. It's because some Stehekin lodgings have off-premises reservation and information numbers. If you want to contact the actual proprietors, you'll need to write a letter.

SILVER BAY LODGING
10 Silver Bay Road, Stehekin, WA 98852
1-800-555-7781 in WA or (509) 682-2212

A sure sense of Stehekin solitude embraces you from the property and grounds of the Silver Bay Lodgings. The two cabins and a 3-unit B&B sit on what must be the prime piece of real estate in the valley—one of the most spectacular in the state. Before you is the ice-blue expanse of Lake Chelan. Behind you, the cleft of the Stehekin Valley frames knife-edged glacial peaks of the North Cascades. And beside you, the Stehekin River flows to its Lake Chelan outlet.

Take your early morning coffee to the deck or lawn to watch and listen to a symphony of wildfowl catch their breakfast: swallows, sparrows, ducks, geese, and blue heron. Play a lazy game of croquet on the flat expanse of lawn ringed with flowers between the inn and the lake. Use one of the complementary canoes to explore the gentle backwaters around your private Eden. Watch the sun set behind the peaks from the spa at water's edge.

Silver Bay Lodging—the unique solar design and exquisite location make it one of the best inns you'll find

Randall and Kathy Dinwiddie, your hosts at Silver Bay, provide the foundation for a memorable stay. The Silver Bay Inn, their passive solar home with 3 B&B rooms, is a study in superlatives. It was the first envelope-design solar home to be built in Washington state—one of the first in the nation. Its location is incredible. And it's one of the most gracious, lovely, and comfortable B&B's in this book.

Decor at the inn is casually elegant, mixing European-style antiques with far eastern and Native American artifacts. The "envelope" solar design results in a sunny "house-within-a-house" with clean lines and a bright and airy breakfast sunroom. The Lake View Suite, ideal for a honeymoon or other special occasion, takes advantage of views from every room. In addition to its spacious bedroom and private bath, it has a sitting room and two decks. It rents for $120 per night. The River View Room has its own convenient entrance, sunny bedroom, private bath, snack preparation area, and a deck overlooking the river. It rents for $95. The smallest room, the Mountain View, has private deck access near the hot tub and rents for $75; its bath is just across the hall. All rooms include a generous continental breakfast. The inn operates May through October; a 2-night stay is required during the summer months.

The Silver Bay Inn shares its idyllic 700 feet of lakefront with two comfortably furnished cabins. Both Silver Bay cabins include a fully equipped kitchen with microwave and dishwasher, an outdoor propane barbecue, a wood stove, and an assortment of books and games. All towels and bedding are provided. The Lake Cabin is private and secluded, with room for up to four in a sleeping loft and main-floor bedroom. The Bay Cabin is larger, with room for six in two queen bedrooms and a sleeping loft. Both the Lake Cabin and the Bay Cabin rent for $135 per night for 2 persons, plus $20 per night for each additional person. The Dinwiddies rent the cabins all year round (5-day minimum in the summer months). Don't forget to bring *all* your food if you plan to stay in a cabin and do your own cooking.

To reach Silver Bay Lodgings, turn left on Silver Bay Road, 1.5 miles up Stehekin Valley Road from the landing. Proceed a quarter mile to the end of the road. The Dinwiddies will provide your initial ride from the landing when the Lady Of the Lake II arrives at 12:30. If you arrive at another time or in another area, such as the airstrip, there will be a $10 fee for transportation. Bicycles (with helmets) are provided for your use at no charge.

No pets, smoking, or children under 8 are allowed at Silver Bay Lodgings.

Highlight: Top-notch B&B and two cabins in Stehekin's most beautiful location.

Inside the Silver Bay Lodging

STEHEKIN VALLEY RANCH
P.O. Box 36, Stehekin, WA 98852
(509) 682-4677

Awake at Cliff and Kerry Courtney's Stehekin Valley Ranch to the distant smell of frying bacon, the promise of hot coffee and crisp mountain air, and the sense of having had a great night's rest. You're as snug as a bug in your cozy bed in your wood-walled, canvas-roofed tent cabin. A valley full of choices awaits you: dayhikes or backpack trips, horseback rides in season, trips into "town," river rafting in season, a bicycling adventure, or lazing in a hammock or deck chair watching the horses graze and reading a good book.

The ranch is a unique, all-inclusive vacation experience (meals, lodging, and transportation all provided). If you are uncomfortable in rustic surroundings or if you want a private hide-a-way for just you and your sweetie, this may not be for you. But if a clean cabin, a comfortable bed, three great meals, and camaraderie with like-minded vacationers appeals to you, don't miss this place.

The ranch is located 9 miles upvalley from the boat landing. Transportation is provided from the landing to the ranch, and from the ranch to other points of interest throughout the lower valley. An informative and entertaining narrative is provided by your bus driver, illuminating many of the questions that this isolated valley may raise in your mind.

At the ranch, your accommodations are simple and comfortable. Of 12 units, most are "tent cabins" with canvas roofs, screened windows, kerosene lamps, and various bed configurations. These units have no heat, electricity, or bathrooms, yet are surprisingly cozy and comfortable. They share a clean, spacious bathhouse and rent for $60 per person per night—ALL MEALS included. Children 7–12 are $50, 4–6 are $35, and 3 or younger $20 (unless you bring your own bedding and towels or they sleep with parents, then they are free). Bring a flashlight along, especially if you're staying in one of these units, for those late-night treks to the potty.

New to the Stehekin Valley Ranch are several cabins with private baths and permanent roofs. These each have a queen bed and two singles, and rent for just $5 more per person per night.

In any of the cabins, you have the option of saving $5 per night by bringing your own sleeping bag (or sheets) and towels.

When budgeting for your trip to Stehekin and selecting your lodging, it is important to remember that the ranch price includes *all* your meals. In fact, it includes an extra meal: lunch is provided the day you arrive and the day you leave.

Breakfasts at the ranch are hearty, varied, and plentiful: eggs (including omelettes) cooked to order, homefries, breakfast meats, hotcakes, and exceptional rolled oats. For lunch, you can eat in the dining room (hamburgers, cheeseburgers, Gardenburgers™, plain or grilled sandwiches) or pack a to-go lunch from the sandwich bar that is set out during breakfast.

Dinners are especially wonderful. Dinner is the only meal at the ranch that is open to non-guests. A limited number of people can sign up to join ranch guests for dinner (see *Dining*, p. 107). As a guest, enjoy all you can eat of your choice of entrees (steak, chicken, fish, and a specialty entree daily), plus homemade bread, vegetables, salad bar, and freshly baked pies.

One of the cabins at Stehekin Valley Ranch

Meals are served in a communal dining room in the main building, which also houses the shared bathroom facilities. The dining room is huge and cheerful, with log beams, pine paneling, and lots of natural light. Take your coffee or water for tea and cocoa from one of the oversized pots on the hearth of the massive stone fireplace. A loft above the dining room provides a lounge area and offers a selection of traditional board games.

Highlight: Three great meals per day included at this "fancy campground"/"rustic resort."

WINKEL'S LINDAL CEDAR HOME
Walter G. Winkel
P.O. Box 14, Stehekin, WA 98852

No one in the valley is a stranger to Wally Winkel. Gray-haired, blue-eyed, and silver-tongued, Mr. Winkel puts on a display of down-home folksiness that is sure to elicit a grin. "Hi, Wally," say the folks at the bakery, pouring him a cup of coffee before he's even in the door. "Wally," murmur the other innkeepers by way of greeting when they all converge on the boat landing to pick up their respective guests. Other drivers smile and wave when they pass him on the road.

Wally is a long-time resident of the valley, and renting this cabin is only one of his many enterprises. Driving heavy equipment is another. You'll see his mark when you least expect it. A handmade cribbage board in the game room at Stehekin Valley Ranch bears his signature.

Wally's Lindal Cedar Home is a spacious cabin with room for six. A double bed downstairs sleeps two, and a roomy loft with double and two twins sleeps another four. The cabin is completely furnished, including bedding, towels, and cooking and

Winkel's is roomy and suited for long stays

eating utensils. The kitchen lacks a few modern conveniences (no dishwasher or microwave), but those who like to cook will be amazed at the array of pots, pans, and hand implements, especially in a place so essentially masculine. The home also includes a laundry room (handy for longer stays), a small freezer, and a wood stove. All laundry and cleaning supplies and many toiletries are provided.

The cabin is fully appointed, but in a no-nonsense manner. It is somewhat rustic and lacks any attempts at cutesy or chic. Decor? Let's just say Mr. Winkel takes "unpretentious" to an art form. You can relax and be yourself in his cabin. You'll want to bring books and games for evening and rainy-day entertainment.

The rate is $100 per night for 2 persons, additional persons $10 each (children under 12, $5). Pets are negotiable (if you're a dog lover, you'll be charmed by Wally's own, who lives across the street with his master). The six-night rate is $500 for 1-6 persons; no maid service. The cabin is available May through October.

Wally's usual arrangement is to pick you up at the landing at a pre-arranged time (usually 12:30 at the boat landing), and drive you out to his property, which is 1.5 miles up Company Creek Road past Harlequin Bridge. Once he has "shown you the ropes," you'll be handed the keys to a vehicle (ours was a sturdy old 4x4 pickup), the use of which is included in the price of your stay if you are a licensed and insured driver.

As with all self-contained cabins in Stehekin, remember to bring *all* your food. Winkel's place is well-suited for a longer stay in this regard, with a full-size refrigerator-freezer as well as a small chest freezer in the laundry area.

Highlight: Use of a vehicle is provided while you stay at this roomy cabin (large enough for six).

STEHEKIN VACATION RENTALS
Mike and Nancy Barnhart
Box 25, Stehekin, WA 98852 or
2101 N. Baker Ave., East Wenatchee, WA 98802
(509) 884-1730

Mike and Nancy Barnhart offer three vacation homes for rent in Stehekin. Two are located on Lake Chelan (accessible only by boat, trail, or float plane), and one is upvalley near the Stehekin River. The Lady of the Lake II can drop you off at either of the lake cabins, and boat shuttles (for a fee) can be arranged to get you back and forth to Stehekin during your stay if necessary.

Flick Creek House is a beautiful post-and-beam cedar structure with a sleeping capacity of 10 (three bedrooms, two baths). It is located two and a half miles downlake from Stehekin Landing (about an hour's walk along the Lakeshore Trail). The completely furnished home has its own sandy beach, boat dock, and row boat, as well as a firepit, a barbecue, and a large deck for enjoying the spectacular views. It rents for $130 per night for two persons, $25 for each additional person. Minimum rental is three nights. Weekly rate is $725 for two, $40 for each additional person. Rental of Flick Creek House comes with a car at Stehekin.

Totem House rents by the week only, for $800. It is also located on the lake, three miles from the landing. A unique design, Totem House has one large bedroom with a king and a queen bed that looks out on Lake Chelan to the south. It features a spacious deck, patio, covered barbecue area, and boat dock with 12-foot rowboat. The house is on a hill, offering great views but no beach (you can swim from the dock). Totem House is not suited for small children (under 12 not allowed), but can sleep up to six persons in the upstairs bedroom and on a downstairs hide-a-bed.

Upvalley, near the end of Company Creek Road, is the Stehekin House. This three-bedroom home sleeps six in a peaceful, private setting near the river. A car is provided to transport you the 7 miles from the boat landing to the house and to trailheads. The house includes a barbecue area and firepit. Rental is $95 per night for two persons, $15 for each additional. Minimum rental is three nights. Weekly rate is $550 for two, $25 for each additional person.

All three houses have complete kitchens, stocked with utensils, pots, pans, and tableware. These houses are ideal for longer stays, but reserve early: the Barnharts' vacation homes are popular, with many guests returning year after year.

Highlight: Three secluded vacation homes, great for longer stays.

CAMPBELL'S RESORT AND CONFERENCE CENTER
104 West Woodin Ave., Chelan, WA 98816
1-800-553-8225 (NW only) or (509) 682-2561

If you will be staying in Chelan before or after catching the boat uplake, try Campbell's. The Campbell family have been innkeepers since 1901. Today, the facility that bears their name is an 8-acre, 150-room resort and conference center, with 1200 feet of beach, boat moorage, two swimming pools, two hot tubs, and two restaurants. Rooms are comfortable, but not plush, and children are welcome. No pets allowed.

Summer rates (June 14–September) range from $106 to $162 for a basic room with one or two beds; from $164 to $170 for a 500-square-foot "Deluxe" room with microwave, wet bar, and small refrigerator. One- and two-bedroom "Terrace," "Beach," or "Cottage" units include kitchen and utensils, sleep as many as six persons, and rent for $150 to $212. Suites, which sleep up to eight, rent for $162 to $298. The Presidential Suite has a whirlpool tub, fireplace, and sitting room; the Penthouse has fireplace, full kitchen, and generous living space.

Campbell's is open year-round, and discounts the above rates in the spring, fall, and winter. If you just need a place to crash the night before you head for Stehekin, you'll appreciate Campbell's convenient location right next to a major grocery store and just down the road from the Lady of the Lake docks. If you plan to stay in Chelan for awhile, doing the resort activity scene, Campbell's is a safe bet for a comfortable stay, with golfing, shopping, casino gambling, and water sports all nearby. Their staff

Campbell's Resort on Lake Chelan

is friendly and informative, their location is convenient, and their rates, while on the high side for eastern Washington, guarantee you a hot shower and a soft bed.

Highlight: 150-room resort in a convenient location for catching Lady of the Lake.

Additional Lodgings

Operating on a permit from the National Park Service, the North Cascades Stehekin Lodge is located right at the boat landing. Because of its location and connection with the Park Service, some sources seem to indicate that it is the only place to stay in Stehekin. While it is an adequate lodging, with 28 motel-type units ranging in price from $71 to $88 ($83 to $98 for units with kitchenettes) for two, it is by no means the best or the only lodging in Stehekin. Call (509) 682-4494 or write P.O. Box 457, Chelan, WA 98816 for information.

Dining

The following is a complete list of dining establishments in Stehekin. *Complete.* Three places. Eat here, or stay in a cabin where you can cook your own meals. If you choose the cabin route, remember: bring *everything* you need. Bring cooking oil, salt, milk. The only store in town is the tiny convenience store at the landing, and its provisions are extremely limited.

The good news is that all three places to eat in Stehekin are excellent.

STEHEKIN VALLEY RANCH
P.O. Box 36, Stehekin, WA 98852
(509) 682-4677

Mention Stehekin Valley Ranch to a local, and you'll likely hear, "Mmm, great food!" They're right! Ranch guests are treated to an incredible three squares a day (see Stehekin Valley Ranch listing under *Lodgings*, pp. 102-103). Those not staying at the ranch can partake of dinner on a reservation basis. Stop at the Courtney Log Office at the north end of the landing area to make your reservation; transportation is $2 per person; $1 for children under 6. During the summer months, reserve early or you'll be out of luck.

The fare is hearty, fresh, creative, and sensationally well-prepared. Grilled chicken breast ($11), halibut steak ($14.95), sirloin ($12.95) and New York ($16.95) steaks are available nightly, along with a specialty entree that varies daily: lasagna, prime rib, barbecued ribs and chicken, and so forth. All dinners include salad bar, starch, vegetable, dinner bread, and beverage (water, lemonade, and coffee—other items available for purchase). Vegetarians can make a meal of side dishes for $8.95. Lighter appetites can have a burger for $5.25 or salad bar for $6.95, but this is no place to come with a light appetite. Plan your Stehekin Valley Ranch meal after your heaviest day of hiking, and come with an appetite like a mama bear in springtime—this is where quality and quantity meet!

Finally, whether you've saved room or not, go back for a $2.50 wedge of pie. Several varieties to choose from daily, all freshly baked.

Dinner, like all meals at the ranch, is served cafeteria-style and eaten elbow-to-elbow with other diners. Make your selection, then cross the sawdust floor and take a seat at one of three extra-long picnic tables in the cheerful, rustic dining room.

Highlight: Hearty, fresh, well-prepared meals for ranch guests; dinners for non-guests by reservation.

SWISSMONT RESTAURANT
AT THE NORTH CASCADES STEHEKIN LODGE
P.O. Box 457, Chelan, WA 98816
(509) 682-4494

The restaurant at the Stehekin boat landing is the choice for most diners in Stehekin. The Swissmont Restaurant is open for breakfast, lunch, and dinner April 1–September 30. During this peak season, avoid dining here between 10:45 A.M. and 2 P.M., when the Lady of the Lake daytrip passengers are in town. Outside of that, it's a good place for a meal.

From November 1 to December 19, the restaurant is open only for lunch during the time when the boat is docked. From December 20 to March 31, it's open for breakfast Saturday and Sunday only, lunch only when the boat is docked, and dinner only Friday and Saturday. A buffet dinner is offered some Sunday nights mid-October through mid-April.

Breakfasts at the Swissmont range from oatmeal at $3.50 to specialties including a spicy breakfast hash, a four-cheese omelette, and a veggie scramble, each at $5.95. Pancakes, French toast, biscuits and gravy, and cold cereals also available at reasonable prices.

Lunchtime features burgers and sandwiches, all served with potato chips and ranging in price from $4.95 to $5.95. Vegetarian sandwiches, chicken burgers, soup, and salad are available.

The evening menu is limited, but well done. When I ate there, four complete dinners were offered: a NY strip steak for $17.95, salmon in a puff pastry with mornay sauce for $16.95, a charbroiled sirloin with honey-peppercorn sauce for $15.95, and shrimp linguine in an alfredo cream sauce for $14.95. These included bread and salad. Three vegetarian entrees were also offered, ranging in price from $7.95 to $9.95, with an additional $3.25 to add bread and salad. One of these, with the amusingly unassuming title, "Italian Pasta" (what other kind is there?), was a delicious combination of sun-dried tomatoes, fresh zucchini, and artichoke hearts in a light pesto, tossed with al dente corkscrew noodles.

Highlight: Limited but tasty menu; hours vary seasonally.

STEHEKIN PASTRY COMPANY

Two miles up Stehekin Valley Road from the boat landing, Stehekin Pastry Company is a must-do. Another holding of the Courtney dynasty (in this case, Cragg and Roberta Courtney), the Pastry Company offers a variety of baked goods (cookies, pies, bars, cinnamon rolls, filled pastries, and more), fresh coffee, and espresso drinks. Savories including pizza and other lunch fare may also be available.

Highlight: A not-to-be-missed Stehekin culinary experience.

Betcha can't eat just one at the Stehekin Pastry Company

Walks and Hikes
Listed in approximate order of difficulty

MCKELLAR CABIN HOMESTEAD TRAIL

Map:	None needed. "Stehekin Landing" map is produced and distributed by the National Park Service; this shows the location of this mini-trail
Distance	0.25 mile round trip
Elevation Gain:	None
Estimated Time:	15 minutes
Highlight:	Quarter-mile stroll to a preserved homestead cabin.

This fun and informative little walk can fit in anytime you have a little extra time at the boat-landing area.

Getting There

From the Lady of the Lake boat landing, turn left (north) and walk up the road a few hundred feet. On your right, you will see the Post Office and Ranger Station. Just past this building, you will cross a creek. Immediately after the creek, you will see the McKellar Cabin Trail on your right, before the road reaches the public shower/laundry/telephone facility.

The Walk

Stroll along a self-guiding tour past an old homestead cabin and a water-wheel generator. Interpretive plaques explain homesteading practices and discuss present-day conservation.

BUCKNER ORCHARD

Map:	None needed; Green Trails #82 "Stehekin" shows the area
Distance:	0.8 mile round trip
Elevation Gain:	None
Estimated Time:	1 hour, including time to wander the orchard and historic buildings
Highlight:	Easy, pretty stroll to a historic apple orchard.

What a gem! Here's an easy walk everyone can, and should, do. You follow a level footpath along a picturesque stream through the trees to the site of a historic orchard. Buckner Orchard, founded by the Buckner family when they moved here in 1917, was one of the first Common Delicious apple orchards in the state, and was a big part of the valley's heritage. The orchard still produces apples, but is now preserved and operated by the National Park Service as a historic site, rather than a commercial enterprise. The project is irrigated the old-fashioned way, with gravity-flow trenches and canvas flaps that, when raised and lowered, regulate the flow. Original buildings and equipment are on display, along with family photo albums detailing the orchard's history.

Getting There

As you head upvalley (northwest) on Stehekin Valley Road, just *before* you reach the Rainbow Falls turnoff, you will cross a bridge over Rainbow Creek. Just past the bridge, a sign on the left marks BUCKNER LANE, a footpath. A wide spot on the Buckner Lane side of the road provides parking for a couple of cars.

The Walk

Head down Buckner Lane, away from the road. On your left, you'll see where water has been diverted from Rainbow Creek into another stream. The resulting aqueduct is the main water source for Buckner Orchard. Walk along this picturesque man-made stream, crossing it several times on quaint little bridges. Watch for the canvas flaps in the stream, installed to control the flow of water.

At 0.3 mile, the path intersects with a road (yes, you can drive to the orchard—but why?) Turn left and walk along the road to enter the orchard. On your left, you will see an outhouse open for public use on the edge of the orchard. Take a moment to wander the orchard, viewing the old-fashioned irrigation system and equipment.

Continuing down the road, you will come to some of the original buildings from the orchard's commercial days. Feel free to enter those that are open and review the historic artifacts on display.

IMUS CREEK NATURE TRAIL

Map:	Interpretive guide published by Northwest Interpretive Center is available at ranger station and Golden West Visitor Center
Distance:	1 mile loop
Elevation Gain:	200'
Estimated Time:	30–60 minutes
Highlight:	Self-guiding interpretive trail offers geologic information and views across Lake Chelan.

A self-guiding interpretive trail, the Imus Creek Nature Trail is a pleasant loop walk beginning at the south end of the landing area and ending at its north end. It gains a bit of altitude en route, affording views of Lake Chelan and its west bank. Be sure to pick up the interpretive guide before you start out.

Getting There

From the boat landing, walk up the hill to your right, to the Golden West Visitor Center (pick up your interpretive guide here). Just past the visitor center, trail signs point uphill toward PURPLE CREEK TRAIL and IMUS CREEK INTERPRETIVE TRAIL, and off to the right toward LAKESHORE TRAIL. Follow the sign uphill to the Imus Creek trail.

The Walk

One of the first sights you will see on the trail is a little weather station, on your right as you ascent the initial incline. During the guided walks offered by the park rangers through the Golden West Visitor Center, visitors have a chance to see the operation of the instruments here.

The first three entries in the interpretive trail book deal with weather and water, presenting a thorough explanation of the difference in precipitation between the east side of the Cascades and the west side, and the resulting differences in vegetation. Stehekin valley residents get their water from wells or pipe it from springs into holding tanks. Those in the Stehekin landing area use a community storage tank; you will pass this cement cistern on the trail.

Climb to the first bridge, crossing Purple Creek. From here, follow the trail along the hillside. The interpretive guide provides information about the geologic forces that formed this area, and about the climate and vegetation of the Stehekin valley.

Views open up over Lake Chelan. The crags of aptly named Castle Rock are across the lake and to your left; the hanging valley of Devore Creek is across and slightly to your right. Farther to your right, upvalley, you can see the "three B's": Boston, Booker, and Buckner. McGregor Mountain looms to your right, on this side of the valley (to hike McGregor, see *Other Hikes and Walks*, at the end of this section).

Two benches provide resting opportunities; bring a book or binoculars.

Cross Imus Creek, named for early settlers Guy and Hazel Imus, near the end of the trail. Just before the trail ends at Stehekin Valley Road and Purple Point Campground, you have an opportunity to recycle your interpretive brochure by dropping it in a trailside box.

COON LAKE

Map:	Green Trails #81 "McGregor Mtn."
Distance:	2.4 miles round trip
Elevation Gain:	300'
Estimated Time:	2 hours, 30 minutes
Highlight:	Short, open hike to a lake.

An easy, open trail to a little lake, this short piece of the Pacific Crest Trail is a pleasant dayhike for the whole family. Nice views of Agnes Mountain to the southwest.

Getting There

Take the shuttle bus or private car upvalley on Stehekin Valley Road to High Bridge. A small, seasonal ranger station is on your right just before the bridge. You'll find the trailhead, which is also the trail to McGregor Mountain (see p. 118), behind and to the right of the ranger station.

The Hike

The trail leaves the ranger station and begins a very gradual ascent. It is a dry, sometimes dusty path without much cover. Hike it in the cool of morning or even on a cloudy or drizzly day.

At 0.8 mile, the footpath intersects with a popular horse trail. This is the trail used twice daily by the folks at Cascade Corrals for their tourist horseback rides (a fun experience if you

Coon Lake

have time; call 509-682-4677, or inquire at the Courtney Log Office at the north end of the landing area). The hiker and horse trails are the same for the next 0.2 mile; bear with the dusty surface.

At 1.0 mile, take the left fork, signed MCGREGOR TRAIL/COON LAKE. The equestrian trail goes off to the right, to its own vantage point above the lake.

Coon Lake is your reward at 1.2 miles. It's not really a swimming lake, as the lakeshore is pretty marshy. But it is a great place to spot wildlife: ducks, deer, and an occasional beaver.

Return the way you came, making sure you do not take the equestrian trail that forks off to your left 0.4 mile down from the lake.

AGNES GORGE

Map:	Green Trails #81 "McGregor Mtn."
Distance:	5.0 miles round trip
Elevation Gain:	300'
Estimated Time:	3 hours
Highlight:	Moderately strenuous, very pretty hike to a raging creek in a deep rock gorge.

A lush, green, rolling trail with big rewards: views of Agnes Mountain, a waterfall, and, finally, a torrential Agnes Creek rushing through the gorge for which the trail is named. Don't miss this one.

Getting There

The Agnes Gorge trailhead is on the left shortly after you cross High Bridge, at the northwestern (upper) end of the valley. Shuttles will drop you off just before the bridge; if you have your own vehicle, the parking area just before the bridge is a good place to leave it, although you could drive the 0.15 mile to the trailhead and park alongside the road.

Cross High Bridge and head up the road. Do not take the first trail on the left, which is a segment of the Pacific Crest Trail leading to Agnes Creek, Suiattle Pass, and Cloudy Pass. Take the second left: Agnes Gorge Trail.

The Hike

A well-maintained path of medium width starts out at a slight incline. Lush for an east side trail, it undulates up and down along the north side of Agnes Creek.

The creek itself is first revealed to you at 1.5 miles, a rushing torrent in a gorge far below. The path winds back into the forest, crossing a small waterfall at 1.75 miles. Just past 2.25 miles, the path forks. The main path goes to the right, away from Agnes Creek. Take a minute to explore the left fork, a short spur out to the edge of the cliff overlooking the creek. A waterfall cascades down the rock wall on the opposite site of the gorge, and you can see the remnants of an old tram—hunks of metal, scraps of cable—on both sides. For some people, this view of the gorge, falls, and old tram might be a suitable turnaround point, for the last 0.25 mile requires light scrambling down to the water's edge. For hikers who don't mind steep, loose surfaces, the best is yet to come.

Returning to the main path, you'll turn left, on what was the right fork when you took the spur fork to see the waterfall. Contour around the back of a hill, then scramble down a steep, dusty goat path to any of several vantage points at or near the water's edge. The convulsing cataract of Agnes Creek is at once peaceful and exciting. You'll want to linger here awhile; bring your camera, a picnic, or a good book.

LAKESHORE TRAIL

Map:	Green Trails #82 "Stehekin"
Distance:	Any
Elevation Gain:	Negligible
Estimated Time	Your choice
Highlight:	Beautiful trail for half a mile or all day; constant lake views.

Take a scenic walk along the shore of beautiful Lake Chelan. Whether you stroll out 0.25 mile and back, or take off for a full-day's workout, this trail offers exceptional views across the lake, as well as views uplake toward the mountains and downlake toward Chelan as it winds along the shoreline.

The Lakeshore Trail offers wide-open views of Lake Chelan

Rattlesnakes are often spotted on the open, sun-baked parts of this trail, but rest assured—the rangers swear that they are very "mellow rattlers." There hasn't been a snake bite reported in Stehekin in over 30 years.

Getting There

From the boat-landing area, walk to the right, past the retail shops and the Golden West Visitor Center. A sign on the far side of the visitor center points uphill toward PURPLE CREEK TRAIL and IMUS CREEK INTERPRETIVE TRAIL, and off to the right toward LAKESHORE TRAIL.

Follow the sign to the right. In about 100 yards, you'll see a post engraved LAKESHORE TRAIL, directing you up a slight incline and to the left. In about 250 feet, you'll reach the trailhead signboard, with its warnings about rattlesnakes and hantavirus, and other words to the wise. Take the fork to the right of the sign. At a final fork, go left at the sign LAKESHORE TRAIL: FISH CREEK 6.6, PRINCE CREEK 17.2.

The Hike

This hiker- and stock-only trail begins in the outskirts of the little village of Stehekin. Within 0.2 mile, you leave civilization behind. At 0.25 miles, a side trail leads down to the right to the first scenic viewpoint. This little point of land makes a nice picnic stop or turnaround point for those with a boat to catch. A second viewpoint spur just after 0.5 mile offers a similar opportunity.

After half a mile, you begin to leave the Stehekin landing daytrippers behind. The farther you go, the fewer hikers will keep you company. The trail rises and falls, dipping into draws formed by Hazard Creek (0.65 mile), Fourmile Creek (2.0 miles—go figure!), and Flick Creek (2.5 miles) as they flow downhill into Lake Chelan. Shaded in parts, exposed to the baking sun in others, the trail is wide and well-maintained, with many opportunities for postcard-perfect photographs of the lake and the peaks of the "three B's"—Booker Mountain, Buckner Mountain, and Boston Peak—nestled in the cleft of the valley to the northwest.

STEHEKIN RIVER TRAIL

Map:	Green Trails #82 "Stehekin"
Distance:	7.0 miles round trip
Elevation Gain:	None
Estimated Time:	3 hours
Highlight:	Lush, level path follows the route of the river to Lake Chelan.

This flat, attractive trail is particularly inviting in the early season. At only 1200 feet above sea level, it is accessible when other trails are not. Spring is also the best time for wildflowers, and for seeing the river at its most dramatic, swollen with early-season snowmelt runoff.

Old-growth fir, cedar, and ponderosa pine line the trail, which meanders next to and away from the river en route from Harlequin Campground to Weaver Point Campground. This is a good hike with kids. Besides being flat, it is cool and shady, and offers a number of diversions, including several footbridges and an airstrip. Mosquitoes like the marshy areas in the summer; bring repellent.

Getting There

Take Stehekin Valley Road to Harlequin Bridge. Turn left across the bridge onto Company Creek Road. In 0.1 mile, look for the DEVORE CREEK TRAIL 3.3, WEAVER POINT CAMP 3.5, FOURTH OF JULY BASIN 12.5 sign. Turn left, entering Harlequin Campground.

Walk along the road through Harlequin Camp until you pass through a gate. If you're driving, there's parking for about three cars off to the right at the gate.

The Hike

The trail proper begins about 100 feet beyond the gate. A sign here reminds you that this is the route to the Devore Creek Trail and to Weaver Camp. The floods of 1996 did some damage to the initial course of this hiker-only trail, but it was quickly restored to usable condition. You may spot some of the older signs, three-quarters buried now.

Cross the first of many footbridges, after which, in a field to your right, you see a landing strip for small aircraft, isolated Stehekin's only means of speedy emergency transport to Chelan.

From the airfield, the path winds through old-growth forest toward the river. The soft, pine-needle path is deeply shaded, lined with vine maple, elderberries, and deadfall in places, and a more marsh-like ecosystem in others. Children will enjoy plucking pieces of snakegrass, which they can pull apart then "put back together" at the "joints."

You will reach the river at 1.5 miles. Watch for evidence of beaver activity along the backwaters.

At 3.3 miles, cross a rocky area where Devore Creek flows to the river. This is also the junction point for Devore Creek Trail #1244, a popular backpacking trail that connects with Company Creek Trail #1243 to form a 23.7-mile loop from this junction back to a point along Company Creek Road near Winkel's cabin.

Less than a quarter-mile past the Devore Creek Trail junction, the Stehekin River Trail ends beside Lake Chelan at Weaver Point Campground.

RAINBOW LOOP TRAIL

Map:	Green Trails #82 "Stehekin"
Distance:	7.3-mile loop
Elevation Gain:	1000'
Estimated Time:	4 hours
Highlight:	Creekside picnic site at 3.0 miles.

The Rainbow Loop Trail is a good leg-stretcher, crossing Rainbow Creek and offering, via short spur trails, views over the Stehekin River Valley. Hikers should be aware of three things before setting out:

1. You will not see Rainbow Falls from the top of the loop. You cross Rainbow Creek nearly half a mile above the falls. You can, however, take a short spur road near the end of the hike and view the falls. Or just see them later. Many of the upvalley shuttle buses stop at the falls, and they are a short bike ride from most of the lodgings.
2. Both rattlesnakes and black bears frequent the Rainbow Loop Trail. Make plenty of noise as you walk, watch where you put your feet, and consider carrying pepper spray. Deer and other wildlife are likely to be seen as well.
3. The trail is a loop only if you don't mind walking a couple of miles on the road. Some people find this objectionable, but it is a very interesting 2.3 miles, passing sites including the old and new Stehekin schools. If you choose not to walk along the road to complete the loop, another option is to hike this trail point-to-point. Have the shuttle drop you off at the north trailhead, walk the 5.0 miles to the road, then catch another shuttle. If none is forthcoming, take the road toward town (southeast). In less than half a mile, you'll come to the bakery, where you can while away the time productively (or at least calorically) until the next shuttle arrives.

Getting There

To begin at the north end of the loop, follow Stehekin Valley Road northwest past its junction with Company Creek Road. (These are really the only two roads in the valley—it's hard to miss their junction!) Company Creek Road crosses a bridge southwest over the Stehekin River, toward Harlequin Campground, and Stehekin Valley Road, which has been paved to this point, loses pavement and continues northwest up the valley along the river's north bank.

About half a mile from the junction, watch for a wooden trailhead marker on the right reading RAINBOW LOOP TRAIL/RAINBOW CREEK TRAIL 2.5, STEHEKIN ROAD 5. Any shuttlebus driver will know where to drop you off. If you have your own car or bike, park it in one of the pull-outs on the left side of the road.

The Hike

The trail is open to horses as well as hikers, resulting in a rocky-dusty surface. The first mile is a gradually switchbacking ascent. It is dry and sparsely forested—a reminder that you are still very much on the east side of the Cascade crest. Vine maple and

Leave the RV at home

dusty ferns provide a thin understory beneath a mixed deciduous and coniferous canopy. This section of the trail is at its best in autumn, when the maples offer up a blaze of color.

After about a mile, the switchbacks cease and the trail turns southeast, contouring around Rainbow Mountain en route to its crossing of Rainbow Creek. The ascent is very gradual for the next half mile, and the path less rocky.

At 1.25 miles, look for a little goat path off to your right: a rocky knoll overlooks the Stehekin River and its valley. Returning to the main trail, the ascent steepens again at 1.5 miles and continues to climb to 2.25 miles, when it opens up into a high desert meadow and levels off. This is rattlesnake territory, where the sun bakes the south-facing hillside.

A must-see: Rainbow Falls

You reach a signed junction at 2.5 miles: RAINBOW LAKE and MCALESTER PASS to the left, STEHEKIN ROAD to the right. Take the right fork, which angles downhill toward Rainbow Creek. The creek comes into view at 2.85 miles; a bridge takes you across just before 3.0 miles. On the far side of the creek, careful scrambling gets you down to the water's edge. This makes the best picnic site on this trail. Rainbow Bridge campsite is on a little spur trail to the right of the main trail just past the bridge.

At 3.25 miles, a trail signed BOULDER AND WAR CREEK doubles back to your left. Stay right to continue on the loop. At 3.5 miles, watch for another spur trail on your right to a viewpoint. From atop a giant boulder, your vista includes a horseshoe bend in the river below, and a commanding view of the lower valley. A similar spur at 3.8 miles reveals much of the same, plus a peek at Lake Chelan to the south.

The next mile drops you down to the Rainbow Creek Trailhead on Stehekin Valley Road at 5.0 miles. To cut your hike short (or if you did not leave a vehicle at the trailhead), turn left on the road and walk to the bakery. To finish the loop, turn right.

Remember, walking along a road in Stehekin is not like walking along a road in the suburbs. I saw more deer as I walked along this road than I did on most deep wilderness hikes. And the people-watching is good, too. As this is the main arterial for Stehekin, you'll see anyone who's going anywhere by car, bike, hoof, or foot as you walk this road.

At 5.5 miles, pass the new (currently-in-use) Stehekin School. This schoolhouse educates all Stehekin children through the 8th grade. For high school, kids choose among home schooling, correspondence courses, and "going out"—moving in with friends or relatives to attend school outside of the Stehekin Valley. The old Stehekin School is on your right just past 5.7 miles. In keeping with the trusting atmosphere of Stehekin, this building is left unlocked, and is filled with historic photos, documents, and other artifacts about the school and the valley, as well as current information about the Stehekin student body.

At 5.8 miles, a short spur road on your right leads to Rainbow Falls. If this will be your only chance to see this 312-foot cascade, it's worth the extra quarter-mile. (Note that the stop sign at the junction of the Rainbow Falls road and the main road is the only stop sign in the entire Stehekin Valley.)

At 6.8 miles, reach the Harlequin Bridge. Continue straight ahead, following the Stehekin River northwest to your vehicle.

Other Walks and Hikes

The floods that wracked Washington state in the winter of 1996 were particularly cruel in Stehekin. The Stehekin Valley Road was washed out in many places, and it remains closed indefinitely above High Bridge (north of the Agnes Gorge Trail and the Stehekin Valley Ranch). For that reason, we concentrated on trails in the Lower Valley. When and if the road re-opens to Park Creek and Cottonwood campgrounds, ask your hosts or the rangers about other favorite dayhike trails including Cascade Pass (to Doubtful Lake, Horseshoe Basin, and/or Sahale Arm), Flat Creek, Park Creek, and the thigh-burning Goode Ridge Lookout.

MCGREGOR MOUNTAIN TRAIL

Speaking of thigh-burners—are you up for a full day of knee-to-chest climbing? Your reward is an 8000-foot summit, but the price is high. This trail has so many switchbacks that on a map it looks like a hacksaw blade. Take the 1.2-mile trail to Coon Lake from High Bridge, then lace up your boots and tuck it in for the grind. After 5.3 more miles and 5000 more feet in elevation gain, you can decide whether to attack the final 0.7 mile hand-and-foot scramble to the summit. Check with the rangers regarding snow before you try this one. Get an early start, pack plenty of water and…maybe make sure you're staying someplace with a hot tub.

Contacts

CHELAN AIRWAYS   (509) 682-5555
Box W, Chelan, WA 98816

CHELAN RANGER DISTRICT   (509) 682-2576
Wenatchee National Forest
Rte. 2, Box 680, 428 W. Woodin, Chelan, WA 98816

NORTH CASCADES NATIONAL PARK   (360) 856-5700
    ext. 515 for General Information
    ext. 340-341 for Stehekin, followed by a message, then
    ext. 14 for Golden West Visitor Center
    ext. 16 for Ranger Station

LAKE CHELAN BOAT COMPANY   (509) 682-2224
P.O. Box 186, Chelan, WA 98816

LAKE CHELAN CHAMBER OF COMMERCE   1-800-4CHELAN

US NATIONAL PARK SERVICE   (509) 682-2549
(shuttle bus and trail information)
Rte. 2, Box 690, 428 Woodin, Chelan, WA 98816

Looking back toward Stehekin on the Lakeshore Trail

Table 5.
Lodgings in the Stehekin vicinity

	SILVER BAY INN	SILVER BAY CABINS	STEHEKIN VALLEY RANCH	WINKEL'S LINDAL CEDAR HOME	STEHEKIN VACATION RENTALS	CAMPBELL'S RESORT
PRICE (1996 RATES, PRE-TAX, 2 PERSON)	$75, $95, $120	$135	Per person, incl. all meals: adult $55-65; age 7-12 $45-55; age 4-6 $30-40; age 0-3, $0-$20	$100	$95-$130	$106-$298
EXTRA PERSON	N/A	$20	see above	$10 (children under 12 $5)	$15-$25	N/A (included)
PAYMENT METHODS	VISA, MC, Check, Cash	VISA, MC, Check, Cash	Check, Cash	Write for info	Check, Cash	VISA, MC, AmEx, Check Cash
# OF UNITS	3 rooms	2 cabins	12 cabins	1 cabin	3 cabins	150 rooms
PRIVATE BATH	Yes	Yes	Yes, 3+ cabins	Yes	Yes	Yes
SHARED BATH	No	No	Yes, 3-6 cabins	No	No	No
BREAKFAST INCLUDED?	Yes	No	Yes—ALL MEALS INCL.	No	No	No
COOKING FACILITIES?	No (mini-kitchenette in one unit)	Yes	No	Yes	Yes	Yes, some units
POOL	No	No	No	No	No	Yes
HOT TUB	Yes	Yes	No	No	No	Yes
CHILDREN	No	OK Oct-June; no children under 8 July-Sept	OK	OK	OK in 2 of the units	OK
PETS	No	No	No	OK by arrangement	No	No
SEASONS OF OPERATION	May-October	Year-round	June-end of first week in October	May-October	April 1-November 1	Year-round

A rest stop along the hike to Agnes Gorge

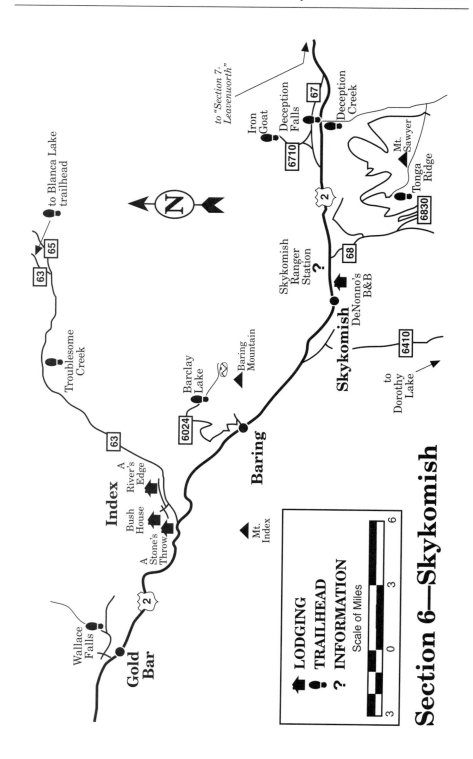

to "Section 7-Leavenworth"

Deception Creek

67

Deception Falls

Iron Goat

6710

Mt. Sawyer

Tonga Ridge

6830

to Blanca Lake trailhead

65

63

N

2

Skykomish Ranger Station

?

68

DeNonno's B&B

Troublesome Creek

Barclay Lake

Baring Mountain

Skykomish

6410

63

6024

to Dorothy Lake

Index

River's Edge

Bush House

Stone's Throw

Baring

Mt. Index

Wallace Falls

2

Gold Bar

LODGING

TRAILHEAD

INFORMATION

? Scale of Miles

6   3   0   3   6

Section 6—Skykomish

Skykomish
(Gold Bar to Stevens Pass, Highway 2 West)

Overview

The western segment of Highway 2, from Gold Bar to Stevens Pass, is a relatively undeveloped stretch of wilderness. There are no tourist-centered towns like Winthrop or Leavenworth, no grand hotels like Salish Lodge or Sun Mountain Lodge. Instead, there are charming, quirky little towns like Index and Skykomish, with warm, wonderful B&B's like DeNonno's and A Stone's Throw. There's a stately, restored, historic inn called Bush House. There's an espresso stand called Espresso Chalet that's almost worth the hour's drive from Seattle. AND, there are dayhikes—*great* dayhikes. What more could you need for a holiday?

From the Seattle area, reach this Highway 2 corridor by taking Interstate 405 north to Bothell. Then take Highway 522 east, past Woodinville and the turnoff to Highway 9, until it intersects with Highway 2 just west of Monroe. Head east on Highway 2, passing through Sultan (8 miles east of Monroe) and Startup (4 miles east of Sultan). The next town you reach is Gold Bar. About 2 miles east of Startup (and less than an hour from downtown Seattle, barring traffic), Gold Bar is the western boundary of this hiking corridor. It is the location of Wallace Falls State Park and the hearty 6.0 mile Wallace Falls dayhike.

Grab a snack, have some espresso, and see Bigfoot on the road to Skykomish

Eight miles east of Gold Bar is the junction road for the town of Index, home to three featured lodgings and the highest-recommended restaurant in the area. Turn left at the INDEX sign and follow the road for one mile to a one-lane bridge on your left (highly controversial at press time, this may expand to two lanes in the near future). Crossing the bridge takes you into the town of Index; continuing straight on the road you are on takes you to Troublesome Creek interpretive trail and the Blanca Lake hike.

Index is a curious little town. Cute as a bug, it's home to a population of about 150. It is named for Mt. Index, a monolithic crag to the south. It is bordered by the North Fork Skykomish River on the south side and a sheer 400-foot granite cliff (known locally as simply "The Wall") on the north side, inhibiting growth in either direction. As with most towns along the Highway 2 corridor, Index owes much of its heritage to the railroad industry; trains still rumble through town many times daily.

Back on Highway 2 heading east, the next "landmark" is Espresso Chalet with its adjacent park and Bigfoot memorabilia. The next "wide spot in the road" is Baring, which is also the turnoff to the Barclay Creek Trail.

The next town is Skykomish. The town itself, just east of the highway, is full of railroad lore. A key stopover for the Great Northern Railway (trains changed engines here before and after the harrowing ascent of Stevens Pass), it was a bustling boom-town of 8000 during the construction of the Cascade Tunnel in the 1920's. Today, it is home to a couple of lodging and dining establishments and more than a few tall tales if you can stir up an oldtimer down at the café or tavern. For the best lodging in the area, however, go just past the town of Skykomish on Highway 2, and take the next right to DeNonno's Bed & Breakfast.

Beyond DeNonno's is the Skykomish Ranger Station, a valuable source of trail information. Always check in here to inquire about trail accessibility and conditions before hiking.

Between the ranger station and the Stevens Pass summit are access roads for several more hikes and walks: Tonga Ridge, Iron Goat, Deception Falls, and Deception Creek.

If you're coming to this area from the eastern part of the state, catch Highway 2 in Wenatchee and travel west. Stevens Pass summit is 55 miles east of Wenatchee, and the hikes and lodgings listed here begin shortly thereafter.

The people of the Index-Skykomish area are interesting. Many are into several enterprises simultaneously. Innkeepers drive school buses, accountants do market-ing, espresso baristas race sled dogs, just about everybody has RV camping space. It's a vigorous sort of ethic that exemplifies the best of the Pacific Northwest. Folks are raised here, or move here, with respect for this little piece of paradise. They make a niche for themselves and live life on their own terms.

It's lucky for us that they do. There are just enough services along this corridor to make it a dayhiking vacation destination. The trails are good, and varied. Being only an hour from Seattle, it's not exactly isolated, but it is less developed than some areas. Trails here are often primitive—true wilderness experiences. Expect, even more so than in other areas of the North Cascades, no trailhead amenities such as dumpsters, toilets, water, or maps. (Notable exceptions are the tourist-friendly Deception Falls and Iron Goat trails.)

As the area grows in popularity—and it will—make your lodging reservation in advance, try to visit on weekdays, and come enjoy a rustic part of the North Cascades.

Lodgings

DENONNO'S BED AND BREAKFAST
P.O. Box 219, 527 Skylane
Skykomish, WA 98288--219
(360) 677-2518

Lou and Pat DeNonno operate a charming in-home B&B on the banks of the Skykomish River just east of the town of Skykomish. They offer three rooms: two with queen beds in the main house ($55 and $65, according to room size, shared bath), and a larger room with queen bed, queen hide-a-bed, private bath, and a separate entrance ($75).

Decor at DeNonno's is sort of "French Country"—lots of florals, colors, and textures mingling in a casual elegance. The walls are decorated with clusters of small and medium-size paintings, many of which were painted by the multi-talented Pat (Mrs.) DeNonno. Pat also maintains the flower and herb garden in front of the home, and is responsible for the lovely DeNonno breakfast, which is as beautiful as it is delicious. Typical fare includes smoked salmon, eggs, baked goods, juice, and a selection of fresh fruits, all garnished with fresh herbs and flowers from the garden and presented in a way that would make Martha Stewart envious.

The DeNonnos are gracious without being intrusive, taking pride in the little "extras" that make your stay truly comfortable: a pitcher of ice water with lemon slices and fresh mint appeared after our hike; piles of fluffy towels encouraged use of the hot tub.

DeNonno's deck with gardens and hot tub

Lou and Pat are New Jersey expatriates who came to the northwest when their daughter was a student at the University of Washington in Seattle. They loved the area so much, they sold everything back home and moved west, leaving 20+ year careers behind without a backward glance. They saw a need for an upscale B&B in the Skykomish area, found this wonderful piece of property right off the highway and adjacent to the river, and the rest is history.

Today, Pat works part-time at the Skykomish Ranger Station just down the road (making her a valuable resource for hiking and other wilderness information), Lou drives a school bus, and, together, they pitch in and run their B&B as a labor of love.

The house is simple and stylish, with a circular gravel drive and garden in front and an expansive deck in the back. Guests will want to linger on the tri-level deck, enjoying the sounds of the river, the sensuous flowers planted all around, and the hot tub. Watch for the DENONNO'S BED & BREAKFAST sign on Highway 2 east of Skykomish. Just east of milepost 49, turn south on Skylane, and theirs is the first home you'll see, right in front of you at the T intersection.

For comfortable rooms, friendly proprietors, good food, and a quiet night's rest, DeNonno's is a solid recommendation.

Highlight: Casually elegant, quiet in-home B&B on the Skykomish River.

BUSH HOUSE COUNTRY INN
300 Fifth Street, Index, WA 98256
(360) 793-2312

When I first discovered Index, a charming little hamlet separated from the rest of the world by a one-lane bridge over the North Fork Skykomish River, I thought, "This place is so darn cute! It's a page out of history! It's so *tiny!* There couldn't possibly be a place to stay..." But there it was. Not just "a place to stay," but a *restored, historic* hotel, as quaint as the little town itself.

The Bush House was established in 1898. Today, it's a restaurant (see also *Dining,* p. 129) and inn with 11 cozy guest rooms, a sitting room, and a cocktail lounge.

Rooms are attractive but

Romantic, historic Bush House

small (except #1, a huge studio suite with king-size bed and sitting area). Each has one double, queen, or king bed. Rates are $59 (for the two smallest rooms), $70 (for most rooms), and $80 (for room #1, the studio suite, or room #11, the one room with a private toilet and wash basin). The rooms are furnished with brass or wicker, lace curtains, and a few antiques. Each has individual baseboard heat; no air conditioning. Hallway decor maintains the turn-of-the-century feel, with tea-rose carpeting and traditional wainscoting. Prices are for two persons, and include a continental breakfast in the dining room.

The 11 rooms at the Bush House share two bathrooms (except, as mentioned, Room #11 has a half bath). One of the shared bathrooms is completely modern, with tub/shower enclosure; the other is a roomy, old-fashioned bath with claw-foot tub and separate, small shower.

Unfortunately, the charm of the past also comes with a few quirks: squeaky pipes, temperamental fuses, vaguely uneven floors. And, oh, yes—the train. It rumbles by several times daily. And nightly.

All that being said, it's a small price to pay for romance, and Bush House has plenty of that. It's a genuine period piece throughout.

To reach the Bush House from the west, take Highway 2 through Sultan, Startup, and Gold Bar. About 8 miles east of Gold Bar, turn left at the INDEX sign. (Coming from the east, it's a right turn about 12 miles west of Skykomish.) Follow the Index-Galena Road one mile. Turn left across the one-lane bridge (which may have been expanded to two lanes by the time you visit). Continue straight ahead two blocks; you literally can't miss the Bush House on your left.

Highlight: Romantic but quirky historic hotel.

A STONE'S THROW B&B
P.O. Box 164, Index, WA 98256
(360) 793-0100

Index is full of surprises. This place is among the best of them.

Your hosts, David and Lynn, welcome you into one of the most inviting, serene, and gracious settings in the North Cascades. Their beautiful home, built in 1912, has been thoroughly hand-restored to its present, gem-like condition. Leave your shoes at the door, and the kids at home—this peaceful retreat is perfect for a single ($65) or a couple ($75) looking to get away from it all.

You'll be the only guest at A Stone's Throw. While there would have been room for two bedrooms upstairs, David and Lynn instead devoted the entire upper floor to one guest suite: bedroom, sitting room, and private bath. Natural fir paneling and hardwood floors surround you, and elegant

A Stone's Throw—the organic garden out back

antiques mingle with a full complement of modern conveniences. The tile bath looks out on a magically abundant organic garden. The private sitting room includes a TV, VCR with movie library, CD player, and coffee bar. A writing desk in the hall faces the granite cliff north of Index, and your room, with queen-size bed and quaint hip roof, has a view of Mt. Index.

The main level of the house is bathed in natural light from the sunbeams that arch through the many windows. Take your breakfast on the sunporch or in the dining room, depending upon the weather and your mood. Enjoy fresh-squeezed orange juice, freshly ground coffee, seasonal fruits, warm homemade muffins, and an entree such as artichoke-bacon frittata, omelette du jour, or a mildly spicy Mexican favorite.

A Stone's Throw is nonsmoking, and accepts cash and checks only; deposit required. To find it, follow the directions to Bush House (above). Turn left at Bush House, pass in front of it and cross the railroad tracks. A Stone's Throw is on your left, just past the tracks. Oh, yes, the train. As with Bush House, the sounds of the train are part of the historic ambiance at A Stone's Throw.

Highlight: Serene gem of a B&B; very private.

A RIVER'S EDGE COUNTRY COTTAGE B&B
Avenue A, Index, WA 98256
(360) 793-0392

Yet *another* lodging in this tiny town of 150? Yes, Dawna Finley's A River's Edge Country Cottage B&B provides a third, totally different type of lodging experience in Index. Accommodations are roomy, where Bush House is cozy, and suitable for families (by prior arrangement), where A Stone's Throw is strictly appropriate for adults.

Dawna offers one unit, which is actually more of a self-contained apartment, for $80 per night for 2 persons (additional persons $10 each). You have a separate entrance, a kitchen, a living room, a large bedroom, and a private bath with over-sized shower. The living room has a queen hide-a-bed, TV, and propane fireplace. A hot tub is on the premises, as is a covered patio area for smoking (indoors is non-smoking). The additional space and the private kitchen make A River's Edge a good choice for a longer stay; ask about discounts.

Of course, there's no need to use that kitchen unless you want to! A generous breakfast is delivered in a basket to your room, and the Bush House Restaurant is just down the road.

To find A River's Edge, follow the directions to Index (see Bush House, above), but immediately after crossing the bridge, turn right onto Avenue A. Follow Avenue A, which parallels the river, almost to its end. Watch for the sign on your left.

Highlight: Separate apartment with kitchen.

Additional Lodgings

Because the recommended lodgings above comprise a small total number of rooms, contact information for the following lodgings is provided. These premises were not thoroughly reviewed by the author.

FLYNN'S SKYKOMISH HOTEL
(360) 677-2477
A funky old semi-restored railroadman hotel right on the tracks in Skykomish; budget rooms (all with shared bath) range $35–$45 for two.

SKY RIVER INN
333 River Drive East, Skykomish, WA 98288-0280
(360) 677-2261
18 standard motel units with one or two double or queen beds; $56–$88; some kitchenettes; pets OK for a fee; midweek discount available.

Dining

Fine dining is not the Skykomish area's forte. The Bush House provides a nice meal, as detailed below, and a couple other cafés allow you to get full after a day of hiking. For the best experience, have breakfast at your B&B (all those featured have great morning fare) or the nearest diner (if you're not staying at a B&B), a midday snack at Espresso Chalet, and an early dinner at Bush House.

BUSH HOUSE RESTAURANT
300 Fifth Street, Index, WA 98256
(360) 793-2312

Housed in the historic Bush House Country Inn, the Bush House Restaurant is probably the best place in the area to sit down to a freshly-prepared meal.

The menu is not exotic, not extensive, but well done, with careful touches like homemade salad dressings. Prices range from about $9 to about $15 for complete dinners including soup or salad and home-baked bread.

Happily, the Bush House makes an effort to cater to vegetarians—one of the soups du jour is vegetable-based, and entrees include a nice primavera pasta and a tasty, chewy, tofu stir-fry (and, alas, the ubiquitous Gardenburger).

Highlight: Well-prepared continental cuisine in a pleasant hotel dining room.

ESPRESSO CHALET
P.O. Box 335, 50000 SR 2 (Milepost 36), Index, WA 98256
(360) 793-7932

Espresso Chalet is a sort of metaphor for the whole Skykomish area; maybe a metaphor for all that's good about Washington state. Owners Mark and Sandy Klein have taken a rough piece of property on Highway 2 between Index and Skykomish and turned it into a thriving little multi-use enterprise by the sweat of their brows and their dedication to the things they enjoy.

The top-notch espresso drinks (six sizes to choose from—up to 32 ounces) are made in a tiny, unassuming travel trailer painted, like the ramshackle shed behind it, an obnoxious yet amusing Crayola green. But espresso and snacks (muffins, cookies, and the like) are only the beginning. The shed behind the trailer houses hysterically kitschy Bigfoot memorabilia (this site was used in filming scenes for the movie *Harry and The Hendersons*). To the east of the shed is a lovely little park, grassy and

shaded, with picnic tables and room for RVs. More remarkable, the park was formerly a dump, cleaned up and landscaped to its present condition by Mark and
Sandy. As if this weren't enough, the Kleins also raise huskies, operate a dog
groomery, and participate in sled-dog rides and races.

Their entire enterprise (espresso shop, RV park, groomery, and sledding) is
known as "Mt. Index Village." Stop by for a latté, at the very least, and stay to enjoy
the park and the company if you can. Get a close-up look at Mt. Index with their on-
site telescope. The Kleins also sell maps, postcards, and visitor guides.

Highlight: Delightful place for a rest and a snack; delicious espresso drinks.

Walks and Hikes
Listed in approximate order of difficulty

DECEPTION FALLS

Map:	None needed
Distance:	0.4 mile round trip to falls (barrier-free)
	0.5 mile nature trail loop
Elevation Gain:	Negligible
Estimated Time:	30 minutes for each trail
Highlight:	Everyone can take the short stroll to this waterfall.

Bring Grandma, Grandpa, and the kids. In fact, bring Auntie, Uncle, and all the
cousins, too—everybody else does! All kidding aside, the short walks here at
Deception Falls are popular, and rightfully so. Besides the falls and the adjacent
nature trail, there's a picnic area with barbecues and a set of composting pit toilets.

A sign at the parking lot explains the layout. The big attraction is Deception Falls,
a showy cascade reached by stairs or a 0.4-mile-round-trip trail that's barrier-free.
Another short walk offers a wooded trail past the confluence of Deception Creek and
the Tye River.

Getting There
The Deception Falls nature trail and picnic area are located on the north side of
Highway 2, eight miles east of Skykomish and 6.5 miles west of the Stevens Pass
summit. It is clearly signed from the highway.

The Walk
From the parking-area map, head down the asphalt trail near the toilets, away
from the parking lot. The trail curves to the right, toward the falls. See these first.
(Party poopers who want to get right to it will quickly realize they can see the falls
just by trotting down a flight of steps from the east end of the parking lot, but this
approach is more appealing.) The barrier-free trail continues across a bridge over
Deception Creek; the falls are immediately on your right (south) as you cross. Those
without mobility impairment can continue a bit farther, crossing under the highway
and up another flight of steps to a platform with a view of the upper falls.

Returning across the bridge, turn right at the first fork to begin the nature-trail loop. The first few dozen feet of this trail area also barrier-free, leading to a photogenic viewpoint of the falls beside Deception Creek.

Continue north along Deception Creek to its confluence with the Tye River. The trail circles counterclockwise, following the curve of the Tye River west, then south, before it turns east to return to the parking lot. The short stroll includes benches, spur trails to the river's edge, interpretive signs, and abundant photo opportunities.

IRON GOAT

Map:	Green Trails #176 "Stevens Pass," or call Iron Goat Trail Information at (206) 283-1440 for brochure
Distance:	Lower Grade: 2.4 miles round trip (barrier-free)
	Upper Grade: 6.8 miles round trip
Elevation Gain:	Negligible
Estimated Time:	1 hour for lower grade; 3 hours for upper grade
Highlight:	Old railroad grade is both historically interesting and beautifully restored.

Named for the mountain-goat logo of the Great Northern Railway, the Iron Goat Trail reclaims land that was once given over to industry (specifically, the abandoned grade of the Great Northern Railway) and returns it to near-wilderness condition for dayhikers' use and enjoyment.

I must admit, I have not been uniformly impressed by old railroad grades turned into hiking trails. Sometimes vapid, overwide, and under-timbered, I feel many are best left to mountain bikers and equestrians. Iron Goat is an exception. A pleasant, verdant walk in the woods, this hiker-only trail is an exhilarating tribute to nature's tenacity. Although man tamed this mountain pass a century ago, routing a railway first by switchbacks, later by a tunnels, nature has (with the help of a good deal of volunteer sweat) reclaimed what is hers.

Iron Goat is a work in progress, with plans for improvements extending to the year 2000 and beyond. As of the summer of 1996, an upper trail extended 3.4 miles, and a lower one 1.2 miles. The lower trail has been graded to be barrier-free, but is in fact moderately difficult for unassisted wheelchair users; an exceptionally wet day could render it muddy and inappropriate.

Besides simply showing up and hiking the trail for pleasure, hikers are encouraged to join in volunteer trail maintenance and construction efforts. Contact the trail association at (206) 283-1440 to find out dates for work parties. Guided interpretive hikes focusing on plant life or history are also offered; call for information.

Getting There

From the west, drive east on Highway 2 to milepost 55, 5.1 miles east of the Skykomish Ranger Station. Turn left (north) onto USFS Road 67. From the east, watch for the right-hand turnoff to the other end of Road 67, 5.8 miles west of the Stevens Pass summit.

From either direction, follow Road 67 to its junction with USFS Road 6710, on which you will turn north. Follow Road 6710 1.5 miles to its end at the Martin Creek trailhead. Parking for 20+ cars and two state-of-the-art composting pit toilets provided.

The Hike

The trail begins on a short boardwalk, which gives way to a well-graded, gravel path lined with alders, ferns, and berry bushes. Near the start, you have a choice of the lower grade (1.2 miles each way), the upper grade (3.4 miles each way), or a loop of about 1.5 miles involving both grades. Those choosing the upper grade or the loop will take the short, steep switchback to the left signed MARTIN CREEK CROSSOVER. After about a half-mile's stroll on the upper grade, take the COREA CROSSOVER down to the lower grade or continue on. These two crossovers are the only ones connecting the upper and lower grades.

The trails, both lower and upper, pass interpretive plaques explaining the history of the area, particularly of the railroad. Even those less than sympathetic to technology will have to marvel at the engineering that went into the Great Northern Railway and the strength and tenacity of the men who labored to build it. Both grades were part of the same route, an upper and a lower switchback that are astonishingly close together. It's no wonder the railmen used to joke about being able to spit from the engine down onto the caboose below.

Tunnels, slag piles, and railway mile markers en route bear witness to the railroad, but in a curious, detached fashion that does not detract from the beauty of the walk. It is as though you were passing through the ancient ruins of some lost civilization. After walking one of the grades, you may find you want to linger and walk the other; it's a surprisingly pretty and peaceful experience.

BARCLAY LAKE

Map:	Green Trails #143 "Monte Cristo"
Distance:	4.4 miles round trip
Elevation Gain:	300'
Estimated Time:	2 hours plus picnic time
Highlight:	Easy hike through old forest to a mountain lake.

Hike a gentle, pleasant trail to a pretty lake tucked behind big, bold Baring Mountain. Stroll along the route of melodic Barclay Creek, through classic old forest thick with deadfall below and fir and pine boughs above. This is a great hike for kids, with plenty of opportunities to study the phenomena of nurse logs, fungus growth, and natural composting. Elevation gain is minimal, and you are rewarded with a fine picnic spot at the end: sandy beaches and cool water at the base of a towering mountain.

Getting There

Find Baring, a little hamlet on Highway 2 about 8 miles east of Skykomish and 6.5 miles west of the Index turnoff. At Baring, turn northeast off the highway (left if

Barclay Lake is a nice reward for a gentle 4.4-mile hike

you're going east, right if you're going west) onto USFS Road 6024, Barclay Creek Road. Cross over the railroad tracks on this crushed gravel road. At 0.3 mile, the road forks. Stay left to continue on Road 6024. After about 4 miles on this winding road, you will see the signed trailhead and a parking area with room for about 10 cars. The trail drops away from the road on the left side.

The Hike

Officially called Barclay Creek Trail #1055, this hiker-only trail is part of the Skykomish District Backcountry; fill out a self-issuing permit at the trailhead.

The narrow, dirt-and-crushed-rock trail descends gently from the parking lot. The walk begins under a bower of sweet-smelling pine and fir. Periodically, the canopy gives way, and you catch glimpses of the pointed peak of Baring Mountain's north face looming ahead and off to your right. Breaking out into a clearing at 0.25 mile, you can also see the crags of Gunn Peak (named for original Index homesteaders Persis and Amos Gunn) and Merchant Peak to the north (on your left).

Most of the walk is in dense, old-growth forest. Ferns and bracket mushrooms abound. Amidst the tangled beauty of snags, young trees, berries, brambles, and fallen logs, the occasional giant—4 to 6 feet in diameter–rises majestically.

Reach Barclay Lake at about 1.7 miles. You'll have your choice of vantage spots along the lake's scenic north bank, where the path continues for another half-mile, for a total hike of 2.2 miles one way. Directly above the lake looms the massive crag of Baring Mountain (best photographed early in the day, while the sun is in the east and striking this northeast face).

Ambitious hikers eager for some additional climbing may wish to continue on past Barclay Lake to Eagle Lake. The less-developed trail from Barclay to Eagle begins where the Barclay Creek Trail ends (at 2.2 miles), and climbs a rigorous 1388 feet to reach the second lake in 1.7 miles, resulting in a total hike of 7.8 miles. Bring plenty of water, and plan an additional three hours.

TONGA RIDGE

Map:	Green Trails #175 & #176, "Skykomish" & "Stevens Pass"
Distance:	4.0 to 9.0 miles round trip
Elevation Gain:	Up to 500' on marked trail; 1200' if ascending Mt. Sawyer
Estimated Time:	2 to 5 hours
Highlight:	Choose from a ridge walk, a mountain climb, or a spur trail to a fishing lake.

This popular hike starts high (4300 feet) and stays high, providing both a forest and a meadow experience, plus views over the Alpine Lake Wilderness. A brief walk through the woods takes you to the ridge, where you stroll along comfortably, enjoying wide-open views to the southeast. The trail itself is 4.5 miles long, and can be done as a one-way shuttle (4.5 miles), a shorter out-and-back hike (4.0 miles or less), or the full 9.0 mile round trip. If you wish, add on a climb up Mt. Sawyer or a spur hike to Fisher Lake. Tonga Ridge offers something for almost all interests and levels of ability.

Getting There

From the Skykomish Ranger Station on Highway 2, go east 0.5 mile. Turn right (south) onto unsigned, paved Foss River Road, USFS Road 68. After 0.9 mile, cross Foss River, after which a sign confirms that you are on Road 68. You reach a fork at 1.1 miles. Stay right, continuing on Road 68 (which loses pavement here) and following the sign for TONGA RIDGE TR.

At 3.6 miles, reach another fork. Take the left branch, USFS Road 6830, Tonga Ridge Road. Proceed 6.9 miles (switchbacking uphill, gaining over 2000 feet in elevation) to a right-hand junction with spur road 310. Turn right, uphill, onto 310 and drive 1.4 miles to the trailhead at road's end, 4300 feet. No parking area per se; the road just sort of expires. Park on either side and continue straight ahead onto the trail.

If you want to do the 4.5-mile point-to-point hike, drop hikers (or your shuttle car) off at the trailhead, return to Road 6830, turn right, and continue to road's end and the other end of the trail.

The Hike

Tonga Ridge Trail #1058 is part of the Alpine Lakes Wilderness trail system, so self-issuing permits are available at the trailhead. The trail is open to hikers only, no stock or mountain bikes; dogs on leashes OK.

Begin with a moderately steep 0.1-mile ascent through low clear-cut remains: young evergreens, berry bushes, and vine maple. The trail then turns right, mellows to a moderate grade, and enters a second-growth forest of slender fir and hemlock. The woods are rife with the chatter of chipmunks and birds.

After about a mile, you emerge onto the meadowed side of a ridge. Views are wide open to the southwest as you continue on this undulating ridgeside full of wildflowers in summer, huckleberries in fall. Those wishing a short out-and-back hike can turn at any time once the ridge has been attained.

Some consider Sawyer Pass, at 3.5 miles, the best destination for an out-and-back hike. Views here are expansive, to be sure.

Mountain goats will want to look for one of several unofficial spur trails on the left of the path, beginning after about 1.5 miles, that lead up to ridgetop vista points. If conditions allow—check with the ranger station—you might be able to scamper to the top of Mount Sawyer, 5501 feet. Any point on the top of the ridge will provide superb views of Mt. Hinman, Mt. Daniel, and, on a clear day, the distant majesty of Mt. Rainier. Stay on established paths as you climb; the high meadows are fragile.

The 4.5-mile point-to-point hike with a shuttle car or a nonhiking driver at the other end is another good option. Nonhikers will enjoy the drive along the north side of the ridge, and the full two-way hike, while nice, is not really worth the time it takes to do 9.0 miles. If you want a hike of that length, consider taking the Tonga Ridge Trail 2.9 miles to a junction with a less-developed 1.5-mile spur trail south to Fisher Lake (bring your rod and reel and a Washington state fishing license). A round trip from the trailhead to Fisher Lake and back is 8.8 miles.

WALLACE FALLS

Map:	Green Trails #142 "Index"
Distance:	6.0 miles round trip
Elevation Gain:	1380'
Estimated Time:	3 hours and 30 minutes
Highlight:	All-season hike with several viewpoints of 265-foot waterfall.

A challenging family hike, the Wallace Falls trail ascends through shaded, ferny forest along the course of the Wallace River to three different viewpoints of a 265-foot waterfall. Not for the very small or the elderly, the trail ascends sharply in places and can be muddy in the spring. Several bridges over creeklets en route give school-age children something to look forward to, and benches all along the way provide opportunities for rest.

Fit hikers could storm this trail in 2.5 hours, while a family with a picnic lunch could make a full day of it. Don't underestimate the climb. The Disneyland atmosphere of the parking lot on a summer weekend could fool you, but some of those folks are just here to picnic in the park. Climbing nearly 1400 feet in 3 miles is a workout.

Because of its low elevation (320 feet above sea level at the trailhead) Wallace Falls is virtually a year-round hike.

Getting There

In Gold Bar, follow the signs to WALLACE FALLS STATE PARK, turning north off the highway on 1st Street. In 0.4 mile, turn right on May Creek Road, continuing to follow the signs to the park. When the road forks, stay left on the road labeled DEAD END. Cross the Wallace River. Arrive at the park entrance after about 1.5 total miles from the highway, all on pavement.

The Wallace Falls State Park parking lot has room for 35–40 cars, a picnic area, and restrooms.

The Hike

The beginning of this hike is enough to make you turn back: a walk on a "path" wide enough to be a road, through an open field, under power lines. But hang in there—after 0.25 miles, the path turns left into forest, and you can hear the Wallace River.

Shortly after entering the forest, you have a choice: turn left to ascend via the longer, gentler incline of Old Railroad Grade, or drop down to the right to climb via the Woody Trail (named in memory of wilderness advocate Frank Woody). These two trails converge 0.25 mile before the first falls viewpoint; Old Railroad Grade takes 2 miles to get to the junction, while Woody takes 1 mile. Many recommend the Railroad Grade on the way up and Woody on the way down. My choice is Woody all the way. I don't come to the forest to walk on wide open, uninspiring trails wide enough for a car!

Now you're on a trail! Despite its huge popularity, Wallace Falls is a beautiful hike, and not just for the falls themselves. Once you're on the Woody Trail, you are surrounded by swordfern and immediately abreast of the surging Wallace River. At about 0.75 mile, the ascent steepens, cranking through a few switchbacks. After 3 bridges and 1.0 mile (1.25 miles from the trailhead), the Woody Trail and Old Railroad Grade converge. The trail goes down a flight of steps before crossing the largest bridge on the route, the North Fork Bridge.

After the bridge, tuck into a steep 0.25-mile climb to the first falls viewpoint. Those who took the Old Railroad Grade and plan to turn after seeing the falls will find this the only steep part of their hike. Reach the viewpoint at 1.8 miles (2.8 for Old Railroad Grade hikers). Many will stop at the picnic shelter here and make this their turnaround point, but the second viewpoint is better. This one gives a view of the pool into which the lower falls drop, and glimpses through the treetops of the falls themselves. Descend a set of steps off the trail to a viewing platform.

Continuing on, the trail is steep and difficult, but offers three more falls viewpoints over the next 1.2 miles, plus sweeping vistas over the Skykomish Valley.

BLANCA LAKE

Map:	Green Trails #143 "Monte Cristo" (#142 "Index" shows access from Highway 2)
Distance:	8.0 miles round trip
Elevation Gain:	2700' gain, 600' loss

Estimated Time: 5 to 6 hours
Highlight: Difficult, rewarding hike to a pale, seafoam-green glacial cirque
                      lake.

The Blanca Lake trail is a steep climb to a meadowed ridgetop and small tarn, followed by a dramatic plunge to a glacial cirque lake like no other. Blanca Lake is milky seafoam-green, fed by Columbia Glacier, which yawns above you at the lake, stretching down between Columbia and Kyes peaks.

This is no hike for kids or first-timers. While the trailhead sign, the US Forest Service handouts, and most guidebooks call it a 3.5-mile hike (7.0 miles round trip), it is closer to 4.0 miles each way. The first miles are a steady, switchbacking uphill grind, devoid of views or respite. But fit hikers will find the ridgetop at 3.0 miles ample reward for their toil, and the lake itself, at 4.0 miles, sublime.

Getting There

Take the turnoff from Highway 2 toward Index. Continue straight ahead on North Fork Skykomish River Road, USFS Road 63; do not take the left-hand turn across the bridge into Index. (If you are coming from Index, cross the bridge, then turn left.)

For the first 9 miles beyond the Index bridge, the North Fork Skykomish River will be on your left. Then you'll cross it and continue along its opposite bank, passing the entrance to Troublesome Creek Campground at 10.2 miles (see *Troublesome Creek* walk, p. 139).

At 14.0 miles, there's a fork in the road. Take the left fork to stay on USFS Road 63; going straight ahead would put you on USFS Road 65. Both forks are gravel from here.

Proceed uphill on Road 63 another 2 miles to another fork. Take the left fork, signed BLANCA LAKE TRAIL #1052, uphill another 0.2 mile to the trailhead and parking area for about 20 cars.

The Hike

You tuck into the switchbacks right away on this long, steep hike. The Forest Service says there are 37 of them, but counting switchbacks is not my idea of the best way to enjoy a hike. And, if you're fit, this one is enjoyable. There are no sweeping vistas to spur you on, but the forest is pretty, and the trail is well-surfaced (except the last downhill half mile, but we'll get to that).

Young cedars and assorted firs line the trail and create constant shade for your climb. Runoff creeklets provide background music, but are largely inaccessible. Bring plenty of water.

Shortly after 2.5 miles, you will sense that you are nearing the top of the ridge. A flat little eagle's nest of a campsite on your right is a good place for a snack and a final chug of water before the ridge.

You break out onto the ridge at about 3.0 miles. The path bends left (west), and traverses a largely open, heathered meadow with scattered stands of evergreens. To your right, vistas at last—including Glacier Peak (at 10541 feet Washington state's fourth tallest mountain).

Stroll the blissfully flat ridgetop path for about a quarter mile. When a sign tells you you're entering Henry M. Jackson Wilderness, you'll begin a short descent. Contour around the east bank of murky little Virgin Lake. (Woe to those who stop here, thinking they're reached "the lake!" Virgin Lake is a suitable destination only if you're a mosquito.)

Watch for a little boot-beaten path continuing north past Virgin Lake through tall grasses and huckleberry bushes, then disappearing into the woods again. It's all downhill from here, and the drop is a doozy in places. Exposed roots, slippery clay, loose talus—you'll wonder if you're still on the path. Take your time, and do your part to keep the nasty trail from deteriorating further. In spots, it's easier to sit on your fanny or put your hands behind you and crab-crawl down.

Could this possibly be worth it? After a quarter mile or so of this torturous descent, look up and see for yourself. You've likely

Blanca Lake—named for its milky green color

never seen a lake this color. The pale, milky, seafoam-green jewel of Blanca Lake, nestled at the base of an honest-to-goodness glacier, is like a tonic for tired quadriceps. Before you know it, you'll be at its banks.

A sand-and-driftwood beach provides the ideal picnic and celebration spot. If you wish to explore further, go left, across the outlet stream, to a few other campsites on the southwest side of the lake.

Other Hike Notes

DECEPTION CREEK

Across the highway from the all-popular Deception Falls picnic area and nature trail is an emerald-green draw that stretches south "practically forever." Along this draw is the Deception Creek Trail. To reach the trailhead, turn south off Highway 2 onto USFS Road 6088, Deception Creek Road, just west of the Deception Falls parking area (and on the opposite side of the highway). The trailhead is one mile down this road. Walk as much or as little as you like. After about 7.5 miles, the trail connects up with the Pacific Crest Trail, eventually crossing Deception Pass. In fact, if you walked 13.5 miles south from the Deception Creek trailhead, you could find yourself at Hyas Lakes (see *Section 9*, "Cle Elum/Roslyn").

TROUBLESOME CREEK

This short, 0.5-mile interpretive trail provides an alternative for nonhikers whose family members are charging up to Blanca Lake. Take the turnoff from Highway 2 toward Index. Continue straight ahead on North Fork Skykomish River Road, USFS Road 63; do not take the left-hand turn across the bridge into Index. After 10.2 miles, turn right into Troublesome Creek Campground. Turn left immediately, and park near the footbridge. The path goes north, up the left side of Troublesome Creek, under the road, and past cascading water, magnificent old Douglas-firs, and commanding viewpoints. Cross a bridge and return down the far side of the creek. Relax, have a picnic, and kill some time amidst this easily attained beauty before you continue up the road to pick up the Blanca Lake hikers you dropped off.

DOROTHY LAKE

This extremely popular trail was inaccessible in 1996 due to construction work on access roads. When it's open, you can hike to the lake and back (4.0 miles), continue along the 2-mile lakeshore before turning back (8.0 miles), or continue around the south shore of the lake and on to Bear, Deer, and Snoqualmie lakes (15+ miles).

From Highway 2, turn south onto Old Cascade Highway/Money Creek Campground Road just east of the tunnel (about 11 miles east of Index and 3 miles west of Skykomish). After 1 mile, turn right (south) on USFS Road 6410, Miller River Road. Continue on this road, which turns into USFS Road 6412 after 4 miles, to its end and the Dorothy Lake Trail #1072 trailhead, about 9.5 miles from Old Cascade Highway.

Contacts

IRON GOAT TRAIL INFORMATION	(206) 283-1440
SKYKOMISH RANGER STATION 74920 Stevens Pass Highway, P.O. Box 305, Skykomish, WA 98288	(360) 677-2414
WALLACE FALLS STATE PARK RANGER Washington State Parks & Recreation	(360) 793-0420

	DENONNO'S B&B	BUSH HOUSE	A STONE'S THROW	A RIVER'S EDGE
PRICE (1996 RATES, PRE-TAX, 2 PERSON)	$55, $65, $75	$59, $70, $80	$75	$80
EXTRA PERSON	$10	N/A	N/A	$10
PAYMENT METHODS	VISA, MC, Check, Cash	VISA, MC, Check, Cash	Check, Cash	VISA, MC, Check, Cash
# OF UNITS	3	11	1 suite	1 suite
PRIVATE BATH	Yes, 1 room	Half-bath in one room	Yes	Yes
SHARED BATH	Yes, 2 rooms	Yes, 10 rooms share 2 baths	No	No
BREAKFAST INCLUDED?	Yes	Yes	Yes	Yes
COOKING FACILITIES?	No	No	No	Yes
POOL	No	No	No	No
HOT TUB	Yes	No	Yes	Yes
CHILDREN	OK	Yes	No	OK
PETS	OK by arrangement	No	No	No
SEASONS OF OPERATION	Year-round	Year-round	Year-round	Year-round

Table 6. Lodgings in the Skykomish vicinity

Wallace Falls (photo credit: Ralph Radford)

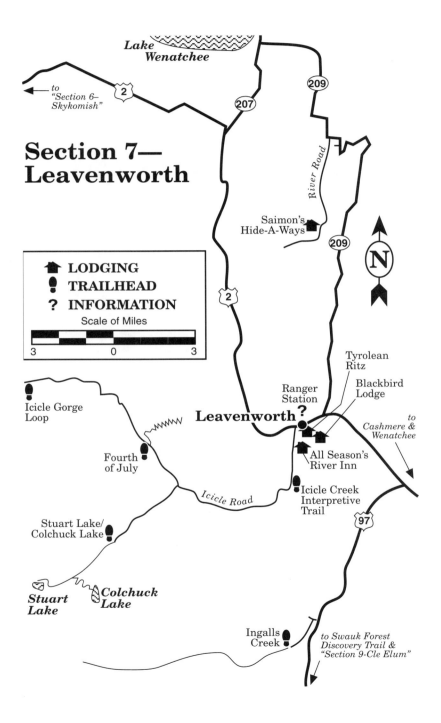

Section 7— Leavenworth

to "Section 6– Skykomish"

Lake Wenatchee

LODGING
TRAILHEAD
? INFORMATION
Scale of Miles
3   0   3

Saimon's Hide-A-Ways

River Road

Icicle Gorge Loop

Fourth of July

Stuart Lake/ Colchuck Lake

Icicle Road

Leavenworth ?

Ranger Station

Tyrolean Ritz

Blackbird Lodge

All Season's River Inn

Icicle Creek Interpretive Trail

to Cashmere & Wenatchee

Stuart Lake

Colchuck Lake

Ingalls Creek

to Swauk Forest Discovery Trail & "Section 9-Cle Elum"

Leavenworth
(Cascade Foothills, Highway 2 East)

Overview

Since the 1960's, Leavenworth has been Washington state's "Little Bavaria." Tourists come by the busload to walk its faux German streets, attend its many festivals, and shop its specialty shops. Need a music box? A teddy bear? A toy Nutcracker? A goofy hat? There's a store specializing in each...and the list goes on.

You have to give Leavenworth credit. Begun as a railroad town in the 1890's (named for Great Northern stockholder Charles Leavenworth), with a turn-of-the-century economy augmented by lumber milling and attempts at irrigated orcharding, Leavenworth might have evaporated when these industries dwindled in the '20s and '30s. But it hung on, and a few decades later, inspired by the success of the re-created Danish village in Solvang, California, Leavenworth turned itself into the Pacific Northwest's answer to Munich.

It's not hard to find a place to stay in this tourist-friendly community. The Chamber of Commerce & Visitor Center (509-548-5807) can provide names and addresses of dozens of lodgings. The four I chose to feature each have unique strengths: All Season's River Inn is one of the most polished B&B's in the state, and is located in an exceptional setting. Saimon's Hide-A-Ways are modern, well-appointed private cabins offering respite from the bustling *gemütlichkeit* of sometimes-overbearing Leavenworth. Blackbird Lodge is a sparkling clean, contemporary-European-styled hotel with an excellent downtown location. The Tyrolean Ritz Hotel is an unpretentious, quirky, old European "pension"-style lodging smack in the middle of the Bavarian village.

All this, and hiking, too? Absolutely. The surrounding forest and alpine scenery was one of the reasons

Leavenworth, a re-created Bavarian village

Leavenworth chose its Bavarian theme. A few strolls are right in town, and dozens of dayhikes are within an hour's drive. Many premier hikes can be accessed from Icicle Creek Road (also known on some maps and signs as, simply, ICICLE ROAD). This road intersects Highway 2 at the west end of town and heads south, then curves west, following Icicle Creek.

Some of the hikes in this area are a part of Alpine Lakes Wilderness, a vast 393,000-acre preserve named for its 700 lakes. Trails in this system are restricted to hiker and equestrian use only; no motorized or mechanized transport is allowed. Use requires a permit. For dayhikers, these permits are generally self-issuing; follow the simple instructions on the boxes at the trailheads. Overnight users must in some cases obtain a permit in person from the Leavenworth Ranger District (509-782-1413) or by calling Reservations Northwest (1-800-452-5687). Advance permits may soon be required for some dayhikes, so check with the ranger station about dayhike plans as well.

Much of the wilderness area near Leavenworth was affected by the Hatchery Creek Fire of 1994, a massive inferno that destroyed 6,000 acres of forest. By the summer of 1996, most of the trails were open, but some lack the full appeal of previous years. Some were not affected. Still others offer a look at the benefits of a post-fire ecosystem while retaining a largely forested hiking experience (these are the best of all, and some have been included). As always, check with the Forest Service for access and trail conditions.

Lodgings

ALL SEASONS RIVER INN
8751 Icicle Road/P.O. Box 788, Leavenworth, WA 98826
1-800-254-0555 or (509) 548-1425

Kathy and Jeff Falconer are living their dream at the exceptional All Seasons River Inn, and their spirit will rub off on you. Helpful and accommodating without being intrusive, the Falconers will provide information about everything from dining and shopping to hiking and biking if you need it. I even caught them offering insect repellent to a pair of guests on the way to a rafting trip.

Don't let the unassuming exterior of the All Seasons River Inn fool you—inside are six spacious and graciously appointed guest rooms, along with common areas so attractive you will understand and appreciate the "no pets/no smoking/no kids under 16" policy. Room rates range from $90-$125. Each room has its own roomy bathroom

All Seasons River Inn is right next to the Wenatchee River

including double shower. Some rooms also have a gas fireplace, three have whirlpool jet tubs, and all overlook the rushing Wenatchee River. Antiques, handmade quilts and teddy bears grace every room at the inn. A well-stocked library includes flower and bird references as well as a fine collection of novels, and the comfortable TV room includes a shared-use refrigerator and a soft-drink honor bar.

All Seasons' elegant interior

Breakfasts at the inn are a special treat. Guests are served family-style in the sunny dining room, surrounded by antiques, with the river and woods beckoning just beyond the deck. Kathy has developed several menus of tasty and filling country fare, some with a mild Southwest flair, and each with enough variety to please everyone at the table.

All Seasons River Inn strikes the ideal balance between a traditional B&B and a fine hotel, embracing guests as though they were extended family, yet providing first-class, upscale accommodations with all the trimmings of a professional lodging establishment (custom-labeled soaps, mints on the pillow…).

The inn is located 1 mile from the Icicle Road/Highway 2 intersection at the west end of Leavenworth. Immediately after crossing the Wenatchee River bridge, look for its entrance on your left as you head south.

Highlight: Deluxe, well-appointed rooms overlooking the Wenatchee River.

SAIMON'S HIDE-A-WAYS
16408 River Road, Leavenworth, WA 98826
1-800-845-8638 or (509) 763-3213

A selection of five completely furnished cabin homes, Saimon's Hide-A-Ways are a short, scenic drive away from Leavenworth, but still offer timely access to all the trailheads in this section, as well as hiking in the Lake Wenatchee and Stevens Pass areas.

From Highway 2, just east of Leavenworth, turn north on the Chumstick Highway (Highway 209, also called Motteler Road on some maps), a winding, well-maintained, pleasant road that takes you to the tiny village of Plain. At 13.9 miles, turn right into Plain, still following Highway 209, which is now called Beaver Valley Road. At 14.4 miles, you will come to a Y in the road. Go left, continuing on Highway 209/Beaver Valley Road and following signs for RIVER ROAD, SEATTLE, LAKE WENATCHEE, and FISH LAKE. Cross the Wenatchee River. At 14.9 miles, after crossing the river, turn left onto River Road. (Note: As you passed through Plain, a road signed RIVER ROAD intersected on your left 0.1 mile before the Y. Do not turn here, as this road dead-ends at a pedestrian bridge. To cross the Wenatchee River by car, you need to continue on Highway 209 as explained above.)

After 3.8 miles on River Road, the Saimon's home and office, 16408 River Road, is on your right (just before the railroad tracks). Cabins 1–4 are 0.7 mile farther down the road, cabin 5 is 3.0 miles back up the road toward Plain, the way you came in.

From the west, you can read Saimon's Hide-A-Ways without going all the way into Leavenworth. Twenty miles east of Stevens Pass on Highway 20, turn left at Coles Corner on Highway 207. Go 4 miles to Highway 209/Beaver Valley Road, and turn right. Proceed 4.5 miles, then turn right on River Road. Continue 3.8 miles to Saimon's home and office as explained above.

Saimon's cabins all have gas-log stoves or fireplaces, and are furnished with linens, towels, TV/VCR with tapes, and telephones. All have complete kitchens including toasters and coffeemakers (dishwasher in cabins 1, 3, 4 and 5), and cooking and eating utensils. Cabins 1, 2, 4 and 5 have a washer and dryer.

Cabins 1, 4 and 5 are the more modern units. Each has a whirlpool tub and rents for $135 per night for two persons, $15 each additional person. Weekly rate for two is $700, additional persons $52 apiece. Cabins 1 and 4 each have two queen bedrooms and a living room hide-a-bed (cabin 1 is all on one level); each sleeps six. Cabin 5 is the newest and most spacious, but lacks the river access of the other four cabins; it sleeps up to 11 in an assortment of queens, bunks, and hide-a-beds.

One of Saimon's charming cabins

Cabins 2 and 3 are more rustic, but still very pleasant, units. They rent for $95 per night for two persons, $15 each additional person. Weekly rate for two is $500, additional persons $52 apiece. Each sleeps up to 8 in queen beds and hide-a-beds.

Additional discounts are available for stays longer than a week, nonholiday midweek stays (Tuesday–Thursday), and in the off season (March–April). All units are nonsmoking; pets and children are welcome. No refunds (roads are plowed and accessible year-round).

Highlight: Quiet, private units away from the hubbub of town.

BLACKBIRD LODGE
305 - 8th Street, Leavenworth, WA 98826
1-800-446-0240 or (509) 548-5800

Just a block south of Leavenworth's bustling Front Street, Blackbird Lodge is a 16-unit hotel with a contemporary European feel. To find it, head south on 8th Street to the corner of 8th and Commercial. Blackbird Lodge is on the southwest corner, nearest Blackbird Island and the river.

Rooms at the Blackbird range from $69 to $98 per night, and include a room-service breakfast. Most have views of the river and surrounding mountains; many have fireplaces and/or private decks. All guests have use of the lodge's hot tub, on a deck overlooking the Wenatchee River and Blackbird Island.

Besides their double, triple, and quad occupancy rooms, the Blackbird operates an adjacent property known as the Daisy Cottage. The cottage rate ranges from $79 (for 2 on a week night) to $125 (for four on a weekend or holiday).

Ask proprietor Bill Brownlee or his staff about their dinner package and golf package, available week nights.

The Blackbird Lodge is an excellent location for those wishing to spend time in town. Its proximity to the strolling path on Blackbird Island makes it a special place to start and end the day. It's probably the best place for a mixed group of hikers and nonhikers to stay when visiting this area.

Highlight: Contemporary European hotel in town near peaceful Blackbird Island.

TYROLEAN RITZ HOTEL
633 Front Street, Leavenworth, WA 98826
1-800-854-6365 or (509) 548-5455

If you want to be right in the middle of the action, with a traditional European feel, choose the Tyrolean Ritz Hotel. Where the Blackbird is "contemporary European," featuring clean lines, and simple, modern furniture, the Tyrolean Ritz is "Old World European," a jumble of quirky but comfy rooms and suites above street-level shops. You'll recognize it by its stucco exterior, doll-house shutters, hanging flower baskets, and HOTEL TYROL painted on the exterior in ornate Germanic script.

Why the name "Tyrolean Ritz?" It's no relation to the Ritz-Carlton—owners are Ron and Sandy Ritz. Their refurbished old hotel includes 16 nonsmoking units, each with cable TV, telephone, refrigerator, coffee maker, and private bath with tub. Basic rooms rent for $65 (2 persons, 1 bed), $75 (4 persons, 2 beds), and $100 (6 persons, 3 beds), and multi-room suites range from $100 to $125 for 4 persons. Discounts may be offered on week nights during the off-season, which varies depending upon snow. Additional persons in any unit are $10 each; a crib is available for $5. Guests share use of a sun deck overlooking the Wenatchee River and Blackbird Island, and have access to a private parking lot that makes shopping in Little Bavaria a lot easier—you can walk everywhere in town from the Tyrolean Ritz Hotel.

Highlight: Traditional European lodge in the heart of "Little Bavaria."

Dining

ANDREAS KELLER
829 Front Street, Leavenworth, WA 98826
(509) 548-6000

When in Leavenworth, you'll have to try at least one of the Bavarian-style schnitzel houses. Might as well pull up your lederhosen and make it Andreas Keller, located downstairs ("keller" means "cellar," after all) toward the east end of Front Street (the main strip of Bavarian-town, across from the park).

In addition to the requisite slabs of pork and some of the town's best wurst (dinner entrees $7.95-$12.95), Andreas Keller offers live accordion music on weekends. Can you beat that for a good time? Domestic and imported draft and bottled beers range mostly from $3 to $4. You won't leave hungry, and you probably won't leave without participating in the Chicken Dance.

Highlight: Totally Bavarian menu and decor.

ALLEY CAFÉ
8th Street & The Alley, Leavenworth, WA 98826
(509) 548-6109

A welcome respite from "Little Bavaria," the Alley Café shares a rabbit warren with Vintage Decadence wine and gift shop (bunnies, bunnies everywhere). They advertise "oriental and continental cuisine," but the night I was there, the entrees were decidedly northern Italian: a house spaghetti at $7.95, a unique and lively seasoned pasta primavera (with red beans and roasted garlic) at $8.95, a chicken cacciatore at $10.95. A signature high-end dish was the filet mignon with gorgonzola cream sauce, served with polenta, for $17.95. Appetizers, on the other hand, were a global experience: from hummus to potstickers, crab dumplings to spanakopetes.

Despite the odd atmosphere of sitting amidst the giftwares, the food is outstanding, fresh with complex and subtle seasonings. With only 7-8 tables you'll want to make a reservation or come at an odd hour, but do come.

Highlight: Lively, fresh renditions of cuisines from around the world.

SIRACO'S OF CASHMERE
106 Cottage Avenue, Cashmere, WA 98815
(509) 782-3444

This place has heart. When you're weary of Leavenworth, mosey east on Highway 2 a few miles to the relaxed little village of Cashmere. And, while you're there, stop in for a meal at Rob & Rhonda Burbank's Siraco's of Cashmere. A full-service dinner house with a Greek flair, Siraco's offers something for the adventurous as well as plenty of choices for the traditional "meat 'n taters" palate that can't be ignored in a small town.

Siraco's is housed in a historic (ca. 1935) structure where formal crown moldings and informal counter seating seem compatible. They serve three meals a day, with standard breakfasts mostly $2.95-$5. Lunches are a good value as well, including six meal-size salads from $6.95 and burgers from $3.35. Sandwich choices include Greek gyros—both regular ($4.75) and vegetarian ($4.35).

But dinner is where Siraco's shines, with generous (though not ridiculous) portions and a few classy touches like original marinades and fresh herbs that place it above your ordinary steak house. Dinners are priced mostly in the $10.75-$16.95 range, with a few pasta dishes less (don't miss Rob's signature Greek spaghetti sauce—not your average marinara!). Try the Greek plate at $11.50 (pasteecho, stuffed grape leaves and Greek salad), or opt for one of the chicken, beef or seafood selections. Special requests are accommodated graciously. Round out your meal with the modest but creative salad bar, which includes Greek olives, feta cheese, and a generous fruit bowl. Beer and wine served.

Highlight: Friendly, low-key dinner house with Greek specialties.

OTHER SNACKS IN CASHMERE...

These don't exactly qualify as "dining," but two other places in Cashmere are worth a stop. The Liberty Orchards Aplets & Cotlets factory (you can't miss it) offers tours of their candy kitchen, lots of free samples, and a gift shop. (For the uninitiated, Aplets & Cotlets are a Washington tradition. Founded at the turn of the century, these confections are combinations of Apple [Aplet] and Apricot [Cotlet] jelly mixed with chopped walnuts and rolled in powdered sugar. Today's factory puts out 2 million pounds of candy a year, and has expanded to over 20 varieties, including pineapple/macadamia and raspberry/pecan. Take the tour, get your little paper souvenir hat—the whole shebang takes less than an hour.)

Finally, the Valley Pharmacy seems an unlikely culinary recommendation, but this drugstore has an old-fashioned soda fountain in the back. You may not luck into the 99¢ banana split special that I did, but you will find malts, phosphates, and an assortment of specialty sundaes at a fair price. The Valley Pharmacy is located on the main drag (Cottage Avenue) in the middle of the block.

Walks and Hikes

ICICLE CREEK INTERPRETIVE TRAIL

Map:	Pick up the handout and map for this short loop at the trailhead, ranger station, or fish hatchery
Distance:	1.0 mile loop
Elevation Gain:	none
Estimated Time:	About an hour, with stops at interpretive checkpoints

Stroll into the past on a self-guiding tour through 12 points of interest explaining the history, environment, and wildlife of the Leavenworth Fish Hatchery and Icicle Creek.

Getting There

Take Icicle Road just over 2 miles south from its junction with Highway 2 at the west end of Leavenworth. Turn left at the sign into the fish hatchery complex. A signed trailhead is adjacent to the fish-rearing ponds.

The Walk

This pleasant mile-long loop is suitable for all ages. History buffs will enjoy

Icicle Creek is a pleasant hike for all ages

tracing the changes in fish and water management since 1939-40, and everyone will appreciate the flora along the paths: wild roses, lupine, yarrow, snakegrass, wild sweet peas, and Oregon grape. Children will be fascinated by the helicopter logging operations that may be in progress on the hills surrounding the hatchery and interpretive trail.

ICICLE GORGE LOOP

Map:	No trail map available at press time; area of hike shows on Green Trails #177 "Chiwaukum Mts"; trail is well-marked and maintained; check with Leavenworth Ranger Station for new map
Distance:	3.0 mile loop
Elevation Gain:	Negligible
Estimated Time:	2 hours

This is an excellent, family-oriented path with two safe river crossings, a well-delineated and maintained trail (even including handrails and YOU ARE HERE signs in places), and numerous stopping points. Footbridges take you over every potentially hazardous or even potentially moist creek crossing (provided no flood damage has occurred recently), making this an ideal route for the elderly or anyone less than sure-of-foot (yet it's still 3 miles). Due to its proximity to flowing water (and the damage it suffered during the floods of 1996), a check with the ranger would be prudent before starting out, especially with kids or older folks.

Getting There

Take Icicle Creek Road south from its junction with Highway 2 at the west end of Leavenworth. Proceed past the fish hatchery (at about 2 miles), Bridge Creek Campground turnoff (at about 8.5 miles), and Fourth of July trailhead (at about 10 miles) The road eventually becomes unpaved; press on. Just past 16 miles, you'll come to a fork in the road. Bear left, passing the Wenatchee National Forest Chatter Creek Guard Station and pit toilet immediately at the top of the rise, followed by the junction of USFS Road 415 to Chatter Creek Campground. Watch for the Icicle Gorge Trail #1596 parking area shortly thereafter on your left. The floods of the winter and spring of 1996 damaged this trail and its trailhead, and repairs and final routing were still in progress when I hiked it, so mileage references may be inaccurate and the trailhead location may change.

The Hike

Heading left from the trailhead to begin a clockwise loop, you enter a wide, well-maintained trail through young forest. Moisture from the creek and its various runoff tributaries makes this a moist ecosystem for an east-side-of-the-Cascades trail; the forest understory is lush and ferny.

The first of two crossings of Icicle Creek is at 0.3 mile, followed by a gentle ascent to a sitting area overlooking the creek, ringed by a low rock wall, at 0.4 mile. Other major and minor stream crossings, all with the help of well-engineered bridges, are frequent along this side of the creek.

Flora and fauna are abundant on this trail. Besides the usual columbine, lupine, desert paintbrush, and Canadian dogwood, see if you can find the spotted coral, a pinkish-rust-colored single-stalk flower about a foot high sporting a cluster of tiny, white, orchid-like flowers marked with maroon. Even a non-birdwatcher will notice

Icicle Creek

the sounds if not the sight of the birds, including the brown creeper with its distinctive downward-hooked bill.

Just after 0.85 mile, the trail leads into a meadow, then back into forest before turning into some open areas that might prove hot on a sunny day.

At 1.75 miles, the trail enters Rock Island Campground, depositing you onto a two-lane dirt road briefly to get you back across the river. Just after joining up with the road and turning right toward the bridge (but before you cross it), you will see a potable-water pump just off the road to your right. Immediately after crossing the bridge (at about 1.8 miles), turn right, following the sign, onto the continuation of the Icicle Gorge Trail.

At about 2.75 miles, you begin a series of downhill switchbacks (which would, of course, be *uphill* switchbacks if you went counterclockwise). These, and the fact that the last part of the hike is within earshot of the main road, are good reasons to do this hike in a clockwise direction.

FOURTH OF JULY PARTIAL

Map:	Green Trails #177 "Chiwaukum Mts"
Distance:	4.0 miles round trip (or extend up to 10.6 miles if you go all the way to Icicle Ridge)
Elevation Gain:	1300' (at 2 miles; hike to Icicle Ridge gains 4500')
Estimated Time:	2 hours, 30 minutes (for the 4-mile version; allow 7+ hours for the whole trail to the ridge)

Virtually every veteran Icicle area hiker with whom I spoke said the same thing about Wenatchee National Forest Trail #1579: "Be sure to go up Fourth of July Creek, but no point going all the way. It's a butt-kicker, and the views are just as good anywhere after the first mile." Following this sage advice, I turned around at 2 miles and cannot attest to the views from the ridge. But the rest of the claim was true: it's a beautiful hike not to be missed, with great views back toward the Stuart Range any time you turn from your knee-to-chest ascent and gaze back.

Hazards on this trail include ticks (especially early in the season) and rattlesnakes (especially when its warm), but I encountered neither. Just be prepared. As with any hike that gains this much altitude, be sure to check with the ranger station if you plan to go very far up; snow and snowmelt conditions can be dramatically different at 6500 feet than at 2500 feet.

This is an Alpine Lakes Wilderness trail; permit required. Fill out your permit at the trailhead and leave Fido at home.

Getting There

Take Icicle Road south from its junction with Highway 2 at the west end of Leavenworth. After a couple of miles, the road changes directions and heads northwest. You'll pass the USFS Road 7601/Bridge Creek Campground turnoff at about 8.5 miles. At about 10 miles, the signed trailhead and a small parking area is on your right.

The Hike

This trail shows its character right from the start: beautiful, verdant, and steep. You'll negotiate two creek crossings within the first 0.25 mile, and more over the next half-mile, especially early in the season when runoff is high. Lupine, desert paintbrush, ragwort, Lyall's star tulip and other east-slope-of-the-Cascades favorites line the lush path.

The switchbacks begin at about 0.75 mile, and the first spectacular, pine-framed view to the south opens up at about 1 mile. Tramp on for a few hundred feet, then stop at this meadow's edge for a snack or at least a breather and a photo opportunity. If you're hiking with kids, this could even be a turnaround point. I suggest tackling one more switchbacky mile for the exercise, the views, and the animal exhilaration of the altitude gain in such a short hike.

STUART LAKE/COLCHUCK LAKE

Map:	Green Trails #209S "The Enchantments," or #177 & #209, "Chiwaukum Mts" & "Mount Stuart"
Distance:	9.0 miles round trip (Stuart); 8.2 miles round trip (Colchuck)
Elevation Gain:	1700' (Stuart); 2200' (Colchuck)
Estimated Time:	6 hours (Stuart); 7 hours (Colchuck); allowing for time to stop and picnic, rest at the lakes
Highlight:	Isolated mountain lake; views of Stuart Range and the Enchantments.

Here are two hikes in one, both offering big payoffs for a moderate effort. Both Stuart Lake and Colchuck Lake, extremely popular dayhikes, are accessed via Mountaineer Creek Trail. The routes share a trail for 2.5 miles, then Colchuck forks to the left and Stuart to the right. The Colchuck Lake route, while shorter, is steeper going and tends to take longer. If you can do only one, opt for Stuart Lake. It's more scenic and a little less difficult, and has exceptional views between miles 3.25 and 3.7.

Birdwatchers will want to keep their eyes peeled for the mountain bluebird, and even the botanically uninitiated will be sure to see the flashy yellow columbine and mountain lupine along the route in season.

As with all Alpine Wilderness trails, a permit is required (see *Overview*, above). No dogs are allowed on the trail.

Getting There

Take Icicle Road about 8.5 miles out of Leavenworth to USFS Road 7601 (signed for Bridge Creek Campground/Stuart Lake Trailhead/Eightmile Trailhead). Turn left onto this hard-packed dirt/gravel road, crossing immediately over Icicle Creek. The route is steep, taking you up 1000 feet in 3.8 miles, with some steep drop-offs on the way. The trailhead for Mountaineer Creek Trail #1599 is at the end of the road.

The Hike

Mountaineer Creek Trail #1599 plunges you immediately into dense forest uphill alongside Mountaineer Creek. Even in the wake of the 1994 fire, the reemerging forest through which you climb is thick with Douglas-fir, noble fir, lodgepole pine and, higher up, both alpine and western larch.

Thanks to the steep drive in (you begin this hike at 3400 feet) your high-country experience comes quickly. By 0.5 mile, you begin to get glimpses of the snowcapped Stuart Range. At 1.6 miles, a sturdy footbridge sunk into boulders at either side takes you across Mountaineer Creek. On the other side of the bridge, less-experienced hikers may have trouble spotting the path; bear left. Over the next 0.5 mile, take care to stay on the main switchbacks, avoiding improper "alternate" routes that have, in most cases, been blocked off by small logs.

After the first switchback following the Mountaineer Creek crossing, you get your first views back to the north. You will see Cashmere Mountain which, at 8500 feet, is likely to sport a snowcap. A steep 0.2-mile series of switchbacks takes you to a table-top-like slab of granite that makes a fine resting spot on a not-too-hot day.

At 2.5 miles, the trail to Colchuck Lake (#1599A) forks to the left, where it begins its serious, switchbacking climb to the lake. Continuing on the right fork toward Stuart Lake, the trail presents its first knock-your-socks-off vistas at 3.25 miles. As you emerge into a grassy meadow, the Stuart Range and the Enchantments loom spectacularly snowcapped and jagged to your left all along the horizon. (At 9415 feet, Mt. Stuart is the sixth highest peak in Washington state.) After this flat and scenic meadow, the climb begins again at 3.7 miles. Watch for a Mountaineer Creek waterfall to your left just before 4 miles.

You will get your first glimpses of the icy black waters of Stuart Lake at 4.4 miles. Continue on a path along the north shore of the lake for up to another 0.5 mile to find your perfect rest, lunch and photo stop.

INGALLS CREEK

Map:	Green Trails #209 & #210, "Mount Stuart" & "Liberty"
Distance:	12.4 miles (to Falls Creek)
Elevation Gain:	1400'
Estimated Time:	6 hours
Highlight:	Lush, colorful creek valley hike.

A feast of wildflowers in season, this creek-draw hike is rewarding without being terribly strenuous (the elevation gain is modest and gradual). The Ingalls Creek trail extends all the way to Stuart Pass, intersecting with other trails there and en route, for a total length of 16 miles each way, and an elevation gain of 4400 feet, but the 12.4-mile round-trip to Falls Creek detailed here makes a nice full-day's hike.

Getting There

From Leavenworth, head east on Highway 2 to its intersection with Highway 97 (about 5 miles). Take 97 south 7.4 miles, then turn right (west) onto Ingalls Creek Road. The road almost immediately forks; you will stay left, briefly paralleling the highway and then heading southwest. Follow this road 1.3 miles to its end and the trailhead.

The Hike

Begin a very gradual ascent, with Ingalls Creek flowing immediately to your left, about 50 feet away. Immediate rewards greet you in the form of deep-pink wild roses, purple subalpine lupine, red-orange desert paintbrush, and white queen's cup. At 0.1 mile, the ascent steepens. As you rise, you may note the effects of recent years' forest fires on the slope to your right; one of the more pleasant effects is the profusion of bright pink fireweed flowers sprouting up in the clearings over the first 0.5 mile.

For being on a south-facing slope, the Ingalls Creek Trail is generally cool and pleasant save for the hottest days of summer. With its protected valley biosphere and only moderate elevation gain, you can pack less clothing than on most hikes, knowing that the weather you end up with is going to be similar to the weather you start out with.

Just past 1.0 mile, you come onto the first of two fields of rocky scree. This being a popular trail, the path through the rocks is clear and easy to follow. Just after the second rock area, begin a steep climb of about 0.3 mile

Your first good stop-and-snack point comes at about 1.75 miles, in a flat area with a number of large boulders. This is followed by a fairly level meadow, which you traverse with Ingalls Creek flowing beside you. The variety of flowers becomes even more interesting as you continue to ascend moderately and leave the burn area behind. (By the 3.0-mile point, no fire damage was visible.) Watch for Lyall's star tulip (three-pointed, slightly fringed white

Mountain Ladies Slipper alongside the Ingalls Creek Trail

petals backed by three smaller, pointed, white sepals and centered with burgundy), yellow stream violets, and, if you're lucky, the precious little mountain lady's slipper (which my stepson unceremoniously refers to as "the bedpan flower").

After 4.0 miles, the trail steepens and becomes rockier, separating "tennis shoe hikers" from the more serious breed. The tread is wet in places; when runoff is high, you won't be able to avoid getting muddy. In other places, you may have to beat a route through the brush where the path is overgrown.

The FALLS CREEK TRAIL #1216 and NEGRO CREEK TRAIL signs indicate the end of the dayhike. Off to the left, a campsite offers a nice place to have lunch and prepare for your descent.

Other Hike Notes
These hikes not personally reviewed or not as highly recommended as the above hikes.

BLACKBIRD ISLAND

Behind the hubbub of Little Bavaria, a lovely city park offers rest and tranquillity within walking distance from wherever you parked to tour Front Street. A nature trail meanders along the Wenatchee River, suitable for all ages. From Front Street (the main tourist strip that parallels Highway 2), turn south on 8th or 9th Street, then right on Commercial. Go to the parking area at the end of the road. You'll see the trailhead sign below.

SKI HILL LOOP

Used for cross-country skiing in the winter, these 2- and 5-mile loops offer views of the Leavenworth valley and a stroll through a meadow. Turn north off Highway 2 onto Ski Hill Drive, and proceed about 2 miles to the parking lot at the top of the hill. The trail begins behind the gate to the right of the shed.

LAKE WENATCHEE/STEVENS PASS AREAS

Hiking trails are so abundant in this area that it's impossible to do justice to all the opportunities. If you stay at Saimon's cabins (see *Lodgings,* p. 145), you may wish to explore the many trails in the Lake Wenatchee and Stevens Pass areas. Check with the Lake Wenatchee Ranger District (see *Contacts,* p. 156) for accessibility of hikes such as Twin Lakes, Dirtyface Peak, and Mount David, and short jaunts such as Hidden Lake and White River Falls. Deception Falls (see *Section 6,* "Skykomish Area"), another short stroll suitable for all ages and abilities, is 27 miles west of the Highway 207 and Highway 2 junction (41 miles west of Leavenworth) on Highway 2.

SWAUK FOREST DISCOVERY TRAIL

This 2.75-mile interpretive loop is virtually equidistant from Leavenworth and Cle Elum (about 25 miles). It is detailed in *Section 9, Cle Elum/Roslyn.* To reach it from

Leavenworth, take Highway 2 east to its intersection with Highway 97 (about 5 miles). Take 97 south to USFS Road 9716 (about 20 miles).

Contacts

CHELAN COUNTY SHERIFF	(509) 782-3770
CITY OF LEAVENWORTH 700 Highway 2, Leavenworth, WA 98826	(509) 548-5275
LAKE WENATCHEE RANGER DISTRICT 22976 Hwy. 207, Leavenworth, WA 98826	(509) 763-3103
LEAVENWORTH CHAMBER OF COMMERCE P.O. Box 327, Leavenworth, WA 98826	(509) 548-5807
LEAVENWORTH RANGER DISTRICT 600 Sherbourne, Leavenworth, WA 98826 or	(509) 782-1413 (509) 548-6977
MT. BAKER-SNOQUALMIE NATIONAL FOREST Alpine Lakes Wilderness Area	1-800-627-0062

Reservations Northwest
  (hiking permits for the Enchantments area and
  some Alpine Lakes Wilderness trails)
	1-800-452-5687

WENATCHEE NATIONAL FOREST HEADQUARTERS 215 Melody Lane, Wenatchee, WA 98801	(509) 662-4335

	ALL SEASON'S RIVER INN	SAIMON'S HIDE-A-WAYS	BLACKBIRD LODGE	TYROLEAN RITZ HOTEL
PRICE (1996 RATES, PRE-TAX, 2 PERSON)	$90–$120	$95–$135	$69–$98 Cottage $79–$125 (for 4)	$65–$100 (up to 6); suites $100–$125 (for 4)
EXTRA PERSON	N/A	$15	$10 (children under 12 $2.50)	$10
PAYMENT METHODS	VISA, MC, Check, Cash	VISA, MC, AmEx, Disc, Check, Cash	VISA, MC, AmEx, Disc, Cash	VISC, MC, AmEx, Disc, Check, Cash
# OF UNITS	6 rooms	5 cabins	16	16
PRIVATE BATH	Yes	Yes	Yes	Yes
SHARED BATH	No	No	No	No
BREAKFAST INCLUDED?	Yes	No	Yes	No
COOKING FACILITIES?	No	Yes	No	No
POOL	No	No	No	No
HOT TUB	No (3 rooms have in-room whirlpool tubs)	No (3 cabins have whirl-pool tubs)	Yes	No
CHILDREN	No	OK	Yes, most rooms	OK
PETS	No	OK	No	Yes (small & medium), $20 deposit
SEASONS OF OPERATION	Year-round	Year-round	Year-round	Year-round

Table 7. Lodgings in the Leavenworth vicinity

Section 8—Snoqualmie West

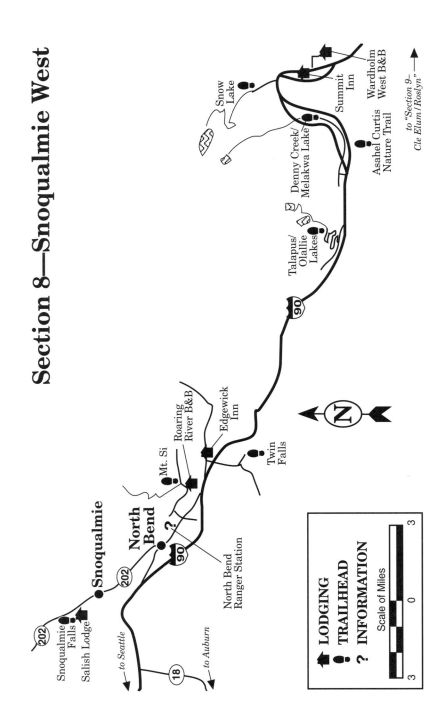

Snoqualmie West
(I-90 from Snoqualmie Pass West)

Overview

The most accessible of all hiking areas for Seattlites looking for a weekend get-away is the western part of the Interstate-90 corridor.

Just 30 miles east of Seattle is North Bend, home of Roaring River B&B and Edgewick Inn motel, and Mt. Si, the most popular hiking trail in the state. Nearby Twin Falls State Park provides another dayhike opportunity. North Bend itself is quaint, with antique stores, bakeries, gift shops, and a good restaurant or two.

Just north of North Bend on Highway 202, Snoqualmie is the site of the Salish Lodge, one of the state's premier luxury hotels. The half-mile stroll to the base of Snoqualmie Falls is a hike almost anyone can, and should, do.

Those seeking the heart of the hiking country will head farther east on I-90 toward the Snoqualmie Pass summit. There, lodging choices are limited (see Summit Inn and Wardholm West B&B under *Lodgings*, below) and services even more so: a couple of eateries, a gas station and two convenience stores. The Trading Post at the summit does multiple duty as a deli, pellet stove outlet, and bus station. On the other hand, you're right at the feet of the area's finest dayhikes: Talapus and Ollalie lakes, Snow Lake, Denny Creek, and others.

Fortunately, the area outlined in this chapter is small enough that any lodging listed is an appropriate base for any dayhike listed. Pamper yourself with a bountiful brunch at Salish Lodge or a decadent breakfast in your room at Roaring River B&B, then drive leisurely to the Snow Lake trailhead; you'll be back in time for dinner at Giuliano's. Now *that's* a relaxing day in the wilderness!

Lodgings

ROARING RIVER B&B
46715 SE 129th Street, North Bend, WA 98045
(206) 888-4834

I, the grate fire, welcome you. Rest here with me. Throw aside the burdens and worries of this and all other days. Draw together the cozy chairs of acquaintance and friendship. Let my cheerfulness impart a real warmth and glow in your hearts. Tell here your tales of road and mart and home, and when you go, take the remembrance of this welcome with you. When you come again, feel that you are welcome here.

This anonymous quote graces the fireplace mantel of Herschel and Peggy Backues' exquisite little home at the Roaring River B&B, a gorgeous find on a peaceful plot of private land overlooking the Middle Fork Snoqualmie River. Operating as a bed and breakfast since 1994, the property includes a rose garden, mountain views, a gift shop, and three—soon to be four— guest rooms.

Each of Roaring River's rooms is unique, but all are beautifully constructed, and furnished with antiques, and each includes a coffee bar, a mini-refrigerator, and a private deck, as well as a packet of information about area dayhikes. All rooms are nonsmoking; no pets or small children.

Roaring River's deck overlooks the river

The Rock and Rose Room has one of the most unusual features I've seen in an inn: a huge granite boulder protrudes into both the bedroom and the private sauna. Herschel and Peggy say it was easier to build and decorate around it than to remove it, and they have done a lovely job. The room, with its king-size bed, sauna, and view of the rose garden and river, is a perfectly elegant honeymoon-style retreat for $100 per night.

The Mountain Room has a kitchenette (wet bar with microwave), giant bathroom with double Jacuzzi tub and double shower, queen bed, and sitting area with elec-

tric-stove heater. Almost a studio apartment, this room has a hip roof, modern decor in ecru and teal, and view of the mountains and river. It rents for $115.

Herb's Place is a detached unit, an old hunting cabin lovingly refurbished as a private retreat for Peggy's uncle. Decorated in a fishing motif, the cabin has a sitting area, a kitchenette with stove, a double sink, and a large refrigerator.

The Rock and Rose Room at Roaring River—built around a giant boulder

Ideal for longer stays, this self-contained unit has a loft with two twin beds, a separate bedroom with full-size bed, and a private bath. Herb's Place rents for $85 for two, additional guests $15.

All rooms include a full breakfast, delivered to your room.

To find Roaring River B&B, head east out of North Bend on North Bend Way until you reach the intersection of Mt. Si Road (going north) and 432nd Avenue (going south). Turn north on Mt. Si Road. After 0.4 mile, cross over the Middle Fork Snoqualmie River. Continue winding along this road until you reach 464th Avenue SE, a gravel road; turn right. Turn left on SE 129th Street. Shortly, you'll see Roaring River's sign on your right; turn into the driveway at the white picket fence.

Highlight: Beautiful, private rooms adjacent to Snoqualmie River.

SALISH LODGE
P.O. Box 1109, Snoqualmie, WA 98065-1109
1-800-826-6124 or 1-800-2SALISH

The soft, piped-in sounds of classical music waft through the hallways, then greet you in your room at one of Washington's premier lodgings, the Salish Lodge at Snoqualmie Falls. Eschewing frills, gold leaf, and anything flocked, decor is simple and classic: goose-down comforters, Shaker furniture, rich woods, and sturdy wicker. And talk about "hot showers, soft beds"—you'll have both in any of the 90 rooms

The Salish Lodge is perched above the Snoqualmie Falls

at the Salish Lodge, plus a private whirlpool spa, woodburning fireplace, champagne-stocked refrigerator, and upscale honor bar.

Four styles of rooms are available with rates ranging from $165 to $245 per night for two; $25 for additional persons. Rooms have one king or two double beds. The four spacious Parlor Suites, located on the corner of the property, are the only rooms with a view of the falls; they rent for $500 to $575 per night. Holiday packages and other specials are available.

Outside your room, a world of luxury awaits. The cozy Asahel Curtis Library—open to lodge guests only—offers complimentary coffee and tea, newspapers, games, books, and a fireplace. The Attic Lounge, with conversation nooks and a view of the falls, serves a pub lunch and microbrews including the private label Fireside Ale. The activity room provides everything you need for a light workout and relaxation: exercise machines, two soaking pools (joined by a waterfall), a lounge with complimentary beverages, even towels and thongs. Mountain bikes, sport courts, guided walks and other activities are available to guests.

For the ultimate experience in pampering, treat yourself to The Spa at Salish Lodge. The result of a $1.5 million remodel, this 4000-square-foot facility across from the activity room offers facials, massage, exfoliations, and other rejuvenating treatments for a fee. Elegant Pacific Rim decor blends cedar and fir with slate for a "Japan meets the Pacific Northwest" look.

If you think you recognize the exterior of the lodge, it might be from TV—this property was used in many shots on the 1980's hit, *Twin Peaks*.

Breakfast is not included with your room, but you'll want to patronize the Salish Dining Room (see *Dining,* p. 164). Extensive room-service menu provides in-room options 6 A.M.–10 P.M.

To reach Salish Lodge, take I-90 to Exit 27, SNOQUALMIE FALLS, or Exit 31, NORTH BEND. Follow the signs for Snoqualmie Falls, which take you to Highway 202 and

through the town of Snoqualmie. Just beyond the town, as you crest a small hill, the lodge is on your left. At this writing, plans were underway to extend Highway 18 north past I-90; completion date was uncertain. When this extension is completed, Highway 18 will be the most direct route to the lodge.

Highlight: Luxury lodge pampers guests with Pacific Northwest elegance.

The two soaking pools at the Salish Spa are joined by a waterfall

SUMMIT INN
P.O. Box 163, Snoqualmie Pass, WA 98068
1-800-557-STAY

The Summit Inn offers 82 clean, modern rooms at the summit of Snoqualmie Pass. Rates vary seasonally, ranging from $69–$85 for a single or double occupancy room with a king bed, and from $75–$99 for a triple or quad occupancy room with two queen beds. Fireplace rooms are available from $99 to $150, and family suites from $125 to $175. All rooms are simple and roomy, and all have showers with bathtubs.

The common areas of the lodge are airy and spacious, with a sort of "hunting-lodge-meets-country" decor. Facilities include ski and bike storage areas, swimming pool, hot tub, and sauna.

Room-service meals are available, and a pancake house adjacent serves simple family fare from 6:30 A.M. to 9:30 P.M. or later daily.

From Seattle, take I-90 east to Exit 52, WEST SUMMIT; turn right at the end of the exit ramp and look for the inn on your left. From the east side, take I-90 to Exit 53; turn left at the end of the ramp, passing under I-90. At the stop sign, turn right and look for the inn on your right.

Highlight: 82 clean, modern rooms near summit-area trailheads.

EDGEWICK INN
14600 - 468th Avenue SE, North Bend, WA 98045
(206) 888-9000

Right off Exit 34, just north of I-90, the Edgewick Inn offers 44 clean, standard motel units in a modern facility. Rates range from $55 for a room with a queen bed to $66 for a room with two queens to $99 for Jacuzzi suites. Rates are based on the room, not the number of people occupying it; double queen rooms easily hold four persons. Each room has a table and chairs, night stand, and bathroom including tub. Commercial, government, senior citizen and other discounts available.

Laundry facilities, a whirlpool spa, sitting areas, and 24-hour coffee/tea bar are available for guests. Children welcome, no pets. Rooms include TVs; VCRs and movies are available to rent.

Highlight: Clean, modern facility at the edge of North Bend.

WARDHOLM WEST B&B
P.O. Box 143, Snoqualmie Pass, WA 98068
(206) 434-6540

If economy and location are your primary concerns, you might consider Wardholm West.

From Seattle, take I-90 east to Exit 52, WEST SUMMIT; turn right at the end of the exit ramp. Pass the services at the summit, including the Summit Inn. Take a left, passing under the freeway to Yellowstone Road. From the east side, take I-90 to Exit 53; turn right at the end of the ramp onto Yellowstone Road.

Follow narrow, pock-marked Yellowstone Road 0.6 mile. The B&B is on your right. Reminiscent of an old European pensione, the big, barn-like structure has a sign in the window advertising ROOMS WITH SHARED BATH $50.

The property includes six rooms and two baths; one room can be rented as a room with private bath for $80. The $50/$80 rate is for two persons in a room; additional persons $10 each. Humble rooms with assorted queen, double, and single beds emphasize economy. Some rooms include microwaves and mini-refrigerators. Continental breakfast in your room is included.

Groups of up to 20 can rent the entire property for $350/night (minimum two nights; single night is $500). This gives them access to all the rooms, the sitting room upstairs, and also the kitchen facility. Bring your own food; cooking and eating utensils are provided, as are cleaning supplies, linens, etc.

Children are welcome. No smoking inside the facility; no pets.

Highlight: Budget lodging at Snoqualmie Summit.

Dining

GIULIANO'S RISTORANTE ITALIANO
101 W. North Bend Way, North Bend, WA 98045
(206) 888-5700

This restaurant opened in 1996 and immediately attracted its share of local fans and media attention. They offer a selection of pasta and specialty entrées including veal, prawns, chicken, and calamari, ranging from under $9.00 to $12.95. At $9.50, Capellini Rosella is angel-hair pasta tossed in a cream sauce with smoked salmon, basil, black pepper, and prawns.

A satisfying lunch menu (weekdays only) includes sandwiches starting at $4.95 and lighter servings of pasta from $5.95 to $6.95. I recommend the Orecchiette di Mia Madre, tender pasta with tomato sauce, cici (garbanzo) beans, basil, onions, garlic, chile flakes, and pancetta for $6.50.

Highlight: Delicious, fresh Italian cuisine.

SALISH DINING ROOM
P.O. Box 1109, Snoqualmie, WA 98065-1109
1-800-826-6124 or (206) 831-6505

The dining room at the Salish Lodge is the perfect site for a celebration meal. Its menu highlights fresh Northwest cuisine, carefully prepared and elegantly served in a dining room with excellent views. A large number of window seats and privacy screening provide an intimate atmosphere.

The Salish Dining Room offers the largest wine selection in Washington state. Three cellar masters preside over 10,000 bottles (over half of which are from the Pacific Northwest), representing 750 foreign and domestic labels.

Dinners at the Salish Lodge will intrigue the most jaded sophisticate. Start with Mediterranean lamb raviolis, or perhaps a goat cheese strudel, followed by a salad of seared spiced rabbit loin, sweet potato confetti, and roast corn vinaigrette over baby mache. Then proceed to your choice of over a dozen entrees, varied seasonally, which may include smoked breast of muscovy duck, hazelnut-crusted fallow venison loin, or pan-seared quail in prosciutto, white truffle puree and fig Port broth.

Perhaps more renowned than their dinners are the Salish Dining Room's breakfasts. If hiking is not your #1 priority on a particular day, or if you have a couple of hours to kill before a moderate afternoon hike, by all means indulge yourself in the upscale hogfest of the $24.95 Celebration Breakfast or the $21.95 Country Breakfast. Guests at the lodge can also choose from an array of lighter a la carte selections such as the $6.95 continental or the $10.50 apple-oat pancakes with multiberry compote, both more reasonable choices for that pre-hike meal. (A la carte menu available to lodge guests only.)

Even the coffee service at the Salish Dining Room is an experience: a fresh Starbuck's Yukon Blend is accompanied by tiny dishes of stiff whipped cream and white and dark chocolate shavings, along with the usual condiments, artfully arranged.

Highlight: Imaginative, upscale dinners; sumptuous, multi-course breakfasts; extensive wine cellar.

Walks and Hikes
Listed in approximate order of difficulty

ASAHEL CURTIS NATURE TRAIL

Map:	none
Distance:	1.25 mile loop
Elevation Gain:	negligible
Estimated Time:	45 minutes
Highlight:	Interpretive trail with wildflowers.

A lush, wooded walk through old-growth timber, the Asahel Curtis Nature Trail is listed by Mt. Baker–Snoqualmie National Forest as one of its best places to see wildflowers. Several crossings of lively Humpback Creek add interest along the way.

Getting There
Take Exit 47 off I-90. Turn south, cross the South Fork Snoqualmie River and proceed to a T intersection, at which you turn left on USFS Road 5590. At the end of the road (0.5 mile), find a large parking lot and trailheads for Annette Lake and Asahel Curtis Nature Trail.

The Walk
Follow this well-marked interpretive loop trail through majestic stands of Douglas-fir, hemlock, and cedar. From early May through July, plant buffs will enjoy trying to spot trillium, salmonberry, dogwood, wood violet, Oregon grape, bleeding heart, vanilla leaf, coral root, queen's cup, and more. Signs along the way during the summer months help identify plants and explain the forest community. Excellent for families with children, this shady, protected stroll is also a good choice on a hot or wet day.

SNOQUALMIE FALLS

Map:	None needed; leave from Salish Lodge (see *Lodging*, p. 161)
Distance:	1.0 mile round trip
Elevation Loss:	500'
Estimated Time:	45 minutes
Highlight:	Spectacular 268-foot falls can be viewed by both hikers and non-hikers.

You need not be a guest at Salish Lodge to enjoy one of its best features: the half-mile walk down to the base of Snoqualmie Falls. Nonhikers should come, too, for they can view the falls from the top at an observation deck, part of a 2-acre park provided by Puget Power, operators of the historic hydroelectric plants at the falls. It is estimated that the lodge and falls are visited by 1.5 *million* guests annually; upwards of 20,000 have been counted on peak weekends.

Getting There

Take I-90 to Exit 27, SNOQUALMIE FALLS, or Exit 31, NORTH BEND. Follow the signs for Snoqualmie Falls, which take you to Highway 202 and through the town of Snoqualmie. Just beyond the town, as you crest a small hill, Salish Lodge is on your left. The best place to park is in the lot across the street from the lodge, on your right. Use the pedestrian bridge to cross the road to the trailhead.

The Walk

A rather steep path leads down through sword ferns, wild thimbleberries, piggy-back plants, and colorful foxglove. Along the way, views open up of the Snoqualmie Valley, a 30-mile stretch from North Bend to Duvall formed by glacial activity as recently as 10–12,000 years ago.

At the halfway point, you will reach a road and hydro Plant 2, built in 1916. Turn left and pass behind the plant on a wooden walkway. The trail continues, less steeply, to a viewpoint at the base of the falls. Those wishing to go beyond the viewpoint to the rocky shores of the Snoqualmie River closer to the base of the falls may do so; proceed with caution, and be sure to bring your camera.

Part of the fascination with these falls is the history of the power plant. Plant 1, recognized as a historic landmark by the American Society of Civil Engineers and listed in the National Register of Historic Places, was built in 1898, and its four original generators are still in use. Care has been taken to preserve the beauty of the area. As you stand at the base of the falls, see if you can make out the small, unobtrusive "cave" to the right of the falls. This is the diversion tunnel from the plant above.

TWIN FALLS

Map:	Green Trails #206 "Bandera" shows State Park; more info available from North Bend Ranger District or State Parks (see *Contacts*, below)
Distance:	2.6 miles round trip
Elevation Gain:	500'
Estimated Time:	1 hour, 20 minutes
Highlight:	Two waterfalls and a bridge; all-season family hike.

This is a short, fairly easy hike to a pair of waterfalls. The well-maintained trail is accessible most of the year, and makes a great off-season walk.

Getting There

Take Exit 34, EDGEWICK ROAD, off I-90. Go south on 468th Avenue SE. After 0.6 mile, and just before the South Fork Snoqualmie River bridge, follow the sign for TWIN FALLS STATE PARK, turning left on SE 159th Street. Trailhead, toilets, and parking for a dozen cars are at the end of the road in 0.5 mile.

The Hike

Scenic, green, and gradual, this is a great family hike. You walk a level path along the South Fork Snoqualmie River, then take a series of long, easy switchbacks up to the first viewpoint of the falls. Another half-mile of gentle climbing leads to a wooden bridge that crosses the river between the two falls. Just before the bridge, steps lead down to an observation deck that affords the best "postcard" photo opportunity and view of the dramatic, 150-foot cascade of the lower fall.

Those wishing a longer hike can continue on this trail for another mile past the falls, where the trail connects to the 100+ mile Iron Horse trail (see *Iron Horse State Park*, p. 187) on the old Milwaukee Railroad grade.

TALAPUS/OLALLIE LAKES

Map:	Green Trails #206 "Bandera"
Distance:	4.0 miles round trip to Talapus Lake, 6.0 to Ollalie
Elevation Gain:	1200'
Estimated Time:	2 hours to Talapus, 3 hours to Ollalie
Highlight:	Gentle climb to two mountain lakes.

A verdant, protected hike in the Mt. Baker-Snoqualmie Forest/Alpine Lakes Wilderness, this hike climbs gently to two lakes, Talapus at 2.0 miles, and Ollalie at 3.0.

Getting There

Take Exit 45 off Interstate 90. At the stop sign, turn north onto USFS Road 9030. After 0.85 mile, turn right, following the sign for TALAPUS LAKE TRAIL #1039. The trailhead, with parking for about 20 vehicles, is at road's end, about 2.5 more winding, uphill miles.

The Hike

This trail is part of the Alpine Lakes Wilderness system, so self-issuing permits are available at the trailhead. Open to hikers, llamas, and dogs on leash only. A modern, wheelchair-accessible pit toilet is at the trailhead.

At the beginning, this looks like a hiker highway—wide enough to pass for a road, or least to walk four abreast. Gentle switchbacks begin after 0.25 mile. A popular, rocky trail, it can be muddy early in the season; boardwalks

Sometimes a cool mountain stream is just the thing for those tired dogs

get you over the worst of it. After the first of these, at about 0.3 mile, the path narrows to a more normal trail width.

As you climb gently through the forest, you are surrounded by ferns, vine maple, devil's club, and Oregon grape. Fir and cedar trees provide thick cover and shade above, making this a good hike for a hot or overcast day (but a bit too squishy for a rainy day).

At 2.0 miles, Talapus Lake comes into view. Several little trails on your left lead down to the lakeshore. Unless you have kids with you or plan to make this your turnaround point, save your picnic for Olallie Lake.

The trail continues along the east shore of Talapus Lake; watch for MAIN TRAIL signs to stay on track. After a couple of switchbacks lead you east away from the lake, you'll see two signs on a tree, one saying OLLALIE LAKE and one saying PRATT LAKE. Both point the same direction; follow them to the right. At 2.5, more signs tell you that the Pratt Lake trail goes straight ahead and Ollalie Lake is to your left up a series of switchbacks.

At about 2.9 miles, the deep green, sparkling pool of Ollalie Lake is visible on your right. Choose from several spots to picnic, rest, nibble on wild huckleberries, and watch the fish jump. The trail continues another 0.3 mile around the west shore of the lake to the talus-sloped north shore.

SNOW LAKE

Map:	Green Trails #207 "Snoqualmie Pass"
Distance:	6.0 miles round trip
Elevation Gain/Loss:	1700' gain, 800' loss
Estimated Time:	3 hours, 30 minutes

Another popular (but worth it) hike, the Snow Lake trail climbs from the Alpental ski area through meadows and forest, up a set of rocky switchbacks, then down into the bowl that holds the lake. To avoid crowds, you might want to do this hike after snow has dusted the ground. But any time of year when its open, this one is a dandy. It can be extra-muddy in early summer.

Elevation gain is moderate but constant to the ridge above the lake. The climb, the rocky footing, and the stream crossings make this a less-than-perfect choice for hiking with small children.

Getting There

From I-90, take Exit 52, SNOQUALMIE PASS/WEST SUMMIT. Turn north, and proceed to Alpental Road, which will be your second right, after 0.25 mile. Turn right on Alpental, and drive to the ski area and trailhead at the end of the road (1.3 miles). Abundant parking on your left; trailhead on your right.

The Hike

A trailhead sign and self-registration box explain the rules for this hiker-only trail (dogs on leash OK).

Begin on a series of steep, terraced steps that keep you out of the mud, which can be considerable during early-season runoff.

After the initial climb, the path levels off, hugging the hillside as you leave the Alpental area and cross Source Creek valley. The footing alternates between rocky and exposed roots, but the trail is easy to follow. Cross several fields of rocky scree before arriving at the signed SOURCE LAKE OVERLOOK junction at 1.5 miles. A 0.5-mile spur trail to the left leads to a view of tiny Source Lake (this spur trail is listed among Mt. Baker–Snoqualmie National Forest's best places to see wildflowers from June to early August: trillium, glacier lily, bleeding heart, vanilla leaf, paintbrush, tiger lily, penstemon). Turn right to stay on the main trail and begin the switchbacks to the ridge.

Gradual at first, then steeper and tighter, the switchbacks take you to the ridge at 2.5 miles and 4800 feet. From here, drop down 800 feet to one of the prettiest (if most crowded), easily accessible lakes in Alpine Lakes Wilderness. Plan time for a picnic before your return.

DENNY CREEK/MELAKWA LAKE

Map:	Green Trails #207 "Snoqualmie Pass"
Distance:	9.0 miles round trip
Elevation Gain:	2300'
Estimated Time:	5 hours
Highlight:	Natural waterslide at 1.4 miles.

Waterfalls, meadows, a mountain lake, and a natural waterslide are all on the itinerary for this popular all-day hike.

Dramatic Keekwulee Falls

Getting There

Take Exit 47 off Interstate 90, ASAHEL CURTIS/DENNY CREEK. At the stop sign, turn north. At the next stop sign, at a T in the road, turn right, following the sign for DENNY CREEK ROAD. Proceed 0.25 mile, then turn left on paved USFS Road 58/Denny Creek Road. Proceed past Denny Creek Campground, staying left when the road forks beyond the campground. At 2.5 miles (total miles from the highway), turn left on USFS Road 5830, signed DENNY CREEK TRAIL #1014. Follow this road to its end, passing several trailheads and crossing a bridge. A parking loop accommodates 25–30 cars: toilets.

The Hike

Another Alpine Lakes Wilderness trail: hikers, llamas, and leashed dogs only. Fill out your permit at the trailhead.

Begin on a wide, gravel-and-pine-needle path sloping ever-so-gently up through old-growth fir and cedar dripping with moss. A lush understory includes vine maple, devil's club, and a carpet of Canadian dogwood. Denny Creek rushes downhill off to your right; at 0.25 mile, a little path affords the first access. Shortly after 0.3 mile, as the concrete curve of I-90 westbound arches above and ahead of you, you cross a footbridge over Denny Creek.

At 1.4 miles, the path dips down to the left, to the side of the creek and the "slide rock" area. When conditions are right, a thin skim of Denny Creek's chilly water washes over these large, flat rocks, providing a sort of natural water slide. Use caution, especially with children.

To continue, cross Denny Creek here. At this writing, the footbridge had been washed out, but the fording was easy.

The path continues through forest, breaking out into a hillside meadow just before 2.0 miles. A steepening climb indicates you are almost at the first significant waterfall, Keekwulee Falls, at 2.0 miles. Snowshoe Falls follows at about 2.25 miles.

Rejuvenated by the views of these falls, continue upward to Hemlock Pass at 4.1 miles, 4800 feet. If you choose, complete the outbound part of the hike by dropping down 0.4 mile to Melakwa Lake.

A thin skim of water over flat rocks makes a natural slide along the Denny Creek Trail

Other Hike Notes

These hikes not personally reviewed or not as highly recommended as the above hikes.

MT. SI

It *is* a nice hike. Steep, switchbacking, and crowded as can be (Washington state's most popular hike, playing host to as many as 50,000 pairs of boots annually), but the views are pretty special. From the west, take Exit 31 off I-90, then go right on North Bend Way. From the east, take Exit 34; go left on North Bend Way. From North Bend Way, turn north on Mt. Si Road. Parking for Little Si (see below) is on the left immediately after crossing the bridge over the Middle Fork Snoqualmie River. For Mt. Si, continue on Mt. Si road about 2 more miles; the trailhead is on the left. The hike to the top is 8.0 miles round trip, with 3900-foot elevation gain. Less energetic hikers might consider turning around at Snag Flat, a viewpoint about halfway up with benches and an interpretive boardwalk. For any segment of this hike, be physically prepared for the steepness and mentally prepared for the crowds. Come on a clear day, when you can make the most of the view.

LITTLE SI

Much less rigorous than its older brother, Little Si is 5.0 miles round trip to a 1575-foot knoll with views over the Upper Snoqualmie Valley. Nevertheless moderately strenuous, Little Si gains 1250 feet in elevation, and much of that gain is achieved in two very steep segments at the beginning and the end of the trail. Follow the directions to Little Si parking in the Mt. Si description, above. From the parking lot, walk 0.25 miles through a residential area to the trailhead.

MT. SI BASE TRAIL

Nonhikers and hikers with limited mobility will appreciate the 500-foot loop trail off the large Mt. Si trailhead parking area. This pleasant stroll takes you through a nonconiferous forest of maple, alder, and oak.

Contacts

NORTH BEND RANGER DISTRICT (206) 888-1421
42404 SE North Bend Way, North Bend, WA 98045

WASHINGTON STATE DEPT. OF NATURAL RESOURCES 1-800-527-3305
P.O. Box 68, Enumclaw, WA 98022-0068   or   (360) 825-1631
  (use telephone menu to reach
  South Puget Sound Regional Office)

	ROARING RIVER B&B	SALISH LODGE	SUMMIT INN	EDGEWICK INN	WARDHOLM WEST B&B
PRICE (1996 RATES, PRE-TAX, 2 PERSON)	$85, $100, $115	$165–$245, suites $500+	$69–85 for 1–2, $75–$175 for up to 4	$55–$99	$50–$80
EXTRA PERSON	$15	$25	Included	Included	$10
PAYMENT METHODS	Check, Cash	VISA, MC, AmEx, Disc, Check, Cash	VISA, MC, AmEx, Disc, Cash	VISA, MC, AmEx, Cash	VISA, MC, Cash
# OF UNITS	3	90	82	44	6
PRIVATE BATH	Yes	Yes	Yes	Yes	Yes, 1 possible
SHARED BATH	No	No	No	No	Yes, 6 rooms share 2 baths
BREAKFAST INCLUDED?	Yes	No	No	No	Yes
COOKING FACILITIES?	Yes, 1 unit has kitchenette	No	No	No	Some w/ micro & mini-fridge; other facilities by arrangement
POOL	No	No	Yes	No	No
HOT TUB	No (1 unit has whirlpool tub, another has sauna)	Yes, 2	Yes	Yes	No
CHILDREN	Older kids OK	OK	OK	OK	OK
PETS	No	OK in some rooms, $50 fee	OK, $10 fee	No	No
SEASONS OF OPERATION	Year-round	Year-round	Year-round	Year-round	Year-round

Table 8. Lodgings in the Snoqualmie West vicinity

Some days the wildlife is more "wild" than others . . .

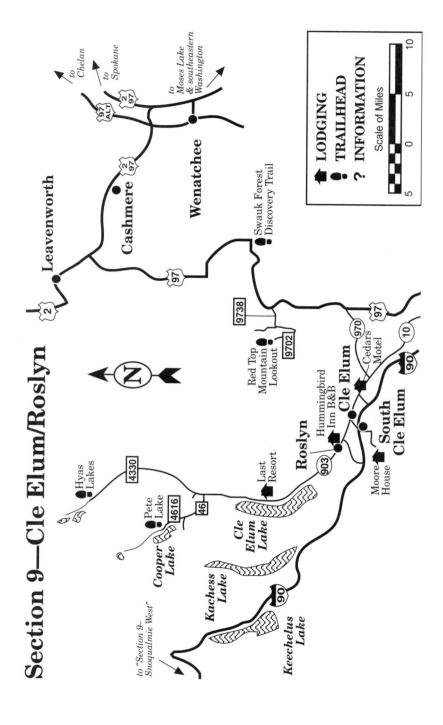

Section 9—Cle Elum/Roslyn

Cle Elum/Roslyn

(I-90 East)

Overview

The Cle Elum Ranger District represents over 500,000 acres of the Wenatchee National Forest. Its 750 miles of trails include a wide range of ecosystems, from parched canyons to forested slopes to high mountain lakes. Good access from Interstate 90 and generally sunny conditions are the major advantages to hiking in this area.

Many of the trails in this district are open to mechanized and motorized use. To avoid these, and to choose amongst the many hikes in this far-flung district, you may wish to pick up a copy of the 113-page spiral-bound trail guide, available from the Cle Elum Ranger District for about $6.00.

We chose to feature hikes within reasonable access from the lodgings of Cle Elum and Roslyn, avoiding those open to motorcycles and favoring the low-lying, creekbed-type hikes. The higher climbs can oppressively hot, windy, or both. While attractive vistas are sure to be attained on Davis Peak or Cathedral Rock (see *Other Walks and Hikes,* below), we found the shady glens of the Pete Lake and Hyas Lakes routes more appealing, and the lakes at the end of the hikes ample reward for our efforts. If it's a mountain goat experience you seek, try the short but stunning Red Top Mountain Lookout hike.

For many people, the reason to come to this area can be summed up in two words: *Northern Exposure.* This area was the site of the filming of much of the popular early 1990's television series. The streets and buildings of Roslyn, Washington, were used to create the fictitious town of Cicely, Alaska, in which the show was centered. Our breakfast companion at the Hummingbird

Roslyn, WA—used as Cicely, Alaska on TV's "Northern Exposure"

Inn flew 3000 miles to spend her holiday along the streets where Dr. Joel Fleischmann pursued his off-again, on-again romance with mail pilot Maggie O'Connell, where Holling and Shelly VanCouer ran The Brick tavern, where Ruth Ann ran the store and Maurice tried to run the town. With a sheepish grin, our cross-continental friend admitted she "pretty much saw everything on her list in the first hour." But don't despair—while the hurried memorabilia-seeker can "do Cicely" in an afternoon, the real Roslyn is a charming little town in which you can while away several days, especially if you've come to hike.

Reach Roslyn by taking exit 80 off I-90, or, if you're coming from Cle Elum, taking Highway 903 north.

The town of Cle Elum sits immediately to the north of I-90. It is home to the Cle Elum Telephone Museum (its official name is the Cle Elum Historical Museum), located at 221 E. First Street. Housed in the original Pacific Northwest Bell Telephone building, the museum contains one of the most extensive collections of telephone history and memorabilia west of the Mississippi. Open Memorial Day to Labor Day; hours vary. This building also houses Cle Elum's Chamber of Commerce.

Lodgings

HUMMINGBIRD INN B&B
106 Pennsylvania Ave. E, P.O. Box 984, Roslyn, WA 98941
(509) 649-2758

Roberta Spinazola's Hummingbird Inn enjoys both an excellent location and a well-deserved reputation as "the" place to stay when visiting *Northern Exposure* country. Just east of the main intersection of Highway 903 and Pennsylvania, the inn provides the perfect jumping-off place for visiting downtown Roslyn on foot. The famous "Roslyn Café" sign (featured in the TV show's introduction) is visible down Pennsylvania Avenue, and The Old Company Store of Roslyn (*the* place for *Northern Exposure* memorabilia, housed in the historic Northwestern Improvement Company building) is virtually across the street.

But there is no TV kitsch inside the Hummingbird Inn. Once you close the garden gate, cross the comfortable porch with its inviting swing, and enter the spacious country foyer, you leave all trace of tacky tourist trappings behind you.

The Hummingbird is a European-style country inn with a gracious elegance that belies its workaday past. The house dates back to the turn of the century, when it was owned by Mr. Murphy, the mine boss for the Northwestern Improvement Company. Subsequent owners included the Sheely family, owners of the dreaded company store from which all the miners were obliged to purchase overpriced goods via payroll deduction. Roberta and her husband purchased the property in 1994 and took on the massive restoration that resulted in the charming blend of old and new that guests enjoy today. Original wood and brick touches remain, along with a restored textured wallpaper in the stairwell.

The foyer/living room area, like all rooms at the Hummingbird, has an airy feeling accentuated by an abundance of natural light, including a north-facing bay window. Hardwood floors are softened by oriental rugs, and a brick fireplace adds warmth in the winter and charm all year round. The proprietors' choice of wallpa-

The delightful Hummingbird Inn

pers and decorative touches are delightful throughout, including a repeating (but not overdone) hummingbird motif.

The inn offers three guest rooms, each with a queen bed, for $60–$70 Monday–Thursday, $65–75 on weekends. The two original rooms, one upstairs and one down, have a country ambiance with floral decor; they share a bath with claw-foot tub on the upper level. The newest room, decorated in a tailored white-on-white fashion and also on the second story, has the option of a private bath. A crib is available at no extra charge, and a rollaway bed is available for $10.00 additional.

Roberta advertises "sun-dried sheets" and "country eats," and lives up to both promises. The full breakfast included with your room rate features fresh seasonal fruits, locally- or home-baked breads, lower-fat entrees ranging from French toast to breakfast burritos, and outstanding fresh coffee. Winter guests may also be treated to a light supper (chili or soup, homemade rolls and the like) at no extra charge; arrange at the time of reservation.

THE MOORE HOUSE
526 Marie Street, P.O. Box 629, South Cle Elum, WA 98943
(509) 674-5939 or 1-800-22-TWAIN (WA & OR only)

Built in 1909 as a bunkhouse for employees of the Milwaukee Railroad, The Moore House is listed in the National Register of Historic Places. It survived as a railroad bunkhouse until 1974. Since then, it has changed hands several times, including ownership by the Moores, who began the remodeling process with their purchase in 1983. Today's proprietors, Eric and Cindy Sherwood, purchased the property in 1991.

The Moore House has been lovingly, although not lavishly, refurbished. While guest rooms and common areas are comfortable, nostalgia, more than luxury, is the draw here. Despite touches of lace and floral wallpaper, a masculine feeling remains in the brickwork, heavy woods, and rust-brown-burgundy tones of the foyer and halls. What would you expect, after 65 years of bunking railroadmen?

The abundant railroad memorabilia are fun and fascinating: an original duty roster board mounted in the lobby; signals, photos, display cases in the halls; antique furnishings and railroad spike doorstops in the rooms. And don't let the conductor mannequin in the hall startle you! (Now do you "get" that toll-free telephone number: "Two-Two Twain?")

The guest rooms have names commemorating some of the railfolk: from the Jim "Tycoon" Benson room and Marvin "the Bird" Canary room to the lavish Brady suite, named for a five-generation Milwaukee Railroad family. Five of the Moore House's rooms (six if you count the little $33 "bunk room," appropriate for older kids with adults in a nearby room) share two large bathrooms; rates range from $45–$65. Three rooms have private baths and rent for $70–$85. The suite, with separate, antique-filled sitting room, four-poster bed with satin sheets, and lace-veiled whirlpool tub, is $115. Rates are for two persons.

The most unusual rooms are the two restored cabooses. Complete with queen bed, private bath, TV, refrigerator, and sun deck, each caboose sleeps up to five people. Rates $105 for 1–3 persons, $115 for 4–5.

"Mystery, intrigue…or at least scrambled eggs for breakfast…" says The Moore House brochure, with the Sherwoods' characteristic understated humor. All rooms

Historic Moore House

*Stay in a restored caboose
at Moore House*

at The Moore House include a country breakfast that is more than mere scrambled eggs. The full country meal, hand-prepared by the proprietors, might be French toast, sausage, and fruit one day, eggs benedict and cinnamon rolls the next. If you're lucky, your meal might be served on genuine Hiawatha Dining Car china from the old railroad.

To reach The Moore House, take First Street (the main street) toward the west end of Cle Elum. Watch for the sign TO SOUTH CLE ELUM, then follow it south under I-90 and over the Yakima River. Turn right on Madison, following signs to Iron Horse State Park. Go two blocks; turn left on Sixth Street. After a zigzag, The Moore House is on your right (you'll see the cabooses as you approach).

THE LAST RESORT
P.O. Box 532, Roslyn, WA 98941
(509) 649-2222

You gotta love a place that advertises "pig roasts" among its amenities.

The Last Resort is a simple, rustic resort complex including 12-unit motel, mini-mart, gas station, and restaurant. Located adjacent to Cle Elum Lake (north of Cle Elum and Roslyn on Highway 903) the Last Resort is in an excellent location for accessing dayhikes in Alpine Lakes Wilderness (such as Hyas Lakes and Pete Lake, below).

Rooms with a single queen bed are $45 per night, two queens $60 per night. Additional people are OK; bring your own sleeping bags and towels. Smoking rooms are available. The simple, standard rooms include TV, mini-refrigerator, and baths with tub and shower.

The restaurant is open for breakfast, lunch, and dinner 7 A.M.–9:30 P.M. Sunday–Thursday, and 7 A.M.–10 P.M. Friday–Saturday (summer hours). Don and Margaret May, owners since 1980, may not roast a pig for you, but they'll do everything else to make sure you feel like family.

CEDARS MOTEL
1001 East First Street, Cle Elum, WA 98922
(509) 674-5535

Nothin' fancy, just 32 clean, basic units for the reasonable price of $30–$48. Cedars Motel is the fresh, friendly-looking place, white with teal trim, at the east end of Cle Elum on the main street. Rooms have one, two, or three beds; doubles and queens are available. No pool, but rooms have telephones, TV's with HBO, and air-conditioning. The premises offer laundry facilities, and are adjacent to a 24-hour café. Both smoking and nonsmoking rooms available.

Additional Lodgings
These premises were not thoroughly reviewed by the author.

STEWART LODGE
805 West First Street, Cle Elum, WA 98922
(509) 674-4548
36 units, $50-$60, smoking & nonsmoking, pool, spa, playground, AC, color TV, laundry, complimentary coffee

Dining

It isn't hard to get a meal in Cle Elum or Roslyn. Most establishments are traditional meat-n-taters joints, with the occasional enchilada or linguine plate thrown in for variety. The B&B's listed above (Hummingbird Inn and The Moore House) are the best places for breakfast if you are fortunate enough to be staying there. Likewise, The Last Resort's restaurant is a hearty and handy option for guests at their motel. The historic Cle Elum Bakery at 501 First Street, established in 1906, is a good place for a bite, and Northern Espresso, a two-sided drive-through coffee kiosk at 1103 First Street, gets my vote for the town's best lattés.

SUNSET CAFE & QUETZAL ROOM
318 East First Street, Cle Elum, WA 98922
(509) 674-2241
Open 24 hours a day, 7 days a week, this Cle Elum institution has served up good food from this location for over 60 years. Begin with a salad from the "one and only coal car salad bar," set up in an authentic mine conveyance once powered by mules. Complete pasta dinners start at $6.95; choose from three sauces (forget the calories and try the creamy garlic). Specialties include a cheesy manicotti (nicely herbed and topped with two sauces, $10.25) and a Sicilian seafood fettuccine (with shrimp, crab, and scallops, $11.75). Steaks and prime rib run $10.25 to $15.75 for a complete dinner, and a selection of "country dinners" such as roast turkey, chicken fried steak, and roast pork, with trimmings, all run about $8.50. A selection of sandwiches and 1/3-pound burgers starts at $4.25. Finally—for the bottomless pits in your party—decadent desserts are available.
Highlight: Pasta and steaks, plus "coal car salad bar."

Walks and Hikes
Listed in approximate order of difficulty

RED TOP MOUNTAIN LOOKOUT

Map:	Green Trails #209 & #210, "Mount Stuart" & "Liberty"
Distance:	1.1 mile loop
Elevation Gain:	480' (fast!)
Estimated Time:	1 hour
Highlight:	Super views and big climb in a 1-mile loop.

This little gem of a trail answers the question, "How can a one-mile trail be a butt-kicker?" The official stats say you climb only 480 feet, but the rapidity of the ascent and the stark promise of the lookout tower looming impossibly high on the cliff in front of you combine to make this climb feel like a real accomplishment. *Stretch your calves* before you set out!

Starting at 4880 feet, you will climb the sun-drenched southwest-facing slope of 5361-foot Red Top Mountain, the only prominent "peak" on the Teanaway Ridge. Views of Mt. Rainier and the Stuart Range greet you on the ascent. The top offers several opportunities to sit and ruminate, take pictures, or just congratulate yourself on the view. (The lookout tower itself is closed to the public.)

Choose from three options on the descent. The 1.1-mile route we detail below affords a real contrast in surroundings for such a small distance.

Depending upon their temperament, this hike might be suitable for children. The climb is short in duration, the lookout tower interesting to see, and the views memorable. A word of caution, however: the talus surfaces are slippery and the dropoffs are steep. If your children are fidgety, inexperienced, prone to bolt, or don't show a proper respect for danger, choose another hike.

This area is renowned for rockhounding: agates, quartz crystals, and thunderegg geodes are plentiful. Walk an additional 2.0 miles to the agate beds as described in this hike, or contact the Cle Elum Chamber of Commerce for more information on this activity.

Getting There

From downtown Cle Elum, take the main street (First Street) east out of town; follow it as it becomes Highway 970 North. (From I-90, take Exit 86, turn right onto Highway 970 North.) About 3 miles from Cle Elum (2 miles from the I-90 exit), Highway 10 forks off to the right toward Ellensburg; stay left on 970. About 7 miles farther, Highway 970 merges with Highway 97; head north on 97. Seven miles north of the 970/97 junction, turn left on USFS Road 9738, also known as Blue Creek Road, and possibly signed for Red Top. From here to the trailhead, the road is one-lane gravel or dirt; passenger cars are fine, but trailers or RV's would be ill-advised. Follow Road 9738 2.8 miles; turn left on USFS Road 9702. Stay on Road 9702 for 4.8 miles, passing several spur roads that provide trail and rockhounding access. A sign at the junction with Dickey Creek Road tells you you have 1.0 mile to go. Park at the trailhead at the end of the road. This area is popular for rockhounding, with many "hikers" taking the level and less scenic trail to the agate beds.

The Hike

The route is measured from the point at the head of the parking lot beyond which vehicles are prohibited (the official signed trailhead is just up the road). Almost immediately, a stunning view of Mt. Rainier appears on your left, and the Red Top Mountain Lookout tower looms high atop a rocky outcropping directly in front of you.

The trailhead sign ("Teanaway Ridge #1364") and a pit toilet are at 0.1 mile. The trailhead sign somewhat misleadingly indicates that the lookout is 1.0 mile to the left (it is actually 0.3 mile from here). The sign more accurately points to agate beds 1.0

mile to the right and Road 2106H 2.0 miles to the right. Our route takes the left fork up to the lookout (we will be returning on the right-hand path, around the back of the mountain).

For the next 0.3 mile, it's hard to say which is more breathtaking: the beauty of the views or the steepness of the ascent. Besides the brooding monolith of Mt. Rainier at "9 o'clock," the snowcapped peaks of The Enchantments—featuring that craggy showoff, Mt. Stuart—appear at "12 o'clock" after about 0.25 mile. On a clear day (and most of them are clear here in the sunny east Cascades), you can also turn around and see the peak of Mt. Adams behind you at "7 o'clock."

Is it possible for a pit toilet to be cute? If so, the A-frame at 0.3 mile gets my vote. By virtue of its setting, it's a little Alpine chalet.

Nearing the top, surfaces can be extremely slippery. Wind around to the left on the main trail, resisting the impulse to cut across the unstable talus field directly to the tower. Once on top, be especially attentive to the sheer drop-off in front of the tower.

Taking a break on the sitting rocks at the base of the lookout tower, you can see the agate-bed trail in the near distance to the north, below. Immediately below you are the zigzagging switchbacks of the next section of this hike, taking you down the talus slopes and basalt face of the back of the mountain.

Those uncomfortable with slippery surfaces may wish to turn around and retrace their steps up the southwest face, for a total hike of 0.8 miles.

For the 1.1-mile loop, descend the goat-path switchbacks along the back side of the mountain, which drop you quickly into shady forest. (Paradoxically, on a windy day, the shady part of the hike can be the warmer part!)

At 0.65 mile, you intersect with the trail to the agate beds, signed BLUE CREEK TRAIL #1364B. A left would take you along this popular route to the agate beds in less than

Near the summit of Red Top Mountain

a mile. Turning right, you return to the trailhead sign at 1.0 mile, and the parking lot at 1.1 miles.

SWAUK FOREST DISCOVERY TRAIL

Map:	Swauk Forest Discovery Trail map, available from Wenatchee National Forest office or the Cle Elum Ranger District, listed under *Contacts*, below; ask for publication R6-WEN-94-001. Also available at trailhead.
Distance:	2.75 mile loop
Elevation Gain:	Negligible
Estimated Time:	2 hours
Highlight:	Gentle interpretive trail explains forest management.

A living, breathing, annotated monument to silviculture (the art and science of managing forest vegetation), the Swauk Forest Discovery Trail is not for everyone. It is too long, and the interpretive plaques and brochure too dry, to hold the interest of small children; it is too short to be a rigorous workout; it lacks the significant vistas of a peak wilderness adventure. And anyone galled by the idea of human forest management should avoid it entirely. Yet, I recommend the trail if you are interested in the science of forest management, the effects of natural and man-made processes on our forests, or the identification of trees in this region. As an armchair scientist, I enjoyed the information presented, and found it useful background for subsequent hikes in the North Cascades.

Getting There
Take Highway 97 north to USFS Road 9716 at Blewett Pass, about 23 miles from Cle Elum. (From the east, catch 97 at Yakima or Ellensburg; from the west, follow the directions for Red Top Mountain Lookout, above, and continue farther north and east on 97.) Turn south (the only option) on 9716, passing a sno park. The trailhead, which includes ample parking, pit toilet, information billboard, and map rack, is clearly marked on your right in less than 0.5 mile.

A North Cascades local

The Hike
Seventeen interpretive signs and 25 interpretive brochure stops make this 2.75-mile loop a mini-museum. Learn to identity Douglas-fir, grand fir, white pine, lodgepole pine, and Engelmann spruce. See examples of various insect- and disease-damaged trees. Learn why fires are necessary to the forest ecosystem. Compare and con-

trast examples of various forest management "treatments" or "prescriptions" for timber harvesting including group selection, seed tree, and commercial thinning.

A cutoff trail after interpretive brochure stop #16 shortens the route by about a mile, eliminating the only steep section of the hike and the only really stunning vista point—a view of Mt. Rainier, Mt. Stuart, and the Enchantments. This shorter route contains most of the informative signs, and results in a gentle, interesting 1.75-mile stroll suitable for most levels of ability.

HYAS LAKES

Map:	Green Trails #176 "Stevens Pass" (access shown in part on #208 "Kachess Lake")
Distance:	5.5 miles round trip
Elevation Gain:	100'
Estimated Time:	3 hours
Highlight:	Two little lakes on a flat, pleasant forest walk.

This lovely hike to two small lakes has so much to recommend it, it's not surprising that its biggest drawback is its popularity. Despite the teeth-jarring 13-mile dirt access road, this trail (which continues on to Deception Pass) and the nearby trails, including Scatter Creek, Paddy-Go-Easy Pass, and Cathedral Rock, draw throngs on a sunny summer weekend. Try for a weekday, or simply go with a smile, a camera, and a friendly attitude—this is not a "wilderness" experience.

That being said, the walk to Hyas Lake and Little Hyas Lake is one of the most pleasant in the area. For the effort expended, it packs a wallop in beauty and ambiance. Families will find this route especially well-suited to hiking with children: flat, scenic, lots of rest opportunities, and no treacherous drop-offs (the creek crossings, however, can be a significant early-season bugaboo—pack those Aqua-Socks for the little ones!)

Both lakes have numerous lakeshore access opportunities and campsites, so even on busy days a degree of privacy can be attained for a scenic lunch. You can shorten the hike by turning around after visiting big Hyas Lake, with access points from 1.5 to about 2.5 miles, or lengthen it by taking the additional 1.75 mile, 800' ascent to Deception Pass.

Getting There

From Roslyn, take Highway 903 north past Cle Elum Lake, the Last Resort restaurant, store and motel (see *Lodgings*), and the Cooper Lake turnoff (see *Pete Lake* hike, below). After about 16 miles from Roslyn, the road forks. Take the right fork, signed TUCQUALA LAKE 10, onto USFS Road 4330. (The left fork would take you across the Cle Elum River to Salmon La Sac Campground and Salmon La Sac Trailhead.)

Road 4330 is a dirt and gravel road that starts off rough and gets progressively worse. As your teeth rattle in your skull, be thankful that such a road might deter the casual trailhead-seeker and reduce the size of the crowds. And rest assured that the Hyas Lakes hike is worth the trouble. Follow this road about 13 miles to its end, passing numerous trailheads (including torturously steep Davis Peak, see *Other Hike Notes*, below) and camping sites including Tucquala Lake.

Lots of parking and a pit toilet are available at the trailhead. As this is an Alpine Lakes Wilderness trail, be sure to fill out the required permit at the trailhead.

The Hike

A wide, well-surfaced path leads you through thick, surprisingly (for eastern Washington) ferny undergrowth and into a cool, green and shady forest.

The walk can be a wet one in the early season. You may be actually walking up a creekbed in places, and you are virtually guaranteed multiple creek-crossings, the first of which is at 0.3 mile.

At just over half a mile, a view of Cathedral Rock opens up to the left. Whether majestically cloaked in early-to-mid-season snow or starkly bare, these dual peaks (appearing as one from this vantage point) are impressive.

Between 1.5 and 1.75 miles, you will get your first glimpse of the aquamarine expanse of Hyas Lake. Access the lakeshore via any of the numerous campsites and paths on your left over the next half mile.

Toward the north end of Hyas Lake, the path winds along the lakeshore, and you can see the lake "shallow up" into reedy marshland, fed by the snowmelt off the ridges to the west (waterfalls may be visible across the lake during the early season). A thin waterway connects Hyas Lake to Little Hyas Lake, just ahead but out of view from the "big" lake.

At the north end of Hyas Lake, the trail leaves the lakeshore and returns to the woods. After 0.1 mile, any path or campsite on your left over the next quarter mile will probably give you a peek at Little Hyas. This smaller lake is definitely worth a look, but has fewer obvious picnic spots to offer.

Continuing beyond 2.75 miles, the trail becomes rapidly steep in its ascent to Deception Pass, and is not really worth the trek unless your main objective is exercise. For the best "bang for the buck," turn around after viewing Little Hyas Lake, take a break (or another break) along Hyas Lake, savoring the way the views have changed in the shifting light since your arrival, and return to the trailhead.

PETE LAKE

Map:	Green Trails #208 "Kachess Lake"
Distance:	9.5 miles round trip
Elevation Gain:	300'
Estimated Time:	4 hours, 30 minutes (allowing for a picnic stop at the lake)

When you're tired of knee-to-chest ascents to mountain lookouts, ridgetops, and high country lakes, consider stretching your legs on the route to Pete Lake. A fairly flat stroll through old-growth forest, this trail utilizes surfaces so well-maintained you could almost jog the route without tripping (not that I'm *recommending* this), and wide enough in places to walk two abreast.

While there are no spectacular views en route to the lake, wildflowers can be abundant in the early season (so, unfortunately, can mosquitoes). A few creek crossings add dimension along the way, and the arrival at the lake, a nice spot for a picnic and a few can't-miss photos, is a fine reward for your efforts.

It is a quiet hike, the hush of the woods broken only occasionally by the rush of a stream or the creaking of a tall tree in the famous Cle Elum wind. It is definitely an "east side" (of the Cascades) hike as well, with that touch of dryness and openness to the understory.

As with all Alpine Lakes Wilderness trails (see *Overview, Section 7*), this one requires a permit, even for dayhikers. These are self-issued at the trailhead.

Getting There

From Roslyn, take Highway 903 north about 15 miles, to its intersection with USFS Road 46, passing Cle Elum Lake en route. Following the sign for Cooper Lake, turn left on 46, a paved road that takes you immediately west across the Cle Elum River then curves north. Follow this road 4.3 miles until you see another sign for Cooper Lake. Following this sign, turn right onto dirt/gravel USFS Road 4616. Cross the Cooper River; note Cooper River and Salmon La Sac trailheads immediately after crossing. After a final, potholed mile, you will come to a fork that is clearly signed for the trailhead: bear left. Plenty of parking and an A-frame pit toilet are available

A fine reward for your efforts—Pete Lake

at the trailhead, which is also the access point for Cooper Lake and Owhi Campground Trail #1327.

The Hike

Listed as Cle Elum Ranger District Trail #1323, the Pete Lake trek is, depending upon your source, 3.0, 4.0, 5.5, or 6.2 miles in length (!) Our experience was, from the trailhead to the first lakeside picnic site, 4.75 comfortable miles.

The route rewards you almost immediately by plunging into old-growth timber and offering a view of the emerald-green backwaters of Cooper Lake. After strolling at a nearly-imperceptible incline for almost a mile, you come to a large basalt boulder immediately to the right of the trail; the first good stop-and-rest point for those with the time and inclination. No great views, but a super spot to soak up some sun.

Shortly after the boulder, at 1.2 miles, is the first of several creek crossings that can be mildly challenging during early-season runoff. At 1.3 miles, Tired Creek Trail (Cle Elum Ranger District Trail #1317) forks to the right; stay left. At 2.5 miles, a trail signed #235 (also known as Cle Elum Ranger District Trail #1323.1) goes off to the right. Mountain bikes, permitted on Pete Lake Trail #1323 up to this point, must turn right here or turn around; the remainder of the trail is hiker/equestrian only.

A variety of white flowers line the path in early summer: queen's cup, Canadian dogwood, vanilla leaf, cow parsnip, wild raspberry. Occasional spots of color include purple lupine and wild rose bushes.

Just past 4.0 miles is the most spectacular creek crossing of all. If the water is high, don't despair. Walk to the edge of the mini-river in front of you, then turn to your right. Just upstream is a sturdy, huge, flat log that is one of the safest you'll ever cross.

As the trail curves around in its final ascent to the lake (the only real "ascent" of any pitch on the trail), notice the huge trees in the area, some upwards of six feet in diameter. At 4.75 miles, you reach the first easy access to the lake, which is on your left. One sign warns against grazing or tethering animals near the water, and another points ahead to Spectacle Lake and behind to Cooper Lake. A third indicates the intersection of Waptus Pass Trail #1329, access to Waptus Lake and Escondido Lake.

Other Hike Notes
These hikes not personally reviewed or not as highly recommended as the above hikes.

IRON HORSE STATE PARK/JOHN WAYNE TRAIL

This trail, most of which is managed by Lake Easton State Park (see p. 188), utilizes the former Milwaukee Railroad right-of-way, resulting in over 100 miles of developed trail open to hikers, equestrians, and mountain bikers. The original 25 miles of trail (from the town of Easton east) is also referred to as the John Wayne Trail.

The John Wayne/Iron Horse trail is easily accessible from the Moore House B&B (see *Lodgings,* above). A 1.5-mile walk (3 miles round trip) takes you to the Yakima River.

DAVIS PEAK

Gaining nearly 4000 feet over 5.5 miles, this zigzagging monster is a great work-out, and a full day's outing. It's open to stock as well as hikers most of the way, but is in surprisingly good shape. You should be, too, if you attempt these 90-plus switchbacks. Follow the directions for Hyas Lakes, above, to USFS Road 4330. On Road 4330, watch for the trailhead on your left in 2 miles. Other dayhikes in the area are more scenic, but few provide this much elevation gain. It's 11 miles round trip to the summit.

CATHEDRAL ROCK

This popular 8.5-mile round-trip trail is accessed from the same trailhead parking area as Hyas Lakes (see above). Where the Hyas Lakes trailhead is straight ahead at road's end, the Cathedral Rock trailhead is back a bit and on the left as you face the end of the road. Flat at first, the trail switchbacks through old-growth forest, then rocky and meadowed areas with forested patches, gaining 2200 feet. You pass several ponds, Squaw Lake at 2.5 miles, and views of Cathedral Rock en route to Cathedral Pass and the intersection with the Pacific Crest Trail at 5600 feet.

Contacts

CLE ELUM CHAMBER OF COMMERCE   (509) 674-5958
P.O. Box 43, Cle Elum, WA 98922

CLE ELUM RANGER DISTRICT   (509) 674-4411
Wenatchee National Forest
803 West Second, Cle Elum, WA 98922

LAKE EASTON STATE PARK   (509) 656-2586
P.O. Box 26, Easton,WA 98925   (509) 656-2230*
   * recorded information on park facilities &
   Iron Horse State Park

WENATCHEE NATIONAL FOREST SUPERVISOR'S OFFICE   (509) 662-4335
215 Melody Lane, Wenatchee, WA 98801

	HUMMINGBIRD INN B&B	MOORE HOUSE	LAST RESORT	CEDARS MOTEL
PRICE (1996 RATES, PRE-TAX, 2 PERSON)	$60–$75	$45–$115	$45–$60	$30–$48
EXTRA PERSON	Rollaway bed $10; crib free	N/A or included	Included	Included
PAYMENT METHODS	VISA, MC, Disc, Cash	VISA, MC, AmEx, Disc, Check, Cash	VISA, MC, Disc, Check, Cash	VISA, MC, AmEx, Disc, Check, Cash
# OF UNITS	3 rooms	11	12	32
PRIVATE BATH	Yes, 1 possible	Yes, 5 units	Yes	Yes
SHARED BATH	Yes	Yes, 6 units share 2 baths	No	No
BREAKFAST INCLUDED?	Yes	Yes	No	No
COOKING FACILITIES?	No	No	No	No
POOL	No	No	No	No
HOT TUB	No	No, 1 unit has whirlpool tub	No	No
CHILDREN	OK	OK	OK	OK
PETS	No	No (Horse paddock available)	No	OK by arrangement
SEASONS OF OPERATION	Year-round	Year-round	Year-round	Year-round

Table 9. Lodgings in the Cle Elum/Roslyn vicinity

Author Notes

Sally O'Neal Coates is a writer, musician, and outdoor enthusiast living in Richland, Washington. A native of the Pacific Northwest, Sally is the author of *Great Bike Rides in Eastern Washington and Oregon,* also from Wilderness Press.

Acknowledgments

Thanks to the following dear friends for being a part of my field work adventures: Dottie and Bob Carrell; Linda Goetz; Geri Leonard; Debbie, Jeff and Aaron Miller; Peggy O'Neal; Terry Owens; Katie Sanborn and Barbara Wright.

Thanks to my husband, Doug, for carrying more than his share of the gear when he was able to join me, and to my stepson, Mitchell, for going along when he might rather have been doing something else.

Thanks, too, to those who helped to keep the home fires burning by watching my house and animals during my frequent and prolonged absences: Dick and Kay Coates; Jeanne O'Neal; Julie, Rob, Melissa and Mandy Hedges; and Mike Rumsey.

Thanks to Shirley Miller and Phyllis Bowersock of The Book Place for being a resource and letting me take time off for research, and to Ken Meek of BB&M Sporting Goods for maintaining an even better map collection than my own.

Finally, thanks to the diligent editorial staff at Wilderness Press. Tom, Caroline, Noelle, and Anne—it is a privilege to work with you.

Index

Your safety is your responsibility

Hiking and camping in the wilderness can be dangerous. Experience and preparation reduce risk, but will never eliminate it. The unique details of your specific situation and the decisions you make at that time will determine the outcome. This book is not a substitute for common sense or sound judgment. If you doubt your ability to negotiate mountain terrain, respond to wild animals, or handle sudden, extreme weather changes, hike only in a group led by a competent guide. The authors and the publisher of this book disclaim liability for any loss or injury incurred by anyone using information in this book.

More Northwest Guidebooks

If you enjoyed *Hot Showers, Soft Beds, and Dayhikes in the North Cascades,* and want to do more exploring in the area, be sure to look for these other Wilderness Press books:

Don't Waste Your Time™ in the North Cascades: An Opinionated Hiking Guide to Help You Get the Most From This Magnificent Wilderness by Kathy and Craig Copeland. The North Cascades offer spectacular hiking opportunities, and this book lets you experience the best that the area has to offer.

How to Rent a Fire Lookout in the Pacific Northwest by Tom Foley and Tish Steinfeld. Spend the night high above the trees in an historic fire lookout. Many of these structures are now available to rent by the public, and this book tells you how to do it.

Great Bike Rides in Eastern Washington and Oregon by Sally O'Neal Coates. The forgotten area east of the Cascade Mountain is ideal for bicycling. The basins and foothills offer wide-open spaces, outstanding scenery, friendly small towns, and miles on end of flat or gently rolling terrain—a great place for your next cycling vacation.

Oregon's Swimming Holes by Relan Colley. Escape from the tension and stress of the everyday world by spending some time submerged in a natural swimming hole, free-flowing lake, or stream. This guide covers swimming holes throughout the state, so wherever you are in Oregon, you're never too far from an inviting swim.

Crater Lake National Park by Jeffrey P. Schaffer. Southern Oregon's High Cascades are a glacier-sculpted, volcanic wonderland with an abundance of recreational opportunities that is bound to please almost every outdoor enthusiast.

Check your local bookstore or outdoor equipment dealer for these books, or write for our free mail order catalog:

Wilderness Press
2440 Bancroft Way
Berkeley, CA 94704
(800) 443-7227